BEYOND ORION'S GATES

Mark A. Finley
Speaker/Director, It Is Written

With Don and Marjorie Gray

HART RESEARCH CENTER
FALLBROOK, CALIFORNIA

Edited by Herbert E. Douglass, Th.D., and Ken McFarland, M.Div.
Page design and composition by Page One Communications
Cover art direction and design by Ed Guthero
Cover illustration by Darrel Tank
Cover photo by Stan Sinclair

Body text set in 12/13 Adobe Garamond
Titles set in 36 pt. Serpentine Bold

Hart Research Center

Except where otherwise indicated, all Scripture references in this book
are from The Holy Bible, New King James Version,
© 1984 by Thomas Nelson, Inc.

The author assumes responsibility for the accuracy of all facts and
quotations as cited in this book.

ISBN: 1-878046-39-X (hardcover); 1-878046-40-3 (paperback)

Contents

Acknowledgments

Producing this book has been a team effort. Without the vital contributions of many people, *Beyond Orion's Gates* could not have been published.

I especially want to acknowledge the work of Don and Marjorie Gray, who provided the original writing that formed the basis of several chapters. Pastor Gray and his wife have spent a long and fruitful career in evangelism, administration, and writing.

And for her skilled assistance in shaping and refining the manuscript, I wish to express gratitude to my sister, Sandra Finley Doran. Her talents as a writer and editor proved invaluable in the preparation of this book.

*"Can you bind the cluster of the Pleiades,
or loose the belt of Orion?"*
—Job 38:31.

Somewhere out there . . .

beyond our solar system,
beyond our home galaxy,
beyond the portals of some starry constellation,
beyond the vast emptiness of intergalactic space—

is the throne of God.

Some have wondered if the place the Bible calls Heaven—the Headquarters of the Universe—might be found somewhere beyond the massive interstellar gates of the Great Nebula (M42) in the constellation Orion.

At least one seer who lived into our own century was convinced that it must be so. Ellen White, a visionary who died in 1915, fervently believed God's throne to be located somewhere beyond "the open space" (generally thought to be the Great Nebula) in Orion.[1]

Astronomer Robert Burnham, Jr., until 1979 associated with the

Lowell Observatory in Flagstaff, Arizona, calls the constellation Orion the "most brilliant of the constellations, and visible from every inhabited part of the earth."[2]

Of the Great Nebula, Burnham wrote that it is "generally considered the finest example of a diffuse nebula in the sky, and one of the most wonderfully beautiful objects in the heavens. . . . In a moderately large telescope its appearance is impressive beyond words, and draws exclamations of delight and astonishment from all who view it. The great glowing diamond-like stars entangled in it, makes a marvelous spectacle which is unequalled anywhere else in the sky."[3]

At least 1,600 light years distant from Earth, Orion's Great Nebula is about 30 light years in diameter—or more than 20,000 times the diameter of our entire solar system.

Yes, somewhere out there, perhaps beyond Orion's gates, is a very real place called Heaven—a place bustling with activity, drama, and anticipation.

Meanwhile on Earth, Heaven is either unknown or ignored by most of the world's billions. The clear impression conveyed by the news media is that the most important events taking place anywhere in the universe are located, not in Heaven, but in Washington, D.C.

Yet compared to what is happening in the real capital of the universe, most of the news out of Washington, D.C. is utterly trivial and irrelevant.

For behind the petty, local headlines of Earth, something is going on that makes even the past century's greatest events pale into insignificance. Behind all wars ever waged on this planet, the greatest war of them all rages on, all but unreported on Earth.

This war—this great controversy, this cosmic conflict—continues *around the clock as we work, play, sleep, and eat here on Earth. It continues even as you read these words.*

What you may not realize is that this great War Behind All Wars is about you! It is a desperate struggle between the true Ruler of the universe and an archrival determined to steal the throne. It is an all-out battle for your loyalties and allegiance.

Whether you realize it or not, whether you choose it or not, you cannot escape personal involvement in this War Behind All Wars. In the countless choices you make every day, you throw your support to one or the other of the two great contenders in this universal war.

The true Ruler of the universe is the Creator of the universe itself and all life in it, the Source of all love, the Author of everything positive.

His archrival is the great destroyer, the source of all selfishness and death, the author of everything negative.

They are polar opposites in character and in action.

And every single day of your life, either by default or by conscious choice, you align yourself with the values and agenda of one of these two great contestants.

Long, long ago, and far, far away, according to the Star Wars movies, a great battle erupted between the Imperial Kingdom and the forces of the Evil Empire led by the evil Darth Vader.

This time, Hollywood almost got it right. Because long, long ago, and far, far away—somewhere, possibly, beyond Orion's gates—a titanic battle did break out between good and evil. The protagonist, however, was not Luke Skywalker but Prince Michael, the Sky Maker. And His rival was not the shadowy Darth Vader, but a fallen angel crazed by selfishness: Lucifer, soon to become Satan.

The great War Behind All Wars has staggered on now for thousands of years. In its wake? Inconceivable misery, pain, suffering, and death. But the good news is that the War is racing to its finish. It is highly possible that those of us now alive on Earth will soon witness its final battle.

This book is the story of the Great War

> *between love and selfishness,*
> *between light and darkness,*
> *between truth and lies,*
> *between life and death.*

It is the story of Michael, Lucifer—and You.

---

1. Ellen G. White, *Early Writings* (Washington, D.C.: Revew and Herald Publishing Association, 1945), p. 41.

2. Robert Burnham, Jr., *Burnham's Celestial Handbook: An Observor's Guide to the Universe Beyond the Solar System* (New York: Dover Publications, 1978), vol. 2, p. 1281.

3. *Ibid.*, p. 1317.

1

Miracle on Death Row

In a war, you can't stay neutral.

You must *choose which side you're on. And in the great War Behind All Wars, choosing can be difficult.*

For one thing, something has gone terribly wrong with those of us born here on Battlezone Earth since the war moved from Heaven to our home planet. We have a natural, inborn preference for the wrong side in the war—the side of selfishness (sin) and Satan.

For another, the prince of selfishness bombards us continually with lies—some open, some subtle—about Prince Michael and God His Father. It's infinitely worse than the mudslinging negative ads that mark the final days of a national election.

According to Satan, God is angry at us. He can barely contain His seething fury as He sees our sins and mistakes. He is all judgment, vengeance, and wrath. He waits to catch us doing wrong so that He can punish us without mercy.

But it's all lies. And God won't respond by launching His own negative propaganda offensive. He responds with the truth.

After the war had played out on the turf of this world for a few centuries, God—speaking through dedicated human penmen—began to set forth the truth about Himself in written form.

Over a period of 2,500 years, the truth emerged, shining forth brilliantly in the sixty-six books of what we today call God's Word—the Bible.

Here is the Book that reveals what is really going on in the universe. Here is the Book that gives meaning and context to the seemingly random and senseless events of our lives. Here is the Book that shows your place in the War Behind All Wars.

10

1

• •

For more than twenty centuries, the Bible has captured the minds and hearts of millions. It cannot be ignored! While Christians have clung to its promises and martyrs have surrendered their lives rather than compromise its principles, skeptics and critics have derided its claims, ridiculed its historicity, scoffed at its prophecies, and laughed at its spiritual authority. But the Bible is still the world's best seller!

The skeptic Voltaire once boasted, "I am weary of hearing people repeat that twelve men established the Christian religion. I will prove that one man may suffice to overthrow it." Yet today a Bible depository stacked with thousands of Bibles stands on the very spot where Voltaire made his prediction!

With the torrent of books available on every topic today, the world's best seller, year in and year out, decade after decade, is still the Bible! Many governments recognize it as the standard by which their country should operate. Presidents take their oath of office on the sacred Word.

What kind of book is it that captures the admiration and loyalty of so many? What lies behind the Bible's obvious power? What does it claim to be? Let's examine its pages and let it speak for itself!

Paul wrote to Timothy, "All Scripture is given by inspiration of God." 2 Timothy 3:16. While most authors clamor for recognition, Bible writers gave all the credit to God for the production of the most significant book in history.

But how did God work through men to write the Bible? "For prophecy never came by the will of man, but holy men of God spoke as they were moved by the Holy Spirit." 2 Peter 1:21. The Holy Ghost did not dictate, verbatim, every word the Bible writers were to pen, but rather moved on their thought processes, allowing them to use their own choice of words to express the concepts being impressed upon them.

◆ Napoleon's stone

Archaeological finds and scientific discoveries through the years shed light on the authenticity of the Bible. Until the nineteenth century, little was known about the ancient past except for the biblical record. History seemed locked forever behind strange picture-writings, such as the hieroglyphics of Egypt. Not a person in Egypt, nor anyone else in the world, could decipher the markings of the ancient language, until the last century.

Then, in 1798, Napoleon led 38,000 soldiers into Egypt. But strange as it may seem, he also took hundreds of artists, linguists, and scientists to help him better understand the history of that intriguing land.

Relics of the past were everywhere with their hidden mysteries of a once-great civilization. Strange inscriptions decorated monuments and temple walls, leaving Napoleon and his scholars wondering what secret messages they contained.

One year later, in 1799, one of Napoleon's soldiers unearthed a black stone four feet long and two-and-a-half feet wide that would unlock the mystery of the picture-writing and reveal secrets hidden for centuries! That slab, known today as the Rosetta Stone, is now housed in the British Museum. The Rosetta Stone bore an ancient decree in three different scripts: hieroglyphics (ancient Egyptian picture-writing), cursive Egyptian, and Greek.

Scholars quickly translated the Greek text, but puzzled over the hieroglyphics. Twenty years later, in 1822, a brilliant young Frenchman by the name of Jean François Champollion startled the world by cracking the ancient code. Discovering that all three inscriptions were identical, he used the Greek to decipher the hieroglyphics and thus opened to the world the vast treasures of Egypt's ancient past. With the language unveiled, scholars were able to verify biblical passages dating back farther than any for which historical corroboration had existed before.

Another fascinating archaeological discovery was that of the Ebla Tablets. Because no historical evidence existed up to the last century to verify whether the Hebrews had developed the art of writing by the time of Moses, Bible critics questioned the credibility of the first five books of the Bible. The discovery of the Ebla Tablets, dating back earlier than Moses, not only proved that the art of writing did exist long before Moses' day, but also revealed the story of creation, the flood, and names and places familiar to all Bible students: Abraham, Esau, Israel, Sinai, Sodom and Gomorrah, and others.

Such historical reference to cities previously only referred to in Scripture confirmed the authenticity of the biblical record. "The entirety of Your word is truth." Psalm 119:160.

Considering the amount of time that has elapsed since the Bible was written, some have questioned the accuracy of our modern translations as compared to the original scrolls. Once again, archaeology provides us with some assuring information.

◆ Dead men do tell tales!

In the summer of 1947, a Bedouin boy, looking for a lost goat near the northwest shore of the Dead Sea, idly tossed a stone through a hole in a cliff. He was startled to hear the sound of breaking pottery!

Unwittingly, Muhammed el-Ehib had stumbled upon the first of the treasures now known as the Dead Sea Scrolls. Other caves nearby revealed more pottery, more scrolls. Portions of every book of the Old Testament, except the book of Esther, were found.

Among the discoveries was the Isaiah scroll—twenty-four feet in length, well preserved, and complete from the first to the last verses. An extraordinary find, the Dead Sea Scrolls were a thousand years older than any complete biblical Hebrew manuscripts in existence. Previously believed by some scholars to have been written by several men over a long time period, the book of Isaiah was confirmed as having always been one book with one author.

With the discovery of the Dead Sea Scrolls, scholars around the world were amazed to learn that the Old Testament has come down to us through so many centuries practically unchanged! Dead men, it is said, do not tell tales. But they do! These long-kept secrets are more fascinating than novels or fiction, confirming the accuracy and reliability of God's Word.

Yet another archaeological discovery verifying the biblical record was made just before the start of the twentieth century. Prior to that time, some historians claimed that the ancient city of Babylon had been built by Queen Semiramis. Yet Scripture credited King Nebuchadnezzar with the construction of this beautiful city. Who was right?

In 1899, Robert Koldewey began excavating the old ruins of Babylon, unearthing tens of thousands of kiln-baked bricks, all bearing the stamp of King Nebuchadnezzar and all taken from the walls and temples of the city! A cuneiform tablet, recounting Nebuchadnezzar's achievements, was among the finds. On that tablet, Nebuchadnezzar remarks, "O Babylon! The delight of mine eyes, The excellency of my kingdom. May it last forever!"

The East India House inscription, now in London, devotes six columns of Babylonian writing to a description of the huge building projects of Nebuchadnezzar. The spade again has confirmed the accuracy of God's Word.

Another mystery unsolved in secular history was the absence of the name of Belshazzar as a ruler of Babylon. Although this ancient king was referred to in Scripture, secular records previously had provided no evidence of his reign. Yet if you visit the British museum today, you will find a cylinder, proving that Belshazzar ruled jointly with his father in Babylon, just as the Bible says.

The prophet Daniel predicted that at the "time of the end, knowledge would be increased." The prophet's words can certainly be applied to discoveries confirming the authenticity of Scripture.

Bricks and cylinders, tablets and manuscripts, are proving that what the Bible says is true and is safe to trust.

◆ Predicting the future

Another compelling evidence that the Bible is God's inspired Word is the Book's ability to foretell the future. "I am God, and there is none like Me, Declaring the end from the beginning, And from ancient times things that are not yet done." Isaiah 46:9, 10.

As God pulls back the curtain of time, giving us a glimpse of history yet unwritten, He demonstrates that the Bible is not just a good book—it is His Book.

Before Babylon reached its zenith of power and glory, God's Book foretold its fall. "And Babylon, the glory of kingdoms, The beauty of the Chaldeans' pride, Will be as when God overthrew Sodom and Gomorrah." Isaiah 13:19.

Even the power that would overthrow this mighty kingdom was identified in Scripture, long before that event came to pass: "The LORD has raised up the spirit of the kings of the Medes. For His plan is against Babylon to destroy it." Jeremiah 51:11.

And the Bible gets even more specific! The name of the man who would lead the armies against Babylon was prophesied 150 years before his birth, as was the very way he would do it: "Thus says the LORD to His anointed, To Cyrus, whose right hand I have held, [I will] open before him the double doors." Isaiah 45:1.

Were the prophecies of the Bible fulfilled? Indeed, they were! In the Persian Hall of the British Museum stands the Cyrus cylinder, found in the ruins of Babylon. On this clay cylinder, Cyrus tells of his conquest of Babylon! The stones indeed cry out, even when men and women have done their best to silence the authenticity of the Bible.

The Bible not only foretold Babylon's destruction but further predicted that "Babylon shall become a heap." Jeremiah 51:37.

So it remains until this day!

We can agree with the prophet of old: "The word of our God stands forever." Isaiah 40:8.

But the Bible is more than just authentic history, more than scientific facts, more than prophecies fulfilled. If it were simply an amazing collection of facts and predictions, its significance would be that it is only a fascinating book! But it is far more—it has been the anchor for men and women in every generation. It speaks divine messages to the human mind and heart.

The theme of the Book—the heart of it all—is the account of what happened on a lonely Palestinian hill more than nineteen centuries ago.

Perhaps the greatest evidence that the Bible is what it claims to be is the power of the Book to change lives. That power is wrapped up in one person—Jesus Christ! Knowing Him and believing His promises opens up a power that men and women never knew existed. This is why the Bible is called the living word of God (see Hebrews 4:12).

Jesus says, "You search the Scriptures, for in them you think you have eternal life; and these are they which testify of Me." John 5:39.

Jesus is referring here to the Old Testament, for the New Testament had not yet been written when Jesus spoke these words. The theme of the entire Bible—both the Old and New Testaments—is a revelation of Jesus Christ. The Old Testament is filled with prophecies which foretold everything about Christ—from His birthplace to the manner of His death—centuries before He came to this earth. The New Testament is filled with the story of His life and why He came to this world to tell the truth about God.

The truth as revealed in the Bible changes men, setting them free from self-destructive habits. There is a power in God's Word—a power that can calm a cannibal, dry out a drunkard, mellow a murderer.

◆ The story of Sam Tannyhill

To those willing to accept the Man in the Book, the Bible offers strength for all circumstances. Sam Tannyhill, a criminal who told his story on death row, is a dramatic example of the power of God's Word to change a man's life completely.

Sam's childhood was far from ideal. His parents divorced when he was five years old, and he was shuttled to a dozen different homes, leaving him feeling bewildered and unwanted. At the age of ten, Sam became involved in a number of minor offenses—pocketing dime-store items, trespassing on private property, one crime after another. And thus his life of crime was established.

Eventually, Sam was convicted of forgery and sentenced to prison. After five years he was released, only to rob a small restaurant in Ohio two weeks later. Forcing the waitress into his car, he sped out of town. Her badly beaten body was discovered the next day.

Sam escaped into Kansas and after several more robberies was captured and sentenced to die in the electric chair. While in prison, he was visited by several Christians. One held out a Bible—a gift from his nine-year-old son—and left Sam with these words. "My boy says you can have it on one condition: you must read it."

Although Sam had little interest in the Bible at first, he eventually opened its covers out of sheer boredom. Soon, he became absorbed. His own words reveal his spiritual journey:

"I found a place where a man named Jesus sent some of His gang to bring Him a mule. For this I thought Him a horse thief. Then I ran across a place where He made wine. For this I called Him a bootlegger. Then I found a place where He raised the dead, healed all manner of sickness, and cast out evil. Now I wondered, What manner of man is this?

"So I started at Matthew, and I read all the part called the New Testament. By that time I found Him, not a horse thief or bootlegger, but the Son of God. I knew of people who prayed and served that God and who lived up to His law, but that wasn't me. I was a convict on death row, a murderer, but I read where people in the Bible were also outside of the law. Then I was troubled; I wanted that peace of mind this God was giving away, but how could I get word to Him? Can He really hear you when you pray? And will He answer a man who has never heard of Him?

"So I tried praying. My prayers never got out of my cell. I prayed for help, but hung onto the world with both hands. . . . I decided to give it one more try. . . . For three days there was no more miserable soul on this earth than I. I prayed, I cried, I prayed, and the longer it went on the more miserable I became.

"On November 4th I made one more try to reach that God who could give me that peace of mind. I got on my knees and truly confessed every wrong I could think of, and asked that God please help me. I told Him if I had forgotten any of my sins to have mercy on me and add them to the list, because I was guilty of them, too.

"Let me tell you I never had such a wonderful feeling in my life. I wanted to shout it to the world. Yes, I felt the Spirit of God as He truly brought His love into my heart. After I settled down to bed along about morning, I slept peacefully for the first time in my adult life. The next morning I got up, I prayed before I even put on my clothes. That day I testified to my fellow men here.

"I am in a cell on death row, but I am more free here than I ever was in the streets. I have no fear of death whatsoever. To me death is one step closer to my Jesus.

"I can truly say there is no sin too black that the blood of Jesus Christ can't wash as white as snow."

Sam's faith was put to the ultimate test. Shortly before his execution at the Ohio State Penitentiary in 1956, he wrote: "There are just four of us on death row at present, but I am glad to tell you that three of us are under the blood of Christ. Please pray that we will be able to get the fourth one before it is too late."

His last audible prayer was, "Lord, don't hold against these guards what they are about to do tonight. What I have done has forced them to do what they are about to do. If it is a sin, Lord, then charge it up to my account, and forgive it just as You have forgiven all the rest of my sins. Amen."

Sam's voice is still today, but the marvelous change the Word of God made in his life continues to be a witness drawing men and women to Jesus Christ.

Never has there been a Book that could so dramatically change the lives of men and women. The challenge for us today, in comfortable and overfed America, is to raise ourselves up out of lethargy and mental numbness and face the implications of just what this Book can mean in our lives. The Bible is more than just a "holy book" to carry to church, more than a Book to decorate tables, more than helpful information or useful advice—it is God speaking to our hearts. It is His love letter to us, His secret of eternal life, His promise of peace of mind now and everlasting happiness to come.

Knowing this, can we do any less than heed the apostle's advice, "Be diligent to present yourself approved to God, a worker who does not need to be ashamed, rightly dividing the word of truth." 2 Timothy 2:15.

Sam's Book will change your life too. ❏

Sam's Book does indeed change lives. But just how well can we get to know the Hero of the Book? Isn't God terribly busy running His immense universe? How much do we really matter to Him? Does He really care?

If you've ever asked these questions—if you've ever felt insignificant and alone—you're ready for the good news coming up in Chapter 2!

2

Lonely No Longer

There's something worse than an angry God.

And that is a God who simply doesn't care. A God who sees that we hurt, who watches us suffer—and it means nothing to Him.

Small children crave the positive attention of their parents. But if it isn't forthcoming, they will often provoke even negative parental attention. Because even negative attention is better than none at all. Nothing is more devastating than being totally ignored. Nothing wounds us so deeply as the thought that we are so worthless that we don't even merit being objects of a Father's anger.

But your Father is like that, Satan says. If you don't sense His anger, it's because you no longer matter to Him. You aren't even worth His trouble to despise. He simply doesn't care.

You've been abandoned, the prince of darkness assures you. You're an orphan on a dying planet. You're all alone.

Don't you believe it, my friend! Satan is incapable of telling you anything but lies. Whatever he tells you, seize its opposite as the truth!

God cares! He cares for you as if you were the only one on Earth. He cares for you more than He cares for His own life—something He proved one horrific Friday afternoon long ago.

You are not alone! You are loved more than you will ever know by One who knows you better than you know yourself. And that love is the exact measure of your worth!

2

• •

Oh, God, I feel so alone!" How often this agonizing cry goes out from people who feel cut off from human companionship. Loneliness is an epidemic of our age. And sometimes, the loneliest are those surrounded by people too busy to care.

Solomon once observed, "Woe to him who is alone when he falls, For he has no one to help him up." Ecclesiastes 4:10.

Psychologists tell us that we need at least one person who cares about us and for whom we care. When that basic sense of human trust and bonding is absent, we soon discover that meaning and significance has vanished from our lives. That kind of life is more than lonely—it soon becomes locked in despair!

If the past holds no meaning, the present no joy, the future no hope, and no one seems to care, what is there to live for?

In their loneliness, people reach out for quick fixes to fill the void. Soon they are doing things, many of which they wouldn't have dreamed of doing before—popping pills, injecting heroin, joining street gangs, guzzling alcohol, vegetating before TV and movie screens, turning to prostitution, acquiring material things—the list goes on.

And when the high wears off, the things wear out, and the music dies down, the loneliness returns, larger and more empty than ever before.

Loneliness is no respecter of persons. We've all hit low points in our lives—times when things looked horribly bleak, when others seemed ruthlessly callous, when the future appeared unworkable. To whom do we turn at such times? Where do we go?

Jacob, in exile, threatened with death by his angry brother, and separated from his loved ones for the first time in his life, hit a low that darkened his very soul. Lying on the ground with a stone for a pillow, this young man so accustomed to the warmth of family felt forsaken by the very God he had been reared to trust.

Then God gave him a dream that has provided hope for lonely men and women ever since. As Jacob slept, he saw a ladder reaching from earth to heaven, with angels ascending and descending it. This ladder represented God's love and care, His accessibility, His never-ending vigilance and involvement with the people He created. Adding to this powerful symbol of God's nearness, the Lord spoke these words of comfort and assurance, "I am with you and will keep you wherever you go . . . I will not leave you." Genesis 28:15.

Do you like that? What God said to Jacob so long ago, He says today to everyone, including you! You are never alone! God is right with you when you need Him. You don't have to stand in line because He is busy somewhere out there running the universe. He is already ahead of you, hearing your cry even before you call.

◆ How can I know You if I can't see You?

But to some today, the words of this promise appear far removed from reality. God seems so far away, so nebulous, so uncertain. How can I trust a Being I cannot see? they ask. Can anyone really know what God is like?

To such, the Bible says, "Now acquaint yourself with Him, and be at peace." Job 22:21.

Wherever you live, the invitation is for you: Get acquainted with God. Get to know Him and find peace of mind and heart. You can look for Him in nature, if that interests you at the moment. The universe is filled with evidences of His handiwork. The prophet Isaiah suggests, "Lift up your eyes on high, And see who has created these things, Who brings out their host by number; He calls them all by name, By the greatness of His might And the strength of His power; Not one is missing." Isaiah 40:26.

Through the centuries, men and women have marveled at the mysteries of the heavens, wondering what secrets lie hidden in the depths of space. During the Dark Ages, the church tried to keep people from looking at the universe through the telescope, afraid that if they studied the heavens too closely, they might discover things that would shake their faith in God! What an irony! As men and women invented bigger and better means of probing the heavens, many found that their faith in God only increased.

James Irwin, an Apollo 15 spacecraft crew member who walked on the moon, found himself awed and humbled before God while tiptoeing across the earth's satellite. About a year after his mission to the moon, he retired from the Air Force and launched the interdenominational Christian High Flight Foundation—an organization dedicated to sharing the good news that "God walking on earth is more important than men walking on the moon."

The universe as we know it is continually expanding, revealing itself in increasingly more intricate detail. Before the invention of telescopes, man counted the stars he could see and concluded that exactly 5,119 stars dotted the night skies. But for centuries the Bible had stated, "The host of heaven cannot be numbered." Jeremiah 33:22.

Today, as we swing our giant telescopes toward the heavens, we discover that many of those tiny dots of light twinkling in the sky are not just stars, but whole island galaxies—made up of millions of blazing suns like our own. And surrounding these innumerable suns are countless planets. Our Milky Way system is but the visible edge of our own island universe.

Astronomer Fritz Conn puts the enormity of it all into perspective with these words, "Our home in the universe is a spiral of 200 billion stars, a unit of suns whirling through space like a fiery pinwheel."

Each twenty-four hours, our galaxy travels a million and a half miles through space at more than sixty-six thousand miles per hour. Beyond our Milky Way system, stretching above, below, and around us, are millions of other milky way systems.

"The 200–inch Hale reflector on Palomar Mountain . . . can see as many as a million galaxies inside the bowl of the Big Dipper alone!" *National Geographic*, May 1974. Imagine what the Hubble space telescope will show us when it begins to count galaxies!

If the island universes are distributed uniformly, we arrive at a figure of 100 billion galaxies—each composed of 200 to 500 billion stars, each star up to one million times as large as our Earth.

◆ The immensity of infinity

Inconceivable? So it seems, until the telescopes start counting them! God used two corresponding illustrations to help us comprehend a little better the immensity of it all. On one occasion, God took Abraham outdoors and challenged him to count the stars, then stated, "So shall your descendants be." Genesis 15:5.

Later, the Lord assured Abraham, "I will multiply your descendants . . . as the sand which is on the seashore." Genesis 22:17.

Interesting comparison—the number of stars in the sky and the number of grains of sand on the beach! Unaware of this biblical analogy, an astronomer recently stated that if you could count all the grains of sand on all the seashores in the world, you would have approximately the same number as there are stars in the heavens!

The finite human mind is boggled by it all! Is it any wonder David said, "When I consider Your heavens, the work of Your fingers, The moon and the stars, which You have ordained, What is man that You are mindful of him?" Psalm 8:3, 4.

Impressive as the innumerable suns and galaxies may be, the size of the universe in which we live is even more awesome. Aside from the sun, the star nearest Earth is Proxima Centauri—more than four light years away, or approximately twenty-four trillion miles from Earth. If we traveled in a rocket ship at the speed of 25,000 miles per hour, it would take us 120,000 years to reach our nearest star! Are you beginning to sense the immeasurable expanse of space?

No wonder the prophet Job said, "See the highest stars, how lofty they are!" Job 22:12.

It is difficult for the human mind to comprehend innumerable worlds, immeasurable space, and the intricate design evident everywhere in the universe. Yet even more astounding is the fact that this incredibly complex universe is as smooth-running as a delicate, finely tuned watch.

The apostle Paul, in revealing the power which keeps this amazing clock in motion, stated, "He is before all things, and in Him all things consist." Colossians 1:17.

Dr. Edwin Frost, director of Yerkes Observatory, wrote: "There is no evidence that the universe is automatic, or that it has within itself the power to make laws which govern it . . . Mere matter cannot be endowed with such capacity. The universe is not a haphazard aggregation of accidental bodies moving without system or order. It is the work of omnipotence."—*Wonder Worlds*, p. 13.

Whether we study tiny atoms or giant galaxies, we find the incredible design and order of a Master Intelligence, a Master Designer. Creation witnesses to a Creator!

The very first sentence in the Bible clearly pinpoints this Creator. "In the beginning God created the heavens and the earth." Genesis 1:1.

And just how did God do that? "By the word of the LORD the heavens were made. . . . For He spoke, and it was done; He commanded, and it stood fast." Psalm 33:6, 9.

God channeled some of His unlimited energy into matter. Jeremiah expounds on the process further: "He has made the earth by His power, He has established the world by His wisdom, And has stretched out the heavens at His discretion." Jeremiah 10:12.

◆ Is God too big to care?

The thought of God's creative power is overwhelming. With all our modern technology, with all our knowledge of computers and space frontiers and neuropsychology, we have never been able to create even one tiny spark of life in the laboratory! But do you ever feel so awed by God's tremendous power that you begin to wonder how

He could possibly look down on this earth and care about the insignificant human beings scattered out here on the edge of space?

The message of the Bible is that the God who created the endless intricacies of the world cares personally for each one of us. He has special time for each of us. Matthew 10:30 tells us that even the hairs of our heads are numbered!

Although damaged by the curse of sin and by man's careless pollution, the world still has breathtaking beauty. The Creator is a God of beauty. He believes in the holiness of beauty as well as in the beauty of holiness.

We catch a glimpse of our Creator's majesty at the most unexpected moments and places: In brilliant sunsets—each uniquely beautiful, crowning the last moments of day. In tiny snowflakes—each with its own intricate, geometric design. In the profusion of fragrant flowers—each delicately tinted, dotting the landscape. In scented pines and autumn maples. In winter's frost and in snowcapped peaks. In every opening bud and tiny seed, we see the prints of the Master's touch covering the whole world.

We can but echo David's praise, "The works of the LORD are great . . . His work is honorable and glorious." Psalm 111:2, 3.

God not only gave men and women a beautiful universe to live in, He is also mindful of all their other needs. "He makes His sun rise on the evil and on the good, and sends rain on the just and on the unjust." Matthew 5:45.

◆ Mastermind of the universe

Consider some of the ways God cares for His creatures.

Have you ever thought that the water you drink is older than the pyramids—as old as the hills? Water may be polluted by chemicals or wastes, but let the sun evaporate it or lift it into the atmosphere, and it becomes clean and usable again and again, distributed back to the earth by rain, dew, or snow. What a tremendous water system God designed!

And then there is God's great powerplant in the sky. If the sun were a little bigger, or a little closer to Earth, our oceans would boil away. If the sun were just a little smaller, or a little further away, our atmosphere would freeze. Either way, life could not exist on Earth. But, you see, God not only created all things, He sustains all things.

The air we breathe is a gift of God, an evidence of His care and love. In designing the atmosphere, God knew just the right mix of oxygen, nitrogen and other elements needed to sustain life and health on Earth. The Bible asks, "In whose hand is the life of every living thing, And the breath of all mankind?" Job 12:10. Clearly, the answer is God.

God did not create this beautiful world simply as a wandering showcase floating in the midst of the universe. He created it for beings who could appreciate and enjoy it! The Bible tells of a God "Who did not create it [the universe] in vain, Who formed it to be inhabited." Isaiah 45:18.

Wonders are anywhere we look in our natural world! There is no end to God's care for His creatures. Think of the migration of the birds—one of the greatest puzzles of nature. How can birds weighing less than an ounce navigate nonstop for thousands of miles to a destination they have never seen before? And then repeat the journey year after year!

How can fish find their natal streams 1,200 miles distant across oceans without highway markers? Who taught the honeybee—with a brain no larger than a pinhead—to make the honeycomb, an engineering marvel? Who is the Mastermind behind it all? "Ask the beasts, and they will teach you; And the birds of the air, and they will tell you; . . . And the fish of the sea will explain to you. . . That the hand of the LORD has done this." Job 12:7–9.

Yes, He did it all! In fact, our duty and privilege to worship God is based on the fact that He is our Creator—to Him all things owe their existence. He knows all our needs, and He has power to supply those needs! Birds, fish, and animals everywhere reproduce themselves under the most amazing circumstances, keeping their genetic stream alive, year after year, all because God cares for them and sustains them.

Doesn't that give you peace of mind, knowing that God is in full control of His universe? And we are part of that universe—in fact, from this Earth's standpoint, we are the most important part of His universe. No problem in our lives is too small to bring to the God of the fantastic atom or the delicate hummingbird; no problem is too large to bring to the God who upholds countless worlds in space and keeps them running "on time"!

But one of the most comforting characteristics of God is that He does not change. He is always the same! "I am the LORD, I do not change." Malachi 3:6. In this rapidly changing world, where people change, relationships crumble, things fall apart, one Person remains the same—God!

What peace and confidence we can have, knowing that nothing can happen in our lives that is too small or too hard for God to handle. And because He is all-wise and always dependable, He will do what is best for us, based on a love that is everlasting.

The theme of this unchanging love of God fills the pages of the Bible. "God is love." 1 John 4:8. "I have loved you with an everlasting love." Jeremiah 31:3. The Bible assures us that nothing in all the world can separate us from that love: "For I am convinced that neither death nor life, neither angels nor demons, neither the present nor the future, nor any powers, neither height nor depth, nor anything else in all creation, will be able to separate us from the love of God that is in Christ Jesus our Lord." Romans 8:38, NIV.

God loves us when we are lovable and when we are unlovable. He loves us whether we are black or white, male or female, flashy or simple. His love is unconditional.

◆ Like Son, like Father

And if any doubt lingers in our minds about His love, God explains it in such simple terms that we cannot help but understand: "Can a mother forget the baby at her breast and have no compassion on the child she has borne?" He asks. "Though she may forget, I will not forget you! See, I have engraved you on the palms of my hands." Isaiah 49:15, 16.

Words and messages are not enough to communicate the all-encompassing, never-failing love of God. Our Father knew that the only way we would ever fully understand His love would be through Jesus, the perfect revelation of the character of God. Jesus said, "Anyone who has seen me has seen the Father." John 14:9.

If we really want to know what God is like and how He feels about us, we need to study the life of Jesus. He took our nature that He might reach our needs. He preached the good news of salvation to the poor; He healed the brokenhearted and gave sight to the blind. He fed the hungry. He forgave their sins and gave them hope for the future. He spread life and joy through scores of villages and towns.

As we see Jesus washing the feet of the one who would betray Him, we see how God does not give up on any one of us—even though we may choose to betray Him: "For God so loved the world that he gave his one and only Son, that whoever believes in him shall not perish but have eternal life." John 3:16.

God gave His Son to a fallen race—to a planet in rebellion. Christ died in your place and in my place. He suffered the cruel lashing, the thorns pushed into His forehead, the nails driven through His hands and feet—without protest. He could have called ten thousand angels to set Himself free—but He could not save Himself and save others, too! This was the ultimate gift of a loving, caring God for guilty men and women. For you—for me.

As His bruised and bleeding body hung on the cross, He prayed, "Father, forgive them, for they do not know what they are doing." Luke 23:34.

That is what God is like! ❏

Indeed, if we see Jesus clearly, we have seen the Father. He came not only to ensure that we could survive the Great War, but to show us what God is really like. He met every devilish lie with absolute truth. Now, in the upcoming chapter, consider Jesus as your risen Saviour and as your great Healer.

3

The
Heart Specialist

Without this,
you'll never make it.

When things go badly, you need it desperately. It's what gets you through the night. If you don't have it, sooner or later you'll give up.

Hope.

After Satan stormed God's perfect Earth and laid it waste, it was as if the lights had gone out in the lives of men and women. A pall of sadness too deep for words settled over the world.

Satan turned Earth into an arena of frenzied hatred, unbounded cruelty, constant suffering, inexpressible sorrow, and all-pervasive death. Men and women were about out of hope.

Then came the promises. Knifing through the thick clouds of gloom, shafts of bright hope reached thousands of believing hearts, chasing away the despair. A Saviour was coming! Satan would not be allowed to make this world his unchallenged personal playground of destruction.

How is it with you today, friend? Are you discouraged? Is the daily battle of living sapping all your resources? Are you weary beyond words with the misery and corruption reported in each day's news? Are you exhausted with the struggle against your own selfishness?

You need hope.

You need the promises. You need to know that the long war between good and evil will not go on forever—that it's almost over. And you need to know that even now, Prince Michael the Saviour can lift you up and fill you with new hope, energy, and optimism.

If that is what you need, this chapter is for you.

3

. . . .

About a hundred years ago, two lawyers were crossing the state of Kansas by train. One was a Christian, the other an agnostic. Time seemed to drag; for the most part, they were wasting it in small talk.

The agnostic lawyer turned to his Christian friend and said, "Lew, we're wasting our time. Why don't we talk about the great themes? Is the Bible inspired? Is Christ divine?"

As the miles went by, the skeptic seemed to be winning the arguments. The Christian lawyer became increasingly embarrassed as he failed to give adequate answers to his friend.

The skeptic pressed his advantage: "Lew, why aren't you a Buddhist, or a Moslem, or a follower of Confucius? Aren't all religions good and equal? Aren't you a Christian simply because of a geographical accident—because you were born in a Christian country?"

The Christian was completely nonplussed by these direct questions.

The questions raised that day by skeptic Robert Ingersoll must be answered. They won't disappear simply by ignoring them. Nor can we hide our heads in the sand and pretend they do not exist. They demand intelligent, sensible answers. Thousands of young people today see little difference between Christianity and Eastern religions. They see little distinction between Jesus Christ, Buddha, and

Confucius. Many searching minds have turned to the Koran or the Bhagavad-Gita for their answers. Interest in Eastern religions has exploded in the United States in recent years.

How can a person be sure that Jesus Christ was all He claimed to be? Is there proof? There surely is—and wise is the individual who builds his faith on the clearly revealed facts of both Scripture and history.

◆ Death-defying confidence

Let's go back about nineteen hundred years to a Roman arena. Ten thousand people are on their feet cheering as Christians are thrown to the lions. The church was not welcome in the Roman world.

Stories of Christians burned at the stake or thrown to the lions are familiar to us today. These chose to die rather than renounce their faith in Christ. They believed that if they were loyal to Him, eternal life awaited them. Such was the faith of the martyrs. But why did they place such death-defying confidence in this particular Man?

Those early Christians saw in Christ the perfect fulfillment of the Messianic prophecies. They recognized Him as the One to whom all Old Testament prophecies pointed and, on the basis of fulfilled prophecy, accepted Him as the Son of God. Throughout the New Testament, the appeal of the early Christians was based on the same foundation as was Philip's faith: "Philip found Nathanael and said to him, "We have found Him of whom Moses in the law, and also the prophets, wrote—Jesus of Nazareth, the son of Joseph." John 1:45. Philip's appeal to Nathanael was essentially this: Jesus is the Messiah of prophecy. He is the One to whom the Old Testament Scriptures point.

Speaking of Apollo, the mighty preacher of Ephesus, Acts 18:28 says, "He vigorously refuted the Jews publicly, showing from the Scriptures that Jesus is the Christ."

Jesus Himself proved His claim to divinity on the basis of His fulfillment of Old Testament prophecy. After His resurrection, He met two discouraged disciples walking on the road to Emmaus. They did not believe He had risen from the dead.

To convince them would have been the simplest matter. Jesus could have drawn their attention to His wounds—the nail holes in His hands and His feet, as well as the spear wound in His side. But instead of doing that, He actually did the opposite. "Their eyes were restrained, so that they did not know Him." Luke 24:16.

Thinking He was a stranger, they confided to Him the cause of their distress; they told Him of their fond hope that Jesus was the Messiah and of how that tragic weekend had destroyed their dreams. It was then that Jesus addressed them as follows: "O foolish ones, and slow of heart to believe in all that the prophets have spoken! Ought not the Christ to have suffered these things and to enter into His glory?" And beginning at Moses and all the Prophets, He expounded to them in all the Scriptures the things concerning Himself." Luke 24:25-27.

Obviously, Jesus wanted to establish their faith, not only on something they had seen, but primarily upon the testimony of the Word of God. So instead of showing them the nail marks in His hands and feet, He reviewed the prophetic forecasts of the coming of the Messiah. He showed what the Old Testament prophets had foretold concerning His birth, His life, His ministry, and His resurrection. Thus, their faith was not based upon the evidence of their senses but upon the certainty of God's Word. They went out to proclaim the Christ of prophecy.

◆ On-target prophecies

Let us review the evidence that led those early disciples to accept Jesus as Lord and Christ. If a study of these prophecies led the early Christians to an all-conquering, death-defying faith, it can do the same for us. If it changed their lives, it can change ours! Thirty-seven remarkably precise prophecies of the birth, life, death, burial, resurrection, and ascension of Christ are in the Old Testament. Let's examine a few of these texts as we study the life of Christ written in advance!

Biographies usually begin with a man's birth. Let us then turn to the prophecy of Micah 5:2: "But you, Bethlehem Ephrathah, Though you are little among the thousands of Judah, Yet out of you shall come forth to Me The One to be Ruler in Israel, Whose goings forth are from of old, From everlasting."

This prophecy was written seven hundred years before the birth of Jesus. Out of the thousands of places in the world where He could have been born, the prophet pointed out the exact place—the little town of Bethlehem.

Most schoolchildren know that the holy family lived in Nazareth, ninety-two miles from Bethlehem. Though only a brief journey by car today, it must have been at least four days' journey in the time of Jesus. Up until a week before His birth, Nazareth would have been His likely birthplace. Yet a decree of Caesar took the family to Bethlehem, where Christ was born the very night of their arrival. Christ is the child of prophecy, born exactly where Micah predicted seven centuries earlier.

We turn now to another amazing prophecy. A biographer usually tells something about a person's parents. In Isaiah 7:14 we read : "Behold, the virgin shall conceive and bear a Son, and shall call His name Immanuel." Some liberal theologians attempt to reason away the virgin birth. Nevertheless, it is a basic Bible truth. The mother of Jesus herself denied that she had ever been with any man. Joseph, her intended husband, denied that the child was his and was preparing to have their engagement quietly annulled. At exactly the right moment, God sent an angel to Joseph and assured him that Christ had no earthly father, but indeed was begotten of the Holy Ghost.

If Jesus Christ had not been born of a virgin, I could not believe in Him. He would not be the Man spoken of by the prophets.

Our text says he was Immanuel—God with us. The apostle Paul put it this way: "And without controversy great is the mystery of godliness: God was manifested in the flesh." 1 Timothy 3:16. We cannot contest it. It is an indisputable fact, it is without controversy. God was manifest in the flesh. "For in Him dwells all the fullness of the Godhead bodily," Paul said in Colossians 2:9.

Speaking to Philip, Jesus Himself declared, "He who has seen Me has seen the Father." John 14:9. On another occasion He said: "I and My Father are one." John 10:30.

In a biography, a man's national background is always of interest. The Bible is not silent on the Lord's genealogy. The 49th chapter of Genesis describes a dramatic deathbed scene. Jacob, the old patriarch, is calling his twelve sons to his side to speak to them his last words and to pronounce on each a special blessing.

He speaks prophetically to Judah: "The scepter shall not depart from Judah, Nor a lawgiver from between his feet, Until Shiloh comes; And to Him shall be the obedience of the people." Genesis 49:10.

In Jewish literature, Shiloh is one of the names of the Messiah. If Jesus, the carpenter from Nazareth, were not a Jew of the tribe of Judah, those looking for the real Messiah would not have given Him a second look. But, true to the Bible's prediction, Jesus Christ of Nazareth traces His lineage back through David's line to Jacob. Indeed, He is "the Lion of the tribe of Judah" (see Revelation 5:5).

If the only information available were what we have just reviewed, we might still have questions. But some of the most fantastic prophecies are yet to come. Seven hundred years before Christ's birth, Isaiah pictured the nature of His ministry. Let's turn to Isaiah 61:1, 2: "The Spirit of the Lord GOD is upon Me, Because the LORD has anointed Me To preach good tidings to the poor; He has sent Me to heal the brokenhearted, To proclaim liberty to the captives, And the opening of the prison to those who are bound; To proclaim the acceptable year of the LORD."

The entire focus of His ministry was on the well-being of people. His entire life was spent ministering to the needs of men and women.

◆ Heart Specialist extraordinaire

In Sydney, Australia, a self-employed repair wizard developed a unique advertising sign to attract customers. It said simply, "Everything mended here." Then followed the subheading, "Except broken hearts."

But this craftsman's exception is our Lord's specialty. Over the centuries He has proven Himself to be a heart specialist without equal.

Someone wrote with special insight:

"When afflictions press the soul,
And the waves of trouble roll,
And you need a friend to help you,
He's the One."

During the last twenty-four hours of Jesus' life, many prophecies—some a thousand years old—met their fulfillment. Take, for instance, His betrayal. Can you not feel the pathos of David's forecast surrounding the treachery of Judas Iscariot—one of Christ's own disciples? Here's what Psalm 55:12-14 says: "For it is not an enemy who reproaches me; Then I could bear it. Nor is it one who hates me who has exalted himself against me; Then I could hide from him. But it was you, a man my equal, My companion and my acquaintance. We took sweet counsel together, And walked to the house of God in the throng."

Several centuries later, the prophet Zechariah took up the story. He predicted the actual price the betrayer would receive and what the money would be used for! Let's read Zechariah 11:12, 13: "Then I said to them, 'If it is agreeable to you, give me my wages; and if not, refrain.' So they weighed out for my wages thirty pieces of silver. And the LORD said to me, 'Throw it to the potter' . . . So I took the thirty pieces of silver and threw them into the house of the LORD for the potter."

Most everyone today knows the rest of the story. More than five hundred years later the bargain was sealed between Judas and the priests, not for twenty-nine or thirty-five pieces, but for exactly thirty pieces of silver.

♦ Blood money

The prophet said the betrayal money would be cast into the house of the Lord for the potter. Judas found, as all who sell their integrity must, that resources gained at the price of betraying Christ, or truth, or principle, are loss, not profit! Such money is too heavy to hold. It cannot salve a guilty conscience. So Judas made his way to the Temple, crying, "I have sinned! I have betrayed innocent blood!" In desperation, he offered to give the money back, hoping to secure the release of his Lord. But the priests had their victim and were not concerned with the conscience of Judas. The agitated traitor threw the money on the Temple floor and went out to commit suicide.

The priests, who had not hesitated to purchase the blood of an innocent man, professed scruples at putting the money Judas left behind into the treasury of the Lord. Since a field was needed in which destitute dead persons could be buried, they decided to use the thirty pieces of silver for this purpose. The land purchased was used for workshops by potters. How very remarkable that both aspects of the prophet's prediction regarding the use of the money should find such exact fulfillment. It was literally cast "into the house of the Lord for the potter."

"They pierced My hands and My feet," David said (Psalm 22:16). Often we find in the Bible that stoning was the Jewish method of capital punishment. Crucifixion was a Roman method of disposing of criminals. Roman soldiers nailed Jesus Christ to the cross of Calvary. His hands and feet were literally pierced, just as David had described.

Verse 18: "They divide My garments among them, And for My clothing they cast lots." Two processes are mentioned here. One, the dividing of His garments; and two, the casting of lots for His clothing. According to Roman custom, the meager belongings of the Lord would become the property of the men who crucified Him. They were busy distributing His clothes between them, when one soldier noticed the seamless robe. To divide it would be to destroy it. So the more practical suggestion was made that lots be cast. Without knowing it, the soldiers of Rome fulfilled Bible prophecy with an accuracy that establishes the identity of their victim as the Redeemer!

David continued: "He guards all his bones; Not one of them is broken." Psalm 34:20. This prophecy also found a dramatic fulfillment before Jesus was taken from the cross. Crucifixion was a slow death. When it became obvious, that Friday afternoon, that the three victims would not be dead before the coming of the Sabbath hours, the Jews insisted that the bodies should not be left on the crosses over the Sabbath day. To hasten death, the legs of both thieves were broken. When the soldiers saw that Jesus was already dead, they refrained from breaking His bones. By not breaking His legs, those Roman soldiers again fulfilled an ancient forecast, thus providing further proof of His Messiahship!

Among the millions of biographies we could read, the biography of Jesus is unique—unique in that it does not end with His death. The Bible predicted that Jesus would rise again. Speaking prophetically of Christ, David declared, "Nor will You allow Your Holy One to see corruption." Psalm 16:10. The prophetic biography of Christ does not stop with His death, because that was not the end. The grave could not hold Him. He burst the bonds of the tomb, and today He lives in heaven as our representative before the throne of God.

Confucius, Buddha, and Mohammed are dead! Thousands pay their respects at their tombs—but the tomb of Christ is empty!

This living Christ, the divine Son of God, desires to change your life. He dwelt in human flesh two thousand years ago as a living demonstration of what happens when divinity is combined with humanity. He desires to dwell in you now by His Spirit. He desires to reshape and remold the direction of your life by again uniting divinity with humanity.

◆ "What have you done to me, Preacher?"

A preacher visited a home in one of the suburbs of a large city. The lady of the house was courteous but firm: "I am not interested in the Bible or in Christianity—not at all," she said, "but if you care to call back some evening, you will find my husband very interested to learn more about it. I would really like you to return and meet him."

The preacher returned on a Saturday evening. Since it was not a working day, the woman's husband had followed his custom of spending the afternoon gambling with friends at a hotel. He was in a talkative mood, but well under the influence of that spirit that makes a man talk much more but say much less.

"I have a Bible," he said. "You must see my Bible. Mother put it in the case when I left home to marry. Where is my Bible, dear?" A long search for the Bible produced only a prayer book. He never did find the Bible.

But alcohol was only one of his problems. Gambling was equally destructive, and he was also a heavy smoker. These, plus other habits, had widened a gap between him and his wife. She had her bags packed, ready to leave home. They were planning to separate. Things were in poor shape.

But a strong desire for something better was in that man's heart. Even strong drink couldn't drown it. The preacher made an appointment to meet him again on Monday evening, and at that time, a series of weekly Bible studies began.

Week by week, as the topics from the Word of God were presented, the appeal of the cross began its work. Christ, by His Spirit, was moving into yet another needy home. Wonderful was that evening when the man said, "You must stay a little longer tonight. My wife will retire now. Can't you and I have a little chat together, man to man?"

Then, frankly, he unfolded to the preacher the sad story of a life that had started well. He had been born into an active Christian home, but had allowed the urges of youth to get out of control. Another prodigal had taken to the road, the ruts of which are deep and lead only to that far country. The church was soon forgotten, the Bible ignored. Christ was appealed to only in idle oaths.

"But what I want to know, preacher, is—what have you done to me? I haven't had a drink or made a bet for four weeks now. Nor have I sworn or used God's name in vain for that long." Then, as he pitched a half-smoked cigarette into the fireplace, he went on. "My cigarettes have become distasteful to me. I know I am about to quit. But there is a greater marvel than even all that. My wife has unpacked her bags. She did it three weeks ago now. This morning she followed me to the gate and, for the first time in years, kissed me goodbye. Yes, she did! I was shocked, preacher, and quite amazed when she smiled into my face and said, 'I like the new Jack.'

"Now, what has happened to me? I am sure it is connected with our Monday evening Bible studies."

The preacher said, "I have done nothing whatever personally, but I do believe that the Bible can explain it all." Then, turning to 2 Corinthians 5:17, he began to read: "Therefore, if anyone is in Christ, he is a new creation; old things have passed away; behold, all things have become new."

Slowly the "new Jack" read the text for himself. "A new creature—a new Jack! That's it! A new Jack! And if you really knew me, preacher, that's exactly what I am tonight."

Yes, friends, Jesus Christ is the divine Son of God, and only He has the power to change men and women.

Perhaps you too may be longing for something you do not have. Perhaps you see more clearly, after reading these pages, that Jesus Christ is the Son of God, that He is the Christ of prophecy, the One who was to come—your Redeemer.

Perhaps you long to turn around and make a new start. Jesus, through His Spirit, can change you as He changed Jack. Let the story of Jesus sink in. He was God, who became man. One of His primary reasons for coming to Earth was to tell the truth about God. When we respond to "the truth" with a willing mind and heart, the change is already taking place. You too can become a "new creature." ❏

Jesus—the Promise of the prophets, the Heart Specialist—could have stayed safely in Heaven when Satan invaded Earth. But the great enemy had taken the entire human race hostage. Jesus couldn't just sit idly by. He would go to the wall for us. He would hold back nothing. He would pay any price.

Coming up: The Highest Ransom Ever Paid.

4

The Highest
Ransom Ever Paid

If I were God . . .

. . . and I had poured my creative best into making men and women in my image, lavishing upon them every possible gift to maximize their happiness . . .

. . . and if after all that, they had chosen to believe the lies of my greatest enemy rather than the truth I had shared with them . . .

. . . and if as a result, they became subject to the inevitable consequences of rejecting me, chief among them, death . . .

. . . if this had happened and I were God, I think I might have just left them to take what they had coming—to write them off along with the whole planet I had created for them—and start over somewhere else.

This is what I might have done if I were God.

Thankfully, I am not. And neither are you.

The real God did not walk away. He did not write us off. But He faced an enormous crisis. He could not suspend the law of sowing and reaping. He could not repeal the law of cause and effect. The natural consequence of our sinful choice was death—nothing could change that.

But neither could God stand to let us vanish into oblivion. He could not bear to lose us.

So Love found a way.

On December 17, 1968, Barbara Mackle and her mother, traveling from Florida, decided to spend a quiet evening in a motel near Atlanta, Georgia. At eleven minutes after four in the morning, someone knocked loudly on the motel door. Awakened from a sound sleep, Barbara's mother went to the door.

Nervously, Barbara pleaded, "Mom, it's too early in the morning. Don't open the door for anybody." The man on the other side of the door said he was a policeman and that Barbara's boyfriend had been in a terrible car accident. He claimed that he needed to talk to Barbara immediately.

Barbara pleaded with her mother, "It's just a hoax, Mom. That's not really a policeman. Mom, please don't open the door!" But Barbara's mother yielded to the insistent pleading.

She opened the door and was immediately chloroformed. After she passed out on the motel room floor, the man and his accomplice, who proved to be a man dressed like a woman, seized Barbara and forced her into their car. They gagged her, tied her securely, and stuffed her into the trunk of the car.

Barbara, the twenty-year-old daughter of a Florida millionaire, was whisked to the Georgia hills. Then her kidnappers stepped off twenty paces from a certain tree and dug a hole.

Barbara was put into a pine box containing some food and water, a battery-operated fan to circulate the air so she wouldn't suffocate, and a battery-powered light to provide some warmth.

Barbara described the horrible experience in these words: "I was lowered into an open grave. As I listened to those shovelsful of dirt covering the box, no words can describe it. The first shovelsful were very loud; after awhile they became muffled. I was still talking, but then I tried to listen. I heard nothing. I thought they were gone. They've left me, I thought. I pushed as hard as I could against the top of the box. I was hysterical. I'd talk—and then I'd be silent, waiting for an answer. There was nothing—only silence."

Barbara's Mackle's father, Frank, was contacted by the kidnappers through a Catholic priest. He was told, "Your daughter is being held safe, but uncomfortable. The battery-powered light and fan will last about forty-eight hours. After that, the life-support oxygen system will be cut off. Barbara will suffocate and die. If you want to see your daughter again, we are demanding a half-million-dollar ransom—$500,000. None of the bills can have serial numbers later than 1950. They can have no more than twenty consecutive serial numbers. The money must be in denominations of tens and twenties. We have put a series of forty-four tests on the bills. If you fail to meet our requirements in any way, you will never see your daughter alive again.

"After you have met the requirements, put an ad in all the Miami newspapers stating, 'Lover, come home.' Take the money and bring it to a specified locker at the air terminal. Place the money in that locker. Don't try to have that locker watched or covered in any way. If you do, you will never see your daughter again."

Frank Mackle knew there was only one way he could see his daughter alive. He knew that his daughter was under a death sentence unless he paid the ransom. Not only was he able, but he was willing to pay the ransom. He withdrew $500,000 and followed the kidnappers' instructions.

First he placed the ad in the newspapers, then placed the money in the locker. The kidnappers were contacted by the priest, who acted as the intermediary.

Soon the phone rang in the home of J. Edgar Hoover, director of the FBI. He was told Barbara's exact location. Mr. Hoover wrote it down very carefully. The FBI sped to that remote farm and discovered the freshly dug grave. They began to dig furiously, wondering whether Barbara would be dead or alive after almost four days. As they lifted the lid off the box, Barbara jubilantly exclaimed, "You are the most beautiful men I have ever seen!"

Her father was contacted: "Barbara is safe. She is on her way home."

Imagine the reunion scene. It's not hard to visualize Mr. Mackle running down that palm-lined sidewalk as his daughter drove up. Bursting away from the FBI agents, she leaps into his arms. They embrace and weep. The ransom had made possible a reunion.

Do we need to wonder whether Barbara ever doubted her father's love after that? Did the $500,000 ransom cause her father to love her, or did it reveal how much he already loved her? The money merely reflected the intense love in the heart of Frank Mackle for his daughter, Barbara.

◆ More expensive than gold or silver

If you were kidnapped, would anybody put up $500,000 for you? Does anyone love you that much? Yes, someone does. A great theme of the Bible is the ransom theme. You cannot understand the golden thread that runs through all the Bible, without understanding the ransom theme.

"You were not redeemed with corruptible things, like silver or gold, from your aimless conduct received by tradition from your fathers, but with the precious blood of Christ, as of a lamb without blemish and without spot." 1 Peter 1:18, 19.

You were redeemed, my friend, not with $500,000, not with a million dollars, but with "the precious blood of Christ." Here is Someone who loves you very much—Someone who cares for you enough to pay your ransom, not in the coinage of gold, but in the coinage of blood. He has done this to enable you to live with Him through all eternity. Truly, a great theme of the Bible is the theme of ransom.

Why is it that the blood of Jesus was shed as a ransom? Why is it that the human race needed to be ransomed?

In Genesis, the first book of the Bible, a story begins of a world that had no taint of sin or disease, a world created without war, without hatred, without bloodshed or strife, a sinless world. Further, from the beginning, God placed within the hearts of men and women the desire to respond to His loving commands.

When God made men and women, He gave them a powerful gift—the ability to choose, to make up their own minds regarding their relationship with Him. He did not want puppets controlled by strings that He would manipulate from some universal control center. No, God didn't want mechanical beings who, every time He pulled a string, would open their mouths with words of praise and worship. He did not want programmed creatures who would worship Him at the pressing of a cosmic computer key.

◆ Robot love

I wonder, how many of you would like a robot child? Before you answer too quickly, listen carefully. How many of you would want a robot child like one of those store models that needs to be wound up every morning? After they are wound up, they behave as programmed: they stand straight and tall and brush their teeth three times a day. When you say, "Johnny, it's time for oatmeal," Johnny (with a little microchip in his brain) chimes, "Yes, Mother," and then marches over to the table. When Johnny sits down, you say, "Johnny, eat," and programmed Johnny immediately eats his oatmeal. Throughout the day, he always responds properly, because he can do no other. He is programmed only one way. With his lips, your most obedient child pecks you on the cheek before leaving for school.

Is that what you want—a programmed child? Or would you rather have a child who, although fussy at times, gets up in the morning, wipes the sleep out of his eyes, looks at you, and says, "Mom, Dad, I love you." Can anything replace the spontaneity of love that comes from the heart—a heart not programmed to say just the right words?

You see, God did not want to create beings who had no capacity to respond spontaneously to His love. He didn't want puppet creatures whose response of love was not thoughtful, sincere, and freely given. You wouldn't want that, and neither did God.

Nevertheless, if you give persons the capacity to choose, they may make wrong choices. But Love was willing to take the risk. In the end, it would be worth it.

As time went by, our first parents, Adam and Eve, listened to the voice of Lucifer, the one who came knocking on the door of Planet Earth. Just as Barbara Mackle's mother made a voluntary choice to let the kidnappers in, so our first parents made a voluntary choice to listen to the voice of the kidnapper rather than the voice of God.

God had told the first couple not to partake of the tree of knowledge of good and evil. If they did, death would follow. The Genesis story continues:

"Then the serpent said to the woman, 'You will not surely die. For God knows that in the day you eat of it your eyes will be opened, and you will be like God, knowing good and evil.' So when the woman saw that the tree was good for food, that it was pleasant to the eyes, and a tree desirable to make one wise, she took of its fruit and ate. She also gave to her husband with her, and he ate. Then the eyes of both of them were opened, and they knew that they were naked; and they sewed fig leaves together and made themselves coverings. And they heard the sound of the LORD God walking in the garden in the cool of the day, and Adam and his wife hid themselves from the presence of the LORD God among the trees of the garden." Genesis 3:4-8.

Why did Adam and his wife hide themselves? They hid because they were guilty. Suddenly, they had no peace. Prior to their disobedience, they were in harmony with God and filled with joy. The cause of their guilt, their restlessness, was their sin.

Further, when Adam and Eve sinned, they hid immediately. Along with their guilt, they were now separated from God. Sin separates man from his Creator.

In Isaiah 59, we learn what happens when sin separates men and women from God. Sin produces guilt within the human heart. Sin produces restlessness. Sin is the root of the guilt problem: "Behold, the LORD's hand is not shortened, That it cannot save; Nor His ear heavy, That it cannot hear. But your iniquities have separated you from your God; And your sins have hidden His face from you, So that He will not hear" (verses 1, 2).

Men and women were created for fellowship with God, to be in harmony with their Maker. When human beings sinned, they ran from God. They could no longer endure His holiness.

But there is more. "Our God is a consuming fire." Hebrews 12:29. The consequence of sin or rebellion against God is death. Paul said it clearly: "The wages of sin is death." Romans 6:23. Like Barbara Mackle in that dirt-covered box, unable to deliver herself, the human race needed a source of help from above.

In the Garden of Eden, two people whom God had created perfect and upright were now condemned to death. The tragic end of their choice was death. What was God to do? A crisis exploded upon the universe. How was this sin problem going to be dealt with? Was the human race to be blotted out like the swatting of a fly?

◆ Mercy finds a way

As God looked at Adam and Eve, He saw creatures that He loved and for whose companionship He longed. Although His justice knew that their sin would end in death, His mercy sought another possibility.

But what could God do? Could He change His law regarding sin? Could He say, "Well, I said the wages of sin is death. But I'm going to change my mind. I'll tell Adam and Eve that they can disobey my law and that they really won't die."

Would God say that? If He had changed His mind at that point, the whole universe would have become insecure, its future placed in jeopardy. God couldn't change His law, because it was not capricious in the first place. God's law was merely the reflection of reality. Justice wouldn't allow Him to be at cross-purposes with Himself—or all created beings would always be in doubt about His predictability and fairness. Still, mercy would not allow Him to destroy those whom His heart loved.

At this crisis moment, Jesus, the One who existed from eternity past and who will exist through eternity to come—the One who is God and equal with the Father, the One who is worshiped by the myriads of the angels—said, "My Father, I will go enter into the arena of human affairs. Yes, the human race has sinned, but I will live a perfect life in human flesh to make up for their imperfect lives. I will die the death that they deserve to die—and in doing so, we shall win back their loyalty."

Out of that decision came the world's ransom—paid in blood for you by a God who loves you.

The story is beautiful as well as awesome—almost too good to be true: God Himself entering into human flesh to live the life I should have lived, to die the death I should have died.

As Paul described it in Philippians: "Let this mind be in you which was also in Christ Jesus, who, being in the form of God, did not consider it robbery to be equal with God, but made Himself of no reputation, taking the form of a bondservant, and coming in the likeness of men. And being found in appearance as a man, He humbled Himself and became obedient to the point of death, even the death of the cross." Philippians 2:5-8.

Here we observe that remarkable cascade of love—God becoming man and dying the death we deserve. When we were condemned to death and deserving death, He left the adoration of angels and the splendor of heaven. Think of it—God Himself leaving the security and peace of heaven to become locked in human form forever!

Why? Because you are precious in His eyes, because He wanted to spend eternity with you. He saw you and me—not only Adam and Eve—when He made His decision to provide the ransom for us all.

The entire human race is afflicted with the cancer of sin. We have a terminal disease. We are condemned to death. Sin will destroy us, not only physically, but mentally and spiritually. This disease is incurable, except for one remedy: the ransom provided by Jesus.

Barbara Mackle did not work her way out of that dirt-covered box. Without a ransom, she was doomed. If a ransom was paid, it had to be paid by somebody other than herself.

We are all in that box without hope—unless a ransom is paid.

That's why the Bible story is such "good news." Someone called Jesus has provided the ransom, paid on Calvary with His own precious blood.

Paul has depicted our Lord's gift to us in several ways. "And you He made alive, who were dead in trespasses and sins. . . . even when we were dead in trespasses, [He] made us alive together with Christ (by grace you have been saved), and raised us up together." Ephesians 2:l, 5, 6.

No matter how deep the hole we're in, Jesus will find us. The cross of Christ will go down as far as any sinner has fallen in human misery. And that same Christ will lift us up to heights, even on this earth, that we could never have imagined. He lifts us from the guttermost to the uttermost, from the depths of despair to the delights of discipleship.

◆ A shattered vase

I think of Shirley, who believed her life was ruined. When I visited her, she said, "My life is kind of like a vase of flowers—beautiful at first, but now shattered into a thousand pieces." She woefully added, "The pieces can never be picked up. I have gone too far in sin."

She rehearsed her sad story. "My marriage was happy for a while," she said. "Then my husband began to spend more time with his friends. While he was out with the fellows, I began to look at another man."

She added, "I was supposed to be a Christian. I knew it was wrong to do what I was doing. But my life was filled with loneliness, and I yielded to my emotions. Soon I began to see the other man regularly. Then my marriage collapsed. For seventeen years I have been filled with guilt. I know I have sinned. It's too late to repair my first marriage—my husband is gone. In my second marriage, I'm happy, but I'm not happy. I'm filled with guilt, filled with remorse. I can't come to God. I have tried to go to church, but I am so filled with guilt and remorse and lack of peace that it makes me miserable. I've been told that Jesus died for me, that He paid the ransom for my sins on Calvary's cross, but I can't forgive myself."

More people than we realize feel as ruined as Shirley. They believe that if they shut their eyes in death, they will be eternally lost because of their sins. People all around us (perhaps even you, my friend) ask, "How can what Christ did on Calvary two thousand years ago affect my life today? How can the death of Christ on Calvary give me peace now? How can it give me freedom from guilt today? How can it give me assurance at this moment? How can I walk with my head up again, knowing that my sins are forgiven, knowing that my hand is in the hand of God, knowing that by His grace I can be saved in His kingdom?"

As Shirley and I talked, I said, "Shirley, I'd like to take you back to Old Testament times. If you lived back in Old Testament days, what would you have to do if you sinned?"

She caught the point right away: "If I lived in Old Testament times, I would probably have to bring a lamb." Encouraging her, I said, "That's right, you would have to bring a lamb. That lamb would have to be without spot and without blemish." Then I suggested, "Let's talk about that lamb for awhile. Shirley, if somebody sinned in Israel, that person brought his or her lamb into the outer court of the tabernacle. Now suppose a man back then had an argument with his wife. He became so angry with his wife that he actually struck her across the face. Later while working, he began to feel guilty. The Holy Spirit pricked his conscience. The man accepted the fact that he had sinned. He accepted the fact that he had sinned against both God and his wife. Therefore, as soon as he could, he brought a lamb to the tabernacle.

"Remember how when John the Baptist saw Jesus, he said, 'Behold! The Lamb of God who takes away the sin of the world!' John 1:29. Jesus was prefigured, or foreshadowed, by the lamb of the Old Testament. So when this man, who has argued with his wife, brings his lamb, he is accepting the fact that he is a sinner and that he cannot save himself. In fact, he knows that because he has broken the law of God, he is a lost man, eternally lost.

"But he senses that this lamb will die in his place. In reverential awe he leads the lamb into the court of the sanctuary, where he meets a priest. Beside the altar of sacrifice, the man places his hand on the head of the innocent lamb. Let's read Leviticus 1:3, 4: 'If his offering is a burnt sacrifice of the herd, let him offer a male without blemish; he shall offer it of his own free will at the door of the tabernacle of meeting before the LORD. Then he shall put his hand on the head of the burnt offering, and it will be accepted on his behalf to make atonement for him.'

"What would the death of that lamb do? It would make atonement for the sinner. This word means 'at-one-ment.' Before the sinner sacrificed the lamb, he was separated from God. When the lamb was killed, that once-guilty husband was made 'at one' with God.

"Did you notice what was said before the words, 'to make atonement for him'? It says that the lamb 'will be accepted on his behalf.' The lamb would take his place!

"Who deserves to die? Does the lamb deserve to die? What did the lamb do wrong? Did the lamb argue with the 'mama' lamb? No, the lamb didn't deserve to die. Who deserves to die? The man deserves to die. But who died? The lamb did.

"Shirley, what is this Old Testament scripture teaching us? When the sinner placed his hand on the head of the lamb, what happened?"

Then I leaned forward, looked Shirley in the eye, and asked, "Where was the sin before the man confessed it?"

"Oh, it was in the man," she replied.

"What did the man deserve?"

Sensing new hope, she responded, "Oh, the man deserved death."

"Where was the sin after the man confessed it?" I asked.

She said, "On the lamb."

"Well, if the lamb had it, who didn't have it?"

"The man."

Light flooded her face, and a new joy washed over her soul as she sensed that Jesus was her sin-Bearer. Shirley had listened carefully. This simple Bible story changed her life. Seventeen years of guilt vanished in thirty minutes! Shirley, for many years, had experienced a self-destroying guilt. But when she placed her hand over her Lamb, her Lord, the Bible story became real to her.

◆ Yes . . . If

So it is for us today. We are either bearing the guilt of our own sins or we've confessed those sins and Jesus is bearing the guilt. If you are living with a load of guilt, if you are filled with a lack of assurance, if restlessness fills your heart, let no more time go by. The Lamb is waiting!

Will you not kneel and confess your sin to Jesus? You will feel the burden lifted. You do not need to bear the burden of your sin. That is what the Lamb is for!

John said it very clearly: "If we confess our sins, He is faithful and just to forgive us our sins and to cleanse us from all unrighteousness." 1 John 1:9. "If . . ." "If we confess"!

Will He forgive you for your dishonesty? Will He forgive you for your anger? Will He forgive you for your adultery? Will He forgive you for your robbery? Yes, if! If you confess!

But in the process, that Old Testament Israelite knew that sin cost something. When he told his children why the lamb was not with the herd anymore, he realized all over again the cost of being forgiven. But even more than a lamb, sin cost the precious blood of Jesus Christ. The ransom for sin was very expensive.

Take a walk with me up Calvary's hill. Look at the crown of thorns pressing down on Christ's bleeding head. Behold His back, lacerated by the lead-weighted Roman whips. Watch as the Son of God, the One worshiped by a myriad of angels, is taunted and pushed through the crowd. Behold as some men spit in His face. Watch Him fall three times, drained of strength. Listen as He is mocked and ridiculed by cursing soldiers. Behold God hanging on Calvary's cross. Look at His outstretched arms, His taut muscles. Behold as the weight of His body hangs from the nails, opening even wider those nail holes in his flesh. See His body heaving in agony.

Why all this, you ask? "Christ was treated as we deserve, that we might be treated as He deserves. He was condemned for our sins, in which He had no share. . .He suffered the death which was ours, that we might receive the life which was His. 'With his stripes we are healed.'"—*The Desire of Ages*, p. 25.

As I see Jesus hanging there, I know He's there for me. It was my lying tongue, my anger, my bitterness, my jealousy, my pride, my wrath, that nailed Him there. He lived a perfectly sinless life, but He gives to me that perfect life. He clothes me with the robe of His righteousness. How does all that happen, you ask?

1. Accept the fact that you never can save yourself.

2 . Believe that Jesus hung on Calvary's cross for you.

3. Come and kneel before that cross and confess your sins to Him.

A well-known poem sums it up well:

> *They borrowed a bed to lay His head*
> *when Christ the Lord came down.*
> *They borrowed the ass on the mountain pass*
> *for Him to ride to town.*
> *But the crown that He wore and the cross that He bore*
> *were His own.*

Yes, the cross was His own.

As Jesus hung on Calvary's cross, He hung there alone. And His cry rang out to echo and reecho to the end of time: "My God, My God, why have You forsaken Me?" Matthew 27:46.

Jesus died the death of a sinner, because He received my guilt and yours. He tasted death for every man—a very lonely death, the death that I deserved.

◆ As He was on the cross, you were on His mind

Hanging there, He thought of you. It was as if He said, "Father, if death means that I'm going to go into the grave and never come out—if it means that Mark Finley, if it means Tony, if it means George or Alice or Mary—if it means that My precious ones will be in heaven with You forever, I am willing to go into the grave. I am willing to bear the penalty of sin. I am willing to bear the guilt of sin. I am willing to die."

Knowing this, we can better understand what Matthew meant: "Just as the Son of Man did not come to be served, but to serve, and to give His life a ransom for many." Matthew 20:28.

Barbara Mackle's father, in love, gave $500,000 for her. Jesus Christ, in love, poured out His life for you. Because of this gift, your sins may be forgiven. You can be saved, my friend. You can live forever.

Friend, behold the hands that were stretched out on Calvary for you. Behold the nails as they are driven in fury through those hands that opened the eyes of the blind, that unstopped the ears of the deaf, those hands that held somebody's child, those hands that brought the dead back to life. The divine hands of the Son of God were nailed on the cross for you. Every drop of blood that flowed from Calvary's cross flowed to cover your sins and opened the gates of heaven.

As I kneel at the cross, I know that Mark Finley can find the peace of forgiveness and the hope of eternal life because of Calvary. I'm free from guilt, but it breaks my hard heart. I kneel at the foot of the cross and say, "Lord, I cannot resist such love. I cannot resist such care, such concern. Lord, I give my life to you, fully and completely. I know that You have given me peace. I know that in You, by You, and through You, I have eternal life. Tonight, Lord, I give my life to You, again."

Will you kneel there with me? Will you whisper, "Lord, I realize that I cannot save myself. I believe Your word to me—that my guilt and my sin are nailed to Calvary's cross"? There is room at the cross for you and me. Enough room for everybody in the world, if only they will come! ❏

At the cross, Jesus proved a lot. He proved that God would hold back nothing to save us—including His own beloved Son. He proved that sin kills. He proved that Satan would sooner murder his own Maker than give up his quest for control of the universe.

The cross was the pivotal battle in the War Behind All Wars. But many other hard-fought battles had gone before, and many others were yet to come. In God's own special kind of history-in-advance called prophecy (up next), He helps us see the Big Picture.

5

A Man of
Mud and Metal

Back to the Future

and its sequel films did well at the box office. These time-travel fantasies had widespread appeal.

But not all time travel is fantasy. Some of it is altogether real. Consider the night an ancient king was transported more than 2,500 years into the future, where he visited not only our own time but the years yet ahead of us.

Previewing the future is the special province of Bible prophecy. And what makes this form of time travel so fascinating is that the future it brings to view is 100 percent accurate. Why? Because it's revealed by the one Person in the universe who knows exactly what the future holds.

No laughable wild guesses of some tabloid psychic or New Age channeler here. Bible prophecy has never missed.

As long as we're all caught up in this long war, it's helpful to know not only what has already happened, but what is yet to come. And it's especially encouraging to know how the war will end—and when.

So come, join an amnesiac king in traveling back to the future.

5

● ●

In an article entitled "Warning: This Planet May Be Harmful to Your Health," Sandra Doran contrasts the cruel realities of life on this planet with the promise of a better land to come. Discussing the environmental hazards of the nineties, she says:

> "The pure joy of plucking a sun-warmed fruit from the plant and popping it into my mouth has been marred by the knowledge of pesticides. . . . I cannot draw a drink of water from the tap anymore without fearing contaminants, lead pipes, and brain disease in children.

> "Being out in the sun too long brings to mind the tear in the ozone layer, and harmful rays. And I arrived at the beach the other day to find a sign straight out of a futuristic novel: 'Seaside Park Closed Due to Unhealthful Swimming Conditions.'"

If our rapid exploitation of this earth is any indication of the future, the prospect is bleak at best. Added to environmental deterioration in the nineties are weighty problems that overwhelm governments. Economic recession and instability in Europe, Russia, Australia, the United States, and South America. Thousands dying daily of starvation in India and Africa. Explosive relations in the Middle East. Is there any hope for the future?

Yes, many reasons for hope! As God draws back the curtain of time, we are able to look through the window of Bible prophecy and see clearly what will take place tomorrow. We are promised, "Surely the Lord GOD does nothing, Unless He reveals His secret to His servants the prophets." Amos 3:7.

◆ Fakers in the palace

God revealed history in advance through a dream to an ancient king who lived in the city of Babylon in 606 B.C. Recorded in the Old Testament book of Daniel, this remarkable dream outlined world history for over 2,500 years. As Daniel tells the story, this dream troubled Nebuchadnezzar because, upon awakening, he could not recall its details. Calling before him his magicians, astrologers, and Chaldeans, the king demanded a recounting of the dream, along with an explanation of the symbolism involved. (After all, that was their business.)

The wise men were anxious to comply with the second half of the request, but were unable to reconstruct the dream. Desperately they stalled for time; however, their hesitancy soon indicated to the king that these men were frauds. Hot with anger, the king commanded: "Execute them! Execute all the 'wise men' of Babylon."

Daniel and his three friends (three Hebrew captives) were listed among the wise men of Babylon and were also subject to the king's death decree.

"So Daniel went in and asked the king to give him time, that he might tell the king the interpretation." Daniel 2:16.

The king agreed, and Daniel returned home to urge his three friends to pray with him that God might reveal the dream to them. God did not fail to honor those earnest prayers.

During the night the mystery was revealed to Daniel, and the next morning Arioch took Daniel to the king. As the king looked intently at young Daniel, he asked if the young man could reveal his dream. A true man of God, giving God the credit, Daniel replied, "The secret which the king has demanded, the wise men, the astrologers, the magicians, and the soothsayers cannot declare to the king. But there is a God in heaven who reveals secrets, and He has made known to King Nebuchadnezzar what will be in the latter days." Daniel 2:27, 28.

Daniel proceeded to relate in detail this most curious dream. Speaking as a prophet of God, he described a great image—a giant statue of a man—comprised of various metals: its head made of fine gold, its breast and arms of silver, its belly and thighs of brass, its legs of iron, and its feet part of iron and part of clay, or mud.

Daniel continued, describing a stone "cut out without hands" (see Daniel 2:34, 45) which struck the image, breaking its feet to pieces, and then becoming a great mountain, filling the whole earth.

In just 150 words, God sketched the next 2,500 years of human history in this dream—from Babylon's day to the end of the world as we know it. Breathlessly, the king waited for the interpretation. What could it all mean?

◆ Golden head of the statue

Daniel began, "You are this head of gold." Daniel 2:38.

Babylon the head! Babylon, a nation of pure gold! A smile of satisfaction crossed the king's face. What a pleasing confirmation for all his hard work!

Babylon's proud monarch apparently gave no thought to the possibility of his kingdom ever being superseded by another. In fact, clay tablets of Nebuchadnezzer's reign recovered by archaeologists are inscribed with these words: "These portals for the astonishment of multitudes of people with beauty I adorned. May it last forever."

Historians confirm that gold was a fitting symbol to represent the Babylonian kingdom, as this precious metal was used liberally in embellishing its architecture. As one historian described fabulous Babylon: "There, with the whole earth prostrate at her feet, a queen in peerless grandeur . . . sat this city, fit capital of that kingdom which constituted the golden head of this great historic image."—Uriah Smith, *Daniel and the Revelation,* p. 49.

But as dazzling and impressive as this great city was, it would be only one of many world kingdoms to come. Courageously, Daniel continued his interpretation of the dream: "But after you shall arise another kingdom inferior to yours." Daniel 2:39.

Daniel lived to see it happen—the silver kingdom replacing the gold. On October 13, 539 B.C., the golden kingdom of Babylon came to an inglorious end. During the reign of Belshazzar, Nebuchadnezzar's proud and arrogant grandson, Cyrus the Mede laid siege to Babylon. Feeling recklessly secure in his capital and foolishly ignoring this aggression, King Belshazzar arranged a great feast for a thousand of his nobles. To show his defiance of the God of the Hebrews, he commanded that the golden vessels taken by his grandfather, Nebuchadnezzar, from the temple in Jerusalem be brought to his table.

"Then they brought the gold vessels that had been taken from the temple of the house of God which had been in Jerusalem; and the king and his lords, his wives, and his concubines drank from them. They drank wine, and praised the gods of gold and silver, bronze and iron, wood and stone." Daniel 5:3, 4.

◆ Mystery message of the bloodless hand

In the midst of this revelry, a bloodless hand began to paint fiery letters across the plastered wall of the banquet hall—the forecast of Babylon's impending doom. Terrified, the people ceased their festivities. The Bible says the king was so frightened that his knees knocked and his legs failed him.

Like his grandfather, Belshazzer summoned the enchanters, astrologers, and diviners to tell him the meaning of the mysterious message. Despite the promise of rewards, no one could read those fateful words. Finally, the queen mother appeared in the banquet hall and reminded Belshazzar of Daniel, who decades before had revealed the meaning of Nebuchadnezzar's dream.

Again, the Hebrew prophet was summoned. And again he was offered wealth and position. The aged Daniel quickly told the king to keep his gifts, for he would do his duty gladly—he would read the writing and tell the interpretation.

Still trembling with fear, the king waited for Daniel's interpretation: "MENE, MENE, TEKEL, UPHARSIN. This is the interpretation of each word. MENE: God has numbered your kingdom, and finished it; TEKEL: You have been weighed in the balances, and found wanting; PERES: Your kingdom has been divided, and given to the Medes and Persians." Daniel 5:25-28.

As Daniel's solemn words ended, a messenger came with the news that the city had been invaded. The Medes and Persians, after diverting the Euphrates River which ran through the city, marched down the river bed into the city, even to discover the massive river gates to be unlocked! The triumphant shouts of the army of Cyrus could be heard above the terrified cries of the revelers.

Through the Prophet Isaiah, God had described the strategy by which the city was to be taken, even naming the general who would accomplish it, 150 years before that general was born: "Thus says the LORD to His anointed, To Cyrus, whose right hand I have held— To subdue nations before him And loose the armor of kings, To open before him the double doors, So that the gates will not be shut." Isaiah 45:1.

So a new superpower rules the then-known world. But like the golden kingdom, Babylon, that went before it, the reign of Medo-Persia, the silver empire, would not last forever. Daniel's interpretation of Nebuchadnezzar's dream went on. "Then [shall arise] another, a third kingdom of bronze, which shall rule over all the earth." Daniel 2:39.

The brilliant young Greek general, Alexander the Great, defeated Persia's Darius III at the battle of Arbela, 331 B.C. At 23, young Alexander became ruler over the most extensive empire the world had known at that time.

The historian Arian said, "I am persuaded there was no nation, city nor people . . . where his name did not reach . . . There seems to have been some divine hand presiding over his work and action."— *Historical Library,* bk. 16, ch. 12.

Much of the armor worn by the Greek infantry was made of brass. The historian Herodotus described Greek pirates as "men of bronze coming from the sea." But this empire, too, was to come to an end. "On June 22, 168 B.C., at the battle of Pydna, perished the empire of Alexander the Great, 144 years after his death." Theodor Mounsen's *History of Rome,* book 3, chapter 10.

The fourth world empire was represented by the legs of iron. Daniel explained, "And the fourth kingdom shall be as strong as iron, inasmuch as iron breaks in pieces and shatters everything; and like iron that crushes, that kingdom will break in pieces and crush all the others." Daniel 2:40.

What great empire overthrew Greece? What nation ruled during the life of Christ? No one disputes the fact that the Roman Empire succeeded the Greeks, thus becoming the fourth world empire, ruling from 168 B.C. to A.D. 476.

Rome was a ruthless nation, ruling with a "rod of iron." Her Caesars called themselves gods and demanded worship and obedience from all men. Rome ruled the longest and reached the farthest of all ancient empires.

But she, too, met her end, but not at the hands of a more powerful kingdom. Surprisingly, no world empire succeeded Rome—just as predicted by Daniel. What did Nebuchadnezzar's dream predict as to what would happen when the Roman empire lost its power? "Whereas you saw the feet and toes, partly of potter's clay and partly of iron, the kingdom shall be divided." Daniel 2:41.

God accurately predicted that ancient Rome would not be followed by another world empire, but that it would disintegrate after six hundred years into smaller kingdoms. Through unparalleled luxury, political corruption, and moral decay, Rome lost its stability and strength, becoming easy prey for tribes of barbarians that began to invade the empire during the fourth century A.D.

By A.D. 476, Rome had been divided into ten segments, listed here with their modern counterparts: Alemanni (Germans), Franks (French), Saxons (English), Visigoths (Spanish), Burgundians (Swiss), Lombards (Italians), Suevi (Portuguese); and the Heruli, Vandals, and Ostrogoths (now extinct.)

The modern nations of Europe developed from these tribes of the divided Roman Empire. Some were strong, some weak.

But there is more to Nebuchadnezzar's dream and its interpretation. As far as we are concerned, the best part of Daniel's interpretation is to understand what happens to those European kingdoms as we get nearer to the end of time: "As you saw iron mixed with ceramic clay, they will mingle with the seed of men; but they will not adhere to one another, just as iron does not mix with clay." Daniel 2:43.

◆ Why no nation will ever rule Europe

Many world rulers have tried to weld the nations of Europe together by royal marriages, mingling themselves "with the seed of men." By the first decade of the twentieth century, virtually every crowned head of Europe was related, but that didn't prevent World War I!

God's prediction of world empires to the end of time has been remarkably accurate. No plan, however grand, to unite the nations into one great empire can ever succeed. Why? God has declared, "They will not adhere to one another." Daniel 2:43.

Charlemagne tried and failed. Charles V and Louis XIV tried and failed. Not even the great Napoleon Bonaparte could cement together the broken parts of the Roman Empire.

At the age of 29, Napoleon overthrew the government of France and set out to conquer the world for France. It seemed that nothing could stop him. At the height of his power, Napoleon decided to defeat Russia. But courageous Russian solders and their fabled winter cold crushed the French army and Napoleon's dreams. We are told that Napoleon left half his army frozen on Russian battlefields.

Napoleon's final defeat at Waterloo came on June 18, 1815, when unusually heavy rain bogged down his artillery in the mud. In a state of despair, Napoleon is reported to have said, "God Almighty has been too much for me."

Yes, God's prophecy stood fast!

Later, Kaiser Wilhelm of Germany in 1914, and then Hitler, in the 1930s and '40s, tried to marshal the world under one flag, but both ended in defeat. A fitting epitaph for all these would-be rulers is, "They will not adhere to one another."

Never again will one nation rule over Europe. The feet partly of iron and partly of clay spell out the ruin of any world leader or nation that shall try to unite these European kingdoms.

But Daniel continues. With obvious joy and confidence, this aged prophet came to the astounding climax of this dream-prophecy: "And in the days of these kings the God of heaven will set up a kingdom which shall never be destroyed; and the kingdom shall not be left to other people." Daniel 2:44.

In the days of the kings represented by the ten toes—the nations of Europe today—God will set up a kingdom to end all earthly kingdoms, one that will last forever.

The next great event in Daniel's forecast is yet future. We may be part of the climax to this remarkably accurate prophecy. The only event yet to take place is the second coming of Jesus Christ and the establishment of His kingdom. The world kingdom, never to be destroyed, is represented by the stone "cut out without hands"—a kingdom founded not by the hands of men but by the mighty hand of God.

When Daniel concluded his interpretation of this sensational vision, King Nebuchadnezzar slowly rose from his throne and humbly prostrated himself before Daniel in honor of Daniel's great God, whose wisdom and power had been so impressively demonstrated. He acknowledged, "Truly your God is the God of gods, the Lord of kings, and a revealer of secrets." Daniel 2:47.

Through this giant metal image seen by Nebuchadnezzar in his dream six centuries before the birth of Christ, God unveiled the course of history to the end of time. The kingdoms represented by the gold, the silver, the brass, and the iron have all passed into history. Where are we living today? What will the next great glorious drama be? Christ and His coming—and eternity! ❑

Everything in Nebuchadnezzar's prophetic dream has already come to pass—exactly on schedule.

Everything, that is, except for the final event in the prophecy— the onrushing stone "cut out without hands" that smashes into the great statue's feet, ushering in the "kingdom which shall never be destroyed."

This spectacular final event is the return of Christ to Planet Earth to end the Great War once and for all. Coming up in Chapter 6—the signs that tell us that Christ's return is imminent.

6

Snoozing Through the Sirens

Now arriving from
somewhere beyond Orion . . .

If in fact the whole universe is caught up in mortal combat between good and evil, which side would you say is winning?

If there's any truth to the daily news, it doesn't look good for the forces of truth and right:

- *Violence grows ever more shocking and sickening.*

- *Morality and decency are buried beneath an avalanche of crudity, obscenity, and cultural toxic waste.*

- *The horror of spouse and child abuse has become common-place.*

- *The self-serving moral bankruptcy of public leaders is matched only by the profound cynicism of their constituents.*

- *Ethnic and religious wars turn much of the planet into zones of unimaginable cruelty, suffering, and death.*

Is evil winning? Is selfishness too strong for love to overcome?

Despite the very real and obvious misery of our dying world, God wants us to know that the Great War is about to end. The universe has seen enough of what Satan would do if he were in control.

The King is about to return and reclaim a hijacked Earth. And here in this chapter are the signs that will tell us His arrival is near.

● ●

The flight of Apollo 12 was normal—normal, that is, for thirty-six seconds. Then it happened! Lightning struck the spacecraft, and warning lights on the control panel flashed all across the instrument board.

Astronaut Dick Gordon later commented on the experience. "If they would have given us something like that in the simulator—the ground model—we would have said it was an impossible situation. Curing a problem of this magnitude seemed impossible."

In space, nothing could be done—for the moment, at least. Once Apollo 12 was in orbit, Dick crawled into the equipment bay, trying to realign the disrupted guidance system. As his eyes finally adjusted to the darkness, he sighted Rigel in the constellation of Orion, and the Dog Star, Sirius. With these two fixed points, he realigned Apollo 12's guidance system, and the astronauts were back on course.

How like the Apollo 12 capsule is Planet Earth—a spacecraft carrying over five-and-a-half billion passengers, hurtling through space at some 65,000 miles per hour, with every warning light on Planet Earth's instrument panel flashing!

We, too, have come to that frightening moment when, everywhere we look, warning lights are flashing reasons for concern. Deep within the hearts of men and women these questions echo across all continents: Have we come to the end of civilization? Is this the last generation to live on Planet Earth? How will it all end? Do we just have to sit and wait for the inevitable? Or is there reason to hope?

One day as Jesus left Jerusalem's magnificent temple, He paused to look at the gold-decorated monument to the highest of Jewish aspirations. Then He said what seemed to be unbelievable: "These things which you see—the days will come in which not one stone shall be left upon another that shall not be thrown down." Luke 21:6.

Later, as He sat upon the Mount of Olives, the disciples came unto Him privately saying, "Tell us, when will these things be?" Matthew 24:3. When will Jerusalem be destroyed, they wanted to know—when will the Temple be overthrown? Thinking that the destruction of this awesome Temple could come only at the end of the world, they asked the next question: What will be the sign of Your coming and of the end of the world?

Down through the ages, the disciples' questions have never lost relevance. Scientists, religionists, atheists, Christians, the old and the young, the educated and the simple, all want to know—how can we know when the end is near?

Christ's response to the disciples in Matthew 24 contains His answer to similar questions that have been raised from New Testament times to the present. Our Lord's description of world events just before the end, His warning lights that flash on the instrument panel of this world, indicate that the end of time has come.

◆ Cults and charlatans

The signs that Jesus Himself gave begin in the fifth verse of the chapter. "For many will come in My name, saying, 'I am the Christ,' and will deceive many." Matthew 24:5. The verse refers to confusion in the religious world—to pretense, sham, hypocrisy, and impersonation. These false Christs are to be no simple charlatans, for the Scripture says they "will deceive many."

The last days will be characterized by voices coming from varying directions, from diverse corners of the religious world, saying, "This is the way," "Follow me," "I am a voice from heaven." Many people will claim divine light, prophetic powers, and equality with the Son of God. Men and women will perform astounding feats and great wonders appealing to the eye, "to deceive, if possible, even the elect." Matthew 24:24.

The deceptions will be so overwhelming that even God's people, unless their minds are fortified with the Scriptures, will be misled.

Cult groups have grown explosively in the United States within the last twenty-five years. Scientology, the Unification Church, and various Eastern religions have captured the attention of thousands. In survey results first released by *USA Today* (November 18, 1993), some 20,000 in a sample group of 113,000 claimed they accepted the theories of the New Age movement. Cult leaders such as Jim Jones and David Koresh have led their unsuspecting followers to horrible deaths. Whether it be the New Age movement admonishing its followers to develop the god within them or cult leaders claiming they are divine, the end result is the same deception. This crescendo of interest in alternative religions and proliferation of religious leaders claiming to be divine reflects the accuracy of our Lord's predictions.

The last days, Jesus went on to explain, would also be characterized by political conflicts. "And you will hear of wars and rumors of wars. See that you are not troubled; for all these things must come to pass, but the end is not yet. For nation will rise against nation, and kingdom against kingdom. And there will be famines, pestilences, and earthquakes in various places." Matthew 24:6, 7.

Jesus looked into the future from His day and foresaw the crisis of our generation. Since 1970 over forty wars and conflicts have exploded in various parts of our world. Annually, the nations of earth spend billions on armaments and defense.

In homes across the world, people lie wide-eyed upon their beds at night, wondering how to pay their bills, fearful of drive-by shootings, in dread over AIDS and needed blood transfusions—the list seems without end. As the Bible predicted, "Men's hearts [are] failing them from fear and the expectation of those things which are coming on the earth." Luke 21:26.

Think of Yugoslavia, Somalia, Armenia, the Middle East, Rwanda,

Nigeria, the former Soviet Union! Regional conflicts have flared up like California brush fires fanned by Santa Ana winds. Ethnic strife is commonplace. Civil war is prevalent in an ever-growing number of countries. The buzz word among career diplomats describing today's world is "destabilization." The changing political map in Europe, Africa, and the Middle East has created a power vacuum.

The restless, strained relations between nations indicate that Christ, indeed, accurately foretold our day. "And you will hear of wars and rumors of wars. See that you are not troubled; for all these things must come to pass, but the end is not yet." Matthew 24:6.

While the history of mankind does reveal that wars have taken place all through time, think of two significant points: First, isolated wars do not constitute any particular sign of the end of the world. But today, war is so commonplace and so widespread that we often take it for granted.

◆ A spinning globe of ash

In the book of Revelation, speaking through the prophet John, Jesus said that He would return to "destroy those who destroy the earth." Revelation 11:18. Never before in the history of mankind has the human race had the power and capability to destroy life on this planet. Orson Welles put it this way: "With thermonuclear bombs, we can make a bonfire of our earth. We can empty our cities and scrape the crust off our planet and blast our habitation into a spinning globe of ash."

Our second point: The Bible predicts that Jesus will come at a time when the human race has the capacity to destroy itself. When atomic scientist Charles Urey witnessed the first atomic explosion in 1945, he tearfully muttered, "I am standing on the place where the end of the world began." We have even invented catastrophic weapons which have not been used. Today's nuclear weapons make yesterday's atomic bombs look like child's toys. One missile launched from one nuclear sub has the capacity to wipe out the majority of cities the size of Washington D.C., Boston, Charlotte, Wichita, or Sacramento.

The breakup of the former Soviet Union has left large nuclear stockpiles without adequate protection and supervision. Clear evidence exists that nuclear weapons are disappearing from Soviet stockpiles. Some intelligence experts predict that some of these will be sold to countries like Iran. The nuclear monster has ascended from the confines of its nuclear prison. It is estimated that close to twenty nations now have the capacity to build nuclear weapons. It's only a matter of time before some madman, oppressive dictator, or fanatical leader uses nuclear blackmail to press his demands. Or imagine an even worse scenario! Nuclear weapons in the hands of demented terrorists!

Surely Jesus must come to deliver us from a nuclear nightmare. We exist in a unique moment in history. In 1 Thessalonians we are told that "When they say, 'Peace and safety!' then sudden destruction comes upon them . . . And they shall not escape." 1 Thessalonians 5:3.

We marveled as Israel's Yitzhak Shamir and the PLO's Yassir Arafat shook hands on the White House lawn in the presence of three living American presidents. Yet implementing the Palestinian peace accord is still more difficult than a handshake. Palestinians and Israelis still kill one another. Whether it is Northern Ireland, Bosnia-Herzegovina, Palestine, Somalia, Rwanda, or a number of other hotspots that make us hold our breath, talks for peace are often followed with more bloodshed and more violence.

All man's plans are transitory. While the ink is still wet on peace documents, factions plan their next move. One United Nations diplomat described man's vain attempt to establish world peace in these words, "We have tried so hard, but we failed so miserably."

A third sign of the end mentioned by Jesus in Matthew 24 relates to the calamities and disasters so prevalent in modern society: "And there will be famines, pestilences, and earthquakes in various places." Matthew 24:7.

Chaos and disasters vie for the headlines of today's papers. Famine on several continents never leaves our front pages. Bangladesh, a country the size of Florida, is home to nearly one hundred million people. In India, seven hundred million exist, two-thirds of them malnourished. In the sub-Sahara region of Africa, between 70 percent and 90 percent of the cattle have died. Some experts have estimated that thousands have starved to death in a continuation of a drought that began a few years ago. The world refugee problem is mounting. Millions are homeless. Some experts estimate millions of deaths due to starvation in Africa in the coming decade. And signs of emotional and giving fatigue on the part of "well-fed" nations are becoming obvious!

But those "well-fed" nations have not escaped the dire predictions of Matthew. Today scourges afflict humans, animals, and crops, seriously affecting the food chain, necessitating chemical-laden sprays and insecticides. A farmer was recently asked, "How many times do you spray your apples?" His response? "Twelve to fifteen times to produce one crop. Pests are so bad the apples would be inedible, otherwise." Insects are developing immunities to deadly pesticide poisons.

Scourges today affect not only the plants in our world, but the human population as well. Cancer, with approximately one hundred different strains, is spreading like an epidemic, destroying babies as well as the aged, cutting down bodies that appear to be strong and invincible. Added to this modern-day leprosy are new diseases, leading off with AIDS, which affects the innocent as well as the perpetrators of their own disease. Society mourns the loss of hundreds of thousands with diseases unknown only a few years ago.

The dooming words of Matthew 24 continue: "And there will be . . . earthquakes" (verse 7). Earthquakes have increased dramatically over the last fifty years. Today more than three thousand major earthquakes are recorded annually. Earthquakes are up a remarkable 2,000 percent in the last quarter century. Whereas in the nineteenth century there were only 2,119 recorded earthquakes during that 100 years, 21,476 were recorded in 1993 alone. According to the National Earthquake Information Center, an average of thirty-five earthquakes occur daily around the world. The Earth's crust has destabilized since the time of the Flood. The Bible says that our world is waxing old! Continental plates are shifting; geologic faults are moving. Imperceptibly, forces are at work under the ground—forces that culminate in tragedy, ruin, and disaster.

Nature is convulsing under the heavy load of sin, as well as under so-called natural disasters. The problems of air and water pollution are staggering. The problem of refuse disposal directly affects our quality of life, never mind the budgets of cities, states, and the nation. The carelessness of one nation soon affects the air and water of another. We live on a fragile planet called Earth.

All the warning lights in the physical world tell us that this is the last generation. Early warning systems indicate that the end is near. The good news is that Jesus will step in before the world destroys itself.

Jesus' description of the last days goes on. "But as the days of Noah were, so also will the coming of the Son of Man be. For as in the days before the flood, they were eating and drinking, marrying and giving in marriage, until the day that Noah entered the ark, and did not know until the flood came and took them all away, so also will the coming of the Son of Man be." Matthew 24:37-39.

"Marrying and giving in marriage . . ." And, we might add, divorcing as well! Notice the following increase in divorce rates in the United States over just the past four decades, as reported by the National Center for Health Statistics:

1950	385,000 divorces
1960	393,000 divorces
1970	708,000 divorces
1980	1,189,000 divorces
1990	1,175,000 divorces

They "did not know." How could they not have known? Noah had been preaching the end of the world for 120 years. His monumental boat—the only one of its kind in the world—was an ever-present reminder of the reality to come.

Yet this description of the people of Noah's generation reveals their unconcern, their apathy. Tuning in only long enough to reject the warning, they sealed their own fate in streams of wine and hollow laughter. Men and women have not changed with the passing of centuries. We still lose ourselves in the thousand distractions of our day. We still hear, but only faintly, the insistent calls of God. And while false christs and false prophets arise all around us, while war and rumors of wars rumble, while earthquakes, scourges, and famines destroy, we fail to discern the signs of the return of Jesus. We are as tuned out as was Noah's generation.

◆ Sleeping through the warnings

A man living in New York City once remarked that he became so accustomed to the fire engines wailing and the ambulance sirens that he could sleep through any disturbance, even those directly beneath his bedroom windows. Have we come to that place? Have we allowed ourselves, in the midst of these warnings, to become so immune to their message that we have fallen asleep?

Let's listen carefully: Jesus said that world conditions at the end of time would resemble those of Noah's day. Looking back at what took place then, we see a far from pleasant picture. "Then the LORD saw that the wickedness of man was great in the earth, and that every intent of the thoughts of his heart was only evil continually." Genesis 6:5.

Noah's days were marked by violence, crime, and lawlessness, much like the corruption that characterizes our own age. Speaking of the moral conditions that prevail when God is ignored, Paul said, "For even their women exchanged the natural use for what is against nature. Likewise also the men, leaving the natural use of the woman, burned in their lust for one another, men with men committing what is shameful." Romans 1:26, 27.

Time is running out! The sins that called for the destruction of the antediluvian world exist today. As Billy Graham was writing his book *World Aflame*, it is reported that he gave the first chapter to his wife, Ruth. After reading it, she handed it back and said, "Billy, if Christ doesn't come soon, He is going to have to resurrect Sodom and Gomorrah and apologize to them."

In addition to world conditions as described in Matthew, Jesus reveals some specific signs in the physical world that would mark that short period known as the time of the end. "Immediately after the tribulation of those days the sun will be darkened, and the moon will not give its light; the stars will fall from heaven." Matthew 24:29.

Jesus predicted that these signs in the sun, moon and stars would occur just before the devastating and accelerating world conditions of war, famine, scourge, immorality, and violence. How do we know we're living in the last days? Because our civilization and world conditions have directly followed these three heavenly signs!

Secular history affirms this fact. On May 19, 1780, the sun arose as usual over the northeastern United States, but by mid-morning it became dark. The cattle came home, and the chickens went to roost. Farmers returned from their fields, and the lamps had to be lighted. The Connecticut legislature, in Hartford, thought the end of the world had arrived. Someone moved to adjourn, and another said, "No, if this is the end, let God find me at my duty. I move the candles continue." That night the moon appeared as red as blood, just as Jesus had prophesied.

Fifty-three years later, on November 13, 1833, the greatest star shower ever recorded in history occurred. Falling meteors streaked through the sky from Maine to Mexico. People said they had no difficulty reading the newspaper even at night (*American Journal of Science*, vol. XXV, 1834).

Observers estimated that at least 200,000 meteors streaked through the sky each hour. Again, people feared the end of the world had arrived. Abraham Lincoln is quoted as saying, "No, it is not the end of the world—the great constellations are still there."

These distinct heavenly signs—the dark day, the moon not giving its light, and the stars falling from heaven—are like signposts marking the eighteenth and nineteenth centuries as forerunners of the end times. They pointed forward to the final generation of false christs, wars and rumors of wars, famines, scourges, earthquakes, and rising crime and violence.

All of these signs are shouting that we are living in Earth's last hour. "Now when these things begin to happen, look up and lift up your heads, because your redemption draws near." Luke 21:28.

◆ The final sign

Climaxing His discussion on the time of the end, Jesus gave the final sign that would be fulfilled before His return. He declares, "And this gospel of the kingdom will be preached in all the world as a witness to all the nations, and then the end will come." Matthew 24:14.

Before the coming of Jesus, despotic regimes crumble. Totalitarian states collapse. The iron curtain and Berlin wall vanish. And the gospel penetrates the heart of atheism.

Even the most astute students of political affairs were overwhelmingly surprised by how rapidly Communism collapsed. The open doors to the preaching of the gospel in our day constitute a modern-day miracle. We have witnessed firsthand as tens of thousands have accepted Christ in Eastern Europe. In recent evangelistic campaigns in Moscow (1991-1993), we witnessed a total attendance of over eighty thousand people in two years. People stood in line for hours to purchase tickets for our Bible lectures in the Kremlin. (Yes, inside the Kremlin—the first Christian services within those walls since Communism muscled in seventy years ago.) We have distributed over 75,000 Bibles, and meeting attendees have completed over 750,000 Bible lessons. Who would have believed a few short years ago that the Kremlin and the Olympic Stadium would be centers of evangelistic activity?

Indications are that soon China, with more than one billion people, may open its doors wider to the gospel.

Beyond all doubt, Jesus is coming soon! We can almost hear the angel call "closing time" for our tired planet. When Christ steps over the threshold of eternity into the arena of human affairs, He will solve all the problems that have eluded mankind for centuries.

And all it takes to be a part of that radiant welcoming party, which will be swept up into the sky by the heavenly paratroopers, is a contrite heart pardoned by the blood of Jesus. None of us has a moment to lose. Won't you lift your heart to God right now and ask Him to help you prepare for Christ's soon coming? ❏

Just as the great enemy meets every truth God utters with a brazen lie, he also meets every genuine act or creation of God with a counterfeit. The devil may be altogether evil, but he is not dumb. He too knows the signs that Jesus is about to return.

So if it's a second coming the world is looking for, Satan decides, a second coming they will get.

7

Beyond
Virtual Reality

Egomania.

This is what Satan has wanted all along: To be the king, to be in charge, to be the uncontested ruler of everything.

So today the Earth, tomorrow the universe.

Millions on Earth expect the triumphant return of the King of kings and Lord of lords? Then they shall not be disappointed.

Before the genuine, the counterfeit. Before Christ can descend from the skies, Satan determines to steal His thunder. So, catering to the very stereotypes of Christ he has himself helped create, the great imposter stages the greatest hoax yet in his long war against Heaven. Conditioned for decades by tales of extraterrestrials and UFOs, the gullible masses, the devil is certain, will swallow the ruse whole.

His reward? The worship and praise of countless millions. And the chance to pass off some of his best lies to a world carried away by the spectacular and prepared to believe anything.

And millions will be deceived. But if you know your Bible, you won't be one of them.

7

Two businessmen sat in an American restaurant waiting to be served. One was Russian, the other American. The conversation flowed freely, touching on lighter topics at first, then becoming more serious.

"I am wondering about this country of yours," the Russian said, turning in his chair to face his friend squarely. "Is it the vast wonderland that we all hear about, or do you, too, have your problems?" The American shook his head, then began to explain, in his best Russian.

"Yes, we have our beautiful parks and wealthy homes. But contrast them with the homeless who wander in the back alleys, bed down in cardboard boxes, and under bridges for the night.

"We have a nation of great families in fine suburbs, but we too, have our broken homes and disillusioned teenagers walking the streets of the big cities, crying out for love and affection.

"We have our health clubs and joggers and marathons, but we also have the drug-addicted, alcohol-dependent, chemical users, searching for an escape. America is a land of contrasts. We have our peace and freedom, but we also have our fears and insecurities—crime, contagious diseases, the threat of nuclear holocaust. . ."

The Russian put up his hand to stop the recitation and asked, "So, your problems are no different from ours. But you Americans, do you have any solutions?"

Without a moment's hesitation the American replied, "Many Americans believe there is only one solution—A KING!"

Shocked, the Russian replied, "A King? For America?

The American quietly replied, "Yes, a King. An extraordinary king. And He is coming soon to settle all the problems in the world. I'm talking about King Jesus."

King Jesus! Men and women have anticipated His reign since His departure two thousand years ago. Clinging to His promise, "I will come again" (John 14:3), Jesus' followers have never given up hope that, yes, there is a solution to all of the crime, sickness, sorrow and hardship so pervasive in our world today.

The Apostle Paul, writing from his prison cell, said he was "Looking for the blessed hope and glorious appearing of our great God and Savior Jesus Christ." Titus 2:13.

Later, as the executioner stood but steps away, Paul triumphantly proclaimed: "I have fought the good fight, I have finished the race, I have kept the faith. Finally, there is laid up for me the crown of righteousness, which the Lord, the righteous Judge, will give to me on that Day, and not to me only but also to all who have loved His appearing." 2 Timothy 4:7, 8.

Paul could face the executioner's sword with confidence, because he had faith in Christ's promise to return, and in the hope that glorious life would be restored to him when Jesus returned to earth.

◆ The Promise

As we face the closing hours of Earth's history, with all its terror ready to unfold, Christians everywhere will find great strength in remembering that our Lord's promise to His disciples belongs to us as well. Jesus will return! That promise is the world's only hope for survival and its only assurance that the future is not in the hands of unpredictable world powers.

Knowing that Satan would attempt to counterfeit His coming, Jesus gave us the exact details of His second coming in the Bible.

Looking down through the ages at this troubled and polluted planet, He warned, "For false christs and false prophets will rise and show great signs and wonders." Matthew 24:24.

If we do not know how to recognize the genuine Jesus or how to spot the counterfeit, we could be deceived by an imposter!

◆ The ultimate deception

Jesus was not referring to a few clumsy deceptions in this passage. He was talking about incredible impersonations, so carefully planned and executed that almost the whole world would be deceived! And such a thought is not too difficult to imagine in our age. The advertising world has perfected the art of influencing the human mind; modern technology has almost perfected subliminal perception. The sights, the senses, the thoughts are carefully bent and shaped toward desired ends. From another angle, we call it "virtual reality," and— fantastic as the computer is in creating illusions that mimic reality today—we haven't seen anything yet!

The Bible even tells us that our five senses will be the focus of impostors in the last days. Our eyes will behold miracles, our ears will hear the unexplainable, our fingers will touch healed flesh—yet such supernatural demonstrations may not be manifestations of a divine power.

Think for a moment: Imagine turning on the evening news and hearing a newscaster reporting that Christ has returned. All networks are focused on Chicago. Pictures are flashed in color, live! We see a noble being healing the sick, performing miracles, speaking words of love and peace and Christian unity. Captured on camera are masses of people, pressing in to see him, to feel him. Never has the world heard such simple words that seem to make so much sense! Everywhere the newscast is seen—Berlin, Beijing, Singapore, Cairo, Moscow, St. Louis—people are reacting with tears, joy, and excitement such as we have not seen in our time.

What do you do? Quickly make a reservation on the next flight to Chicago? Rush out to see him? Bow down and worship him?

Without a clear understanding of just what to expect when Jesus comes again, we are vulnerable to almost any clever deception, especially if masterminded by the ace of deception, Satan himself.

Jesus said, "Therefore if they say to you, 'Look, He is in the desert!' do not go out; or 'Look, He is in the inner rooms!' do not believe it." Matthew 24:26.

Christ advises us not to even check out the claim. "Do not go out." Rather than put ourselves in a position where we might be deceived by miracles or charisma, it's best to just stay home, He says. Our Lord's warning is unambiguous: A man might teach like Christ. He might heal like Christ. He might sound like Christ. He might even come close to deceiving "the very elect." But guess what? That person will be a false Christ, a super deceiver.

So you see, then, why it is so important not to trust even our own senses! In regard to the second coming of Jesus, the Bible is the only safe guide by which we can distinguish between counterfeit christs and our Lord Jesus. And the Bible is very clear as to the signs that precede His return to this earth, as well as about the manner in which Jesus will return.

First, Christ's return will be visible to all: "For as the lightning comes from the east and flashes to the west, so also will the coming of the Son of Man be." Matthew 24:27.

We will not have to turn on our televisions to catch the news of Christ's return; everyone will know about it! We will literally see Him coming, for the Bible says, "Behold, He is coming with clouds, and every eye will see Him." Revelation 1:7.

Every eye! Imagine it. The tired eyes of the old and weary. The shining eyes of the child. The discerning eyes of the young adult. The glazed eyes of the blind. The happy eyes of the saved. The downcast eyes of the lost.

◆ Too many angels for a UFO

Christ is not going to suddenly appear in some distant city, or quietly step out of a flying saucer. He is coming back in the clouds with power and great glory, and every eye will see Him! The Bible says it will be a glorious coming: "When the Son of Man comes in His glory, and all the holy angels with Him." Matthew 25:31.

Jesus is not coming back by Himself! When He comes, He will be accompanied by all the holy angels, filling the skies with glory and songs indescribable! When just one angel rolled back the stone from Christ's tomb, the Roman guards fell down in a daze. And that was the glory of just one angel! Think of the glory of "ten thousand times ten thousand, and thousands of thousands" of angels (see Revelation 5:11) who will accompany Jesus.

The Bible says it will not only be a glorious, visible event, but it will also be a dramatic, audible coming. All nature will join forces to create an impact never before heard or seen: "And there were noises and thunderings and lightnings; and there was a great earthquake, such a mighty and great earthquake as had not occurred since men were on the earth. . . . Then every island fled away, and the mountains were not found." Revelation 16:18, 20.

The crash of thunder and the rumble of earthquakes will be punctuated by the clear, full tone of heavenly trumpets as they announce the melodious, commanding voice of God, calling the saints to come forth from their graves. "For the Lord Himself will descend from heaven with a shout, with the voice of an archangel, and with the trumpet of God. And the dead in Christ will rise first." 1 Thessalonians 4:16.

The Lord Himself will descend! But what kind of a Lord will that be? What will Jesus be like when He returns? A spirit, without substance and flesh? A being indescribable, seen only as dazzling light?

The Bible makes it clear that when Jesus returns at His second coming, He will be the same Jesus whom thousands of Palestinians will remember well—the traveling Teacher, the carpenter from Nazareth, the remarkable Healer, the great Friend of all.

After our Lord's resurrection, He spent a few weeks with His disciples sharing His final instructions and assuring them of His love and presence "even unto the end of the world" (see Matthew 28:20, KJV).

As the time came for Christ to ascend to His Father's throne, He stood with hands outstretched in blessing, slowly ascending heavenward. The disciples stood gazing upward, straining their eyes for that last glimpse of their Lord, and suddenly, "While they looked steadfastly toward heaven as He went up, behold, two men stood by them in white apparel, who also said, 'Men of Galilee, why do you stand gazing up into heaven? This same Jesus, who was taken up from you into heaven, will so come in like manner as you saw Him go into heaven.'" Acts 1:10, 11.

This same Jesus! Jesus with flesh and bones. Jesus with nailprints in His hands and feet. Jesus with a wound in His side. The same Jesus who talked and walked and prayed with the disciples. The same Jesus who went away in the clouds will return the same way!

Do you see how the counterfeits pale in comparison to the actual picture of what the second coming of Christ will truly be like? If He isn't seen by every human eye, if there is no glorious descent to earth, no call that pierces even the sleep of death, no retinue of dazzling angels—it isn't Jesus! It's as simple as that.

Such an understanding is crucial to our eternal destiny. If we are deceived and don't prepare for Christ's coming, we lose everything. No replays—no reruns! When that thunder crashes and those trumpets play, the destiny of every human being will have already been decided!

When Jesus comes, judgment for all the living and the dead will already have been settled. That's why the angels know to which graves they should go in the first resurrection—they know who will arise first and join the redeemed from among the living.

How insignificant are the earthly treasures we now prize so highly! One earthquake, one tornado, one nuclear bomb, one doctor's diagnosis, one threatening phone call from a stranger in the night—and our security is shattered. That is why Paul said, "Set your mind on things above, not on things on the earth." Colossians 3:2.

◆ Where will you be when Jesus comes?

Can there ever be anything more important than being ready to meet Jesus? Today we can still decide. Today we can still choose. What a precious privilege! In choosing Jesus as our Lord, we are choosing everything that matters most in this life and in the life to come.

Where will you be, and what will you be doing, when Jesus comes? When all nature is in turmoil—the earth convulsing, mountains and islands disappearing, cities toppling—how will it be with you?

When a small cloud appears on the horizon, growing in size, getting brighter every moment until everyone in the world is aware of this compelling Person and His entourage in the skies, how will it be with you?

◆ An invitation with your name on it

All the shadows of Earth disappear—the glory is almost overwhelming! Nothing else then will be on our mind. As He draws nearer the Earth, every eye beholds Christ—not as a man of sorrows, but as a mighty conqueror! Not with a crown of thorns, but with a crown of glory. And with Him, the armies of heaven—all the holy angels! No human pen can portray the scene; no mortal mind is adequate to conceive its splendor (we have been given only a flashlight peek): "And He has on His robe and on His thigh a name written: KING OF KINGS AND LORD OF LORDS." Revelation 19:16.

At the sound of a heavenly chorus, at the spectacle of a sky filled with the glory of our returning Lord and His heavenly paratroopers—criminals will drop in their tracks, armies the world over will lay down their guns, the battlefields will be still. Only one thing matters to those who have rejected the wooing voice of the Holy Spirit. And that is to pray for the rocks to fall on them rather than look upon the face of Him whom they have rejected or neglected.

A loud but friendly call pierces the air, and trumpets echo the summons; graves open, and the redeemed dead rise out of those graves or are gathered from the depths of a hundred seas. The saved among the living are caught up together with them to meet the Lord in the air and are taken to those "mansions" prepared by our Lord for a one-thousand-year vacation (see Chapter 24).

Could anything be more thrilling, if we are prepared? I am beginning to feel the excitement even now!

Are you ready for Jesus to come? Why not decide right now to be a part of that grateful number who sing their joy: "Behold, this is our God; We have waited for Him, and He will save us." Isaiah 25:9.

Back comes Jesus' invitation: "Come, you blessed of My Father, inherit the kingdom prepared for you." Matthew 25:34.

Your name is on that invitation! ❏

Yes, someday soon, look for Satan to stage a phony second coming. Meanwhile, though, sensing that his time is running out, he pulls out all the stops in his effort to make God look bad. If he can just convince the people of Earth that God is against them, that He is isn't fair, that He doesn't care, that He is to blame for all the bad things that happen to good people—then he wins. Because no one will ever want anything to do with that kind of God.

Chapter 8 takes us behind the scenes to expose who is really to blame for the evil on Earth.

8

. . . .

Why Insurance
Companies
Are Wrong

Two pictures of God.

It probably seems as if Satan's greatest goal and delight is to tempt, harass, hurt, and destroy human beings. Quite definitely, all this is gratifying enough to him. But tormenting the innocent is only a means to an end.

What the devil is really out to do is to assassinate the character of God. So he savagely attacks us, then works overtime to get us to blame it all on God.

When we suffer, he wants us to conclude God is to blame.

When death rips our loved ones from us, he wants us to blame God.

When tragedy or disaster or disease strike, it is—he tells us— God, always and only God, who is to blame.

If he can fill our lives with misery and suffering and death, then convince us that it's all God's fault, we're his.

This is the great central issue of the Great War—this is what it is all about.

What is the real truth about God? Is it what Satan would have us believe? Or is it what Jesus showed us in His life and words?

Only one side in this war is right. And not a day goes by in which we don't vote our own conviction as to which side that is.

I n 1981, Harold S. Kushner wrote a book that promised to answer a question that has been asked from the time of Job to the
present. *When Bad Things Happen to Good People* instantly cata-
pulted to best seller fame.

Kushner's answer to the universal question, however, was limited
by his own narrow idea of God. Beginning with a denial of God's
power in the creation of this world, Kushner went on to reject the
literal accounts of miraculous Old Testament occurrences. Bad things
happen to good people, he concluded, because the God who set this
universe in motion is powerless to intervene in natural law.

Is this the solution to the timeless question, Why pain? Do we
serve a God who suffers with us at injustice and sorrow but who has
no power to reverse the trend of a cancer cell, the law of gravity, or
the randomness of nature? Why *do* bad things happen to good people?

Every few minutes in America, a young girl is raped, a life is snatched
away amidst the screech of metal on pavement, and a new victim falls
prey to a deadly disease. Deep within every human heart arises the
nagging question that will not be quieted: "If God is so good, why do
we have such a bad world?"

An incident in Lake Worth, Florida, a few years back will focus
our thoughts on the source of evil in the universe. A man made a
claim to his insurance company, based on an unfortunate accident

he'd had in which he was shocked by a high-power electrical line. The insurance company refused to pay, on the grounds that the incident was an "Act of God." The courts agreed.

◆ Suing God

The man then responded creatively. He filed a suit against "God and Company," implicating fifty-five Christian churches in his city. During the court proceedings, one minister spoke out saying, "I believe the expression, 'An Act of God,' is wrongly used. God was not responsible for this accident. It should be called, 'An Act of Satan.'"

According to the Bible, this clergyman was absolutely correct—and the insurance companies are wrong! Two opposing forces exist in the universe: one good and one evil, the powers of heaven and the powers of hell. As the author of love and order, God is in no way responsible for any or all evil on Planet Earth. This is Satan's domain. Hate, suffering, guilt, shame, pain, remorse—all can be fairly charged to the grand usurper.

God's love is eternal. He never changes. "I have loved you with an everlasting love; Therefore with lovingkindness I have drawn you." Jeremiah 31:3.

But why would a God of love permit a planet to be held captive by evil? The Bible gives a clear explanation of the origin of sin and suffering on this Earth. When God created our world, He made it perfect—without a flaw. He fashioned a perfect man and woman and placed them in an ideal environment. He desired that this special couple should enjoy their Eden home without anything to mar their happiness.

Sickness, suffering, and death were not part of God's plan. Where, then, did all the evil on this earth come from? How did God's plan for this world get upset? The book of Revelation gives this urgent warning: "Woe to the inhabitants of the earth and the sea! For the devil has come down to you, having great wrath, because he knows that he has a short time." Revelation 12:12.

Satan is humanity's enemy! He is the guilty one responsible for all the evil we find on Planet Earth.

You and I are caught in the center of a bewildering cosmic drama—a conflict between right and wrong, between the Creator and Satan, the rebel angel. We are not spectators—we are involved whether we want to be or not!

The idea that Satan is only a myth or a costume-party character with tail and horns leaves us totally unprepared to confront him as the intelligent being he actually is.

Peter warned, "The devil walks about like a roaring lion, seeking whom he may devour." 1 Peter 5:8.

If we are to effectively combat this power that so negatively affects our lives, it is important that we understand exactly who he is and where he came from. Surprisingly enough, Satan's origins are not found in some disadvantaged corner of the universe. The Bible tells us: "I saw Satan fall like lightning from heaven." Luke 10:18.

A devil in heaven! Incredible, but true! The Bible unravels a most tragic story. Satan, or Lucifer as he was then called, walked the streets of heaven as a powerful, dazzling, beautiful angel.

Using the symbolism of the King of Tyre, the prophet describes this angelic "Lucifer"—his name before he became "Satan," the devil. "You were the model of perfection, full of wisdom and perfect in beauty. You were in Eden, the garden of God; every precious stone adorned you . . . . You were anointed as a guardian cherub, for so I ordained you. You were blameless in your ways from the day you were created till wickedness was found in you." Ezekiel 28:12-15, NIV.

Lucifer held the highest position of all the angels in heaven. Why would he defect? Because this beautiful, exalted angel coveted the glory and homage due God alone. He was power hungry. "Your heart was lifted up because of your beauty; You corrupted your wisdom for the sake of your splendor." Ezekiel 28:17.

In fact, this created angel had the boldness to challenge his Creator for the rulership of the universe! "For you have said in your heart: 'I will ascend into heaven, I will exalt my throne above the stars of God; I will also sit on the mount of the congregation On the farthest sides of the north; I will ascend above the heights of the clouds, I will be like the Most High.'" Isaiah 14:13, 14.

It wasn't long before Lucifer began to spread the spirit of discontent among the other angels. Insidiously, he undermined God's love and justice; he cleverly raised doubts about how God was running the universe.

Obviously, God could have eliminated Lucifer and the angels who chose to join his rebellion, in one blinding flash; but had God done that, all of His creatures would have served Him out of fear. A God of love could make no such choice—not a God who longed for His created beings to love Him freely.

The deadly virus of doubt and deception spread by Satan infected one-third of the angels of heaven, leading to open rebellion. "And war broke out in heaven: Michael and his angels fought with the dragon; and the dragon and his angels fought, but they did not prevail, nor was a place found for them in heaven any longer. So the great dragon was cast out, that serpent of old, called the Devil and Satan, who deceives the whole world; he was cast to the earth, and his angels were cast out with him." Revelation 12:7-9.

◆ Battlezone Earth

Heaven, of all places, became the battleground of the first war, and Satan and his angels were thrown out of heaven. But the conflict between Christ and Satan was not over—it just changed theaters! The battle that began in heaven moved to Planet Earth. Earth became the stage upon which the great controversy between good and evil would be dramatized, where Satan would demonstrate his kind of government with all of its sad, miserable consequences.

Planet Earth—that uncontaminated environment fresh from the hand of the Creator—now became headquarters for the most sinister being in the universe! Evidently Satan saw this world as a prize worth capturing—a planet of rare beauty, a world newly born.

Although Adam and Eve were created perfect, they were not placed beyond the possibility of wrongdoing. Free to love and follow God, they could also choose to ignore His instructions. As the story unfolds, their loyalty would be tested on a simple issue. God warned,

"You are free to eat from any tree in the garden; but you must not eat from the tree of the knowledge of good and evil, for when you eat of it you will surely die." Genesis 2:16, 17, NIV.

The request seemed reasonable. The sweet juice of a thousand fruit trees awaited this new couple. All the delights cultivated by the Master Gardener were theirs—save one.

But the time of testing came. Walking in the garden one day alone, Eve stopped to look at the forbidden tree. The beauty, the fragrance, the appeal of a special taste attracted her. Then it happened! Satan, disguising himself as a gorgeous snake (not like snakes we know), complete with iridescent wings, boldly wooed her and asked, "Has God indeed said, 'You shall not eat of every tree of the garden'?" Genesis 3:1.

Spontaneously loyal, Eve quickly replied, "We may eat the fruit of the trees of the garden; but of the fruit of the tree which is in the midst of the garden, God has said, 'You shall not eat it, nor shall you touch it, lest you die.' " Genesis 3:2, 3.

As if the idea were ridiculous, the serpent scoffed, "You will not surely die." Genesis 3:4.

As Eve stood there listening to the serpent, she hesitated, encountering for the first time a contradictory note in her perfect environment. Sensing her confusion, the serpent moved in for the kill. "For God knows that in the day you eat of it your eyes will be opened, and you will be like God, knowing good and evil." Genesis 3:5.

The insinuation was far from subtle. "God is holding out on you. There's even more joy and wonder beyond the limited confines of what God has given you in this garden. You can be like God Himself!"

The all-consuming desire for equality with God that drove Satan to rebel in heaven, he now foisted on Eve. And she, too, was attracted to the thirst for this new, strange power. In her dallying, she sold out. "When the woman saw that the tree was good for food, that it was pleasant to the eyes, and a tree desirable to make one wise, she took of its fruit and ate. She also gave to her husband with her, and he ate." Genesis 3:6.

So Adam and Eve, that gifted couple with the promise of all eternity before them, failed God's test of love and loyalty. The consequences of their decision were not long in coming. For the first time in their lives they were plagued by strange, dark feelings of hopelessness, shame, guilt, and despair.

Slowly, the realization dawned. Their disobedience had cost them everything: happiness, perfect love, fellowship with God, their garden home, and the dominion of Planet Earth. Gone!

No longer masters, they had become slaves!

◆ A hijacked planet

Satan had hijacked the newly created world! Exultant with his victory in deceiving this first pair, he established himself as ruler of a planet in rebellion, claiming dominion and power as prince of the planet.

As this most tragic day drew to a close, God came in the cool of the evening, calling for Adam and Eve. Until now the evening hours in communion with God had been the most cherished moments of the day. But God was no longer a welcomed guest! Guilty, ashamed, acutely conscious of their own nakedness and vulnerability, the couple hid! In fear and shame, they hid!

Finally, Adam slipped slowly from behind some shrubs in the garden and confessed, "I heard Your voice in the garden, and I was afraid because I was naked; and I hid myself." Genesis 3:10.

Adam had never before experienced fear. But sin produces fear—even of the One who is our chief Protector. And fear produces a number of other reactions, not the least of which is excuse-finding, rationalization, "passing the buck," and self-justification. The next few minutes of this sad story provide a classic profile of how men and women ever since have blamed someone else for their own bad choices. Today we hear it when young and old say, "It's not my fault. I'm just the victim of a poor home, not enough schooling, bad breaks, and a government that doesn't care about me. I'm not to blame!"

As God questioned Adam about what had happened, Adam became the victim, not responsible for his part of the problem. It didn't take him long to find someone to blame: "The woman whom You gave to be with me, she gave me of the tree, and I ate." Genesis 3:12.

A few hours before, Adam loved Eve dearly. Now he blames her for his problems. Further, he blames God for creating Eve! How sin shatters the best relationships!

Eve is no less accusing. "And the LORD God said to the woman, 'What is this you have done?' The woman said, 'The serpent deceived me, and I ate.'" Genesis 3:13.

In attempting to justify herself and to blame someone else, Eve puts the blame on God Himself. "It's the serpent You made that led me astray." Like Adam, she grapples with the sin problem and struggles to find a scapegoat.

So death, in spite of Satan's lie, became the fate of this couple of so much promise. Immortality had been promised on condition of obedience. By disobeying, Adam and Eve forfeited eternal life and faced the inevitable. They were evicted from their Eden home, witnessed the murder of their son at the hands of his own brother, suffered emotional and physical pain, worked, sweat, cried, agonized, and eventually died.

A perfect world, blighted with the curse of sin. Planet Earth—a cauldron of disease, cruelty, and death. Who is to blame? When will it end?

Perhaps nowhere in the Bible is Satan's strategy more clearly exposed than in the first chapter of Job. Here we find God being very kind to us. He gives us the background as to who is behind the troubles on earth.

The story opens with drama in heaven. The sons of God presented themselves before the Lord. And in their midst, present without invitation, appeared Satan, fresh from "going to and fro on the earth, and from walking back and forth on it" (Job 1:7), jeering at the others, claiming control over the hearts and minds of men.

"Then the LORD said to Satan, 'Have you considered My servant Job, that there is none like him on the earth, a blameless and upright man, one who fears God and shuns evil?'" Job 1:8.

"His allegiance to You is all based on things," Satan responded. "Why shouldn't he worship You? You've given him riches and honor. He's the greatest man of the East! Take away all the things You've given him, and he'll curse You to Your face."

The Lord responded in confidence. "Behold, all that he has is in your power; only do not lay a hand on his person." Job 1:12.

Satan left, eager to get his hands on Job's possessions. The blows began to fall, fast and furious! First, the Sabeans stole Job's cattle and murdered his cowhands. Next, lightning struck, killing his sheep and shepherds. Then the Chaldeans came and plundered Job's camels. But the most heartbreaking news of all was yet to come. A tornado demolished the home of Job's oldest son, killing all ten of Job's children in one merciless stroke.

Although overcome with grief, Job's loyalty to God was unchanged. "The LORD gave, and the LORD has taken away; Blessed be the name of the LORD," he uttered through his sorrow (Job 1:21).

But Satan's cruelty would extend even farther, sparing nothing. After afflicting Job with painful sores from the bottom of his feet to the top of his head, this enemy of humanity waited—waited eagerly for the string of curses he expected from a man who has seen his whole world come tumbling in!

Deprived of his possessions, grieving the loss of his family, suffering with the breakdown of his health, Job remained loyal to God. "In all this Job did not sin nor charge God with wrong." Job 1:22.

◆ The true source of all evil

Through this series of events, the character of Job is clearly revealed. But he is not the only one whose character is suddenly thrown into the limelight of the universe. The master of evil, too, shows his true colors!

Who was it that plagued Job? Satan. Who was it that stole his livestock and killed his servants? Satan. Who brought the tornado that destroyed Job's sons and daughters? Satan.

Down through the ages, it has always been Satan, plotting and planning and scheming for the outworking of evil in the universe. Working through the jealous mind of King Herod, Satan tried to destroy the Christ-child at Bethlehem.

Coming to Christ in the wilderness, masquerading as an angel from heaven, he attempted to divert the mission of the Son of God and thus gain dominion over Planet Earth forever. Spreading the glories of all the kingdoms of the world before our emaciated Lord, he had the audacity to declare that all this "property" was his property and that he could give it to whomever he chose! "All these things I will give You if You will fall down and worship me." Matthew 4:9.

But his most sinister energies to control this earth were marshaled at Calvary. All his power was bent on preventing Christ from restoring man's lost dominion. Christ was humanity's last chance for survival.

Finally, Satan managed to have Christ betrayed into the hands of the murderous religious leaders—who killed Him on Calvary. However it appeared to all, behind everything, God was the one in control. God gave His only Son over to the evil powers; Jesus gave Himself to die, to reverse your fate and mine.

Jesus did die, but not as a partner with Satan. He died as One who faced Satan down, even while He was suffering the worst that Satan could throw at Him. Calvary was the day that spelled freedom for all the prisoners of the devil. That day Satan became a defeated foe! Christ, by His unsullied life and awesome death, earned the right to destroy Satan and to end all evil and suffering.

Satan had demonstrated before all the intelligences of the universe what kind of being he is. That evil mind may now be fully disclosed to heavenly intelligences, but that is not so on earth! He still works under disguise, and what he really does is still cloaked in mystery. In fact, what he does, others get blamed for—others such as God!

The Bible tells us, "And no wonder! For Satan himself transforms himself into an angel of light." 2 Corinthians 11:14.

Prince of darkness. Master of evil. Artist of deception.

The problem of pain in the universe? Why do bad things happen to good people? The answer does not need two hundred pages or more written in heavy theological language. The thirst for power, ambition, and equality with God has led one being in the universe to make the misery of mankind his entire chief reason for existence. In fact, to cause humanity to rebel is Satan's last hope to save himself. Thus we suffer.

And while God has chosen to allow sin to run its course in this theater of the universe, the day will come when He will say, "No more!" This celestial planet, hijacked by Satan, is soon to be rescued. And God's justice will put an end to Satan's game. "I will destroy thee, O covering cherub . . .. Therefore will I bring forth a fire from the midst of thee, it shall devour thee, and I will bring thee to ashes upon the earth." Ezekiel 28:16, 18, KJV.

Gone forever will be sin and suffering. Jesus Himself will descend from the clouds, not as a lowly Galilean, not as One ridiculed, spat upon, denied, hanging on a cross, but as King of Kings with the right to reign. And the problem of pain will be forever vanquished. Because Satan will be destroyed. ❏

The great controversy—the mighty war between Christ and Satan—is over the character of God. Is He love and only love? Is He totally on our side?

Unknown to almost everyone on Earth, an investigation is going on at this very moment in Heaven to determine which side of the great controversy each of us has chosen.

Chapter 9 describes your day in court.

9

· ·

When Your Case
Comes to Court

The jury is still out—
but not for long.

In recent years, several high-profile trials have attracted national and even international attention. Whether it be the fictional courtroom episodes of "Perry Mason" or "L.A. Law," or the real-life drama played out on cable's CNN or "Court TV," viewers seem to have developed an intense fascination with the judicial process.

Unknown to most, however, the greatest courtroom drama ever has been in session now for just over 150 years.

We've been saying all along in this book that in the great War Behind All Wars, each of us has a part to play. Your part—and mine—is to choose each day which of the two great combatants in the war we will support. Will we support Prince Michael (Jesus), who stands for love and truth and life? Or will we—either by choice or default—give our loyalties to Satan, who stands for selfishness and lies and death?

The Bible says that shortly before Christ returns, Heaven will be the scene of a judicial inquiry called the judgment, in which the lives of all who have ever lived or will yet live are to be investigated to determine which side of the Great War they are on.

This investigative judgment is also Christ's chosen forum to defend Himself against Satan's false charges before an onlooking universe.

Open your subpoena, then. Heaven's court is in session!

E very man or woman who has ever lived has a case pending before the judgment bar of God—the Supreme Court of the Universe. Every person has an appointment. No one will be excused. No one can escape the summons. "For we must all appear before the judgment seat of Christ." 2 Corinthians 5:10.

Whether we believe it or not! Whether we like it or not! Whether we profess to be Christians or not! Whether we are rich or poor, black or white—we must all appear! God has no favorites. When a person is summoned by the court in heaven, he must appear to "give account of himself to God." Romans 14:12.

The decision of heaven's court will forever seal each person's destiny. The verdict will be irrevocable, for there is no higher court of appeal. But before the final sentence is passed, a thorough investigation will take place in heaven's court.

The prophet Daniel describes the awesome court, presided over by the Ancient of Days and attended by "ten thousand times ten thousand" angel witnesses (Daniel 7:10). Standing before the Ancient of Days is the Son of God, the Advocate of mankind. And who is on trial? As we continue reading the seventh chapter of Daniel, we find that, although human beings are not present, books are opened.

Evidently "the books" contain the records of the deeds of those who stand trial, for Solomon wrote, "For God shall bring every work into judgment, with every secret thing, whether it be good, or whether it be evil." Ecclesiastes 12:14.

Malachi, the last book in the Old Testament, refers to a "book of remembrance" (Malachi 3:16), and King David also writes about a book of God (Psalm 56:8).

In this age of computers and technology, we can imagine a heavenly computer containing the precise, exact, all-inclusive record of a life. But why would an all-knowing, omniscient God need a "hard copy" history of men and women? Obviously, He has total awareness and knowledge.

But these heavenly records are kept, not to jog God's memory, but for the benefit of the universe. These records will provide clear evidence of God's love and justice as the destiny of each person who has ever lived is decided.

The records leave out nothing, as Solomon pointed out: "For all these God will bring you into judgment." Ecclesiastes 11:9. And not only are our deeds recorded, but our words as well. Matthew wrote, "Every idle word men may speak, they will give account of it in the day of judgment. For by your words you will be justified, and by your words you will be condemned." Matthew 12:36, 37.

◆ Speaking volumes

It has been estimated that the average person speaks enough words in one week to fill a book of 320 pages! In sixty years, that could mean more than three thousand such books! What will your library of books "say" in the judgment? And more than that, even the motives behind those words and actions will be open to view: "[God] will both bring to light the hidden things of darkness and reveal the counsels of the hearts." 1 Corinthians 4:5.

No erasures, no cover-ups in that day. We might be able to fool our friends and even our families, but no one can fool God. He reads the secrets of the heart!

On the day of judgment, we will find ourselves in one of two positions: either our entire record of past failures will be covered by the blood of Jesus, or our record will stand to condemn us. Not what we profess, but what we have done, will make the difference. We are told that when Jesus comes, "He will reward each according to his works." Matthew 16:27.

Such an understanding is not contradictory to the Bible teaching that we are saved by grace. While works cannot atone for our sin, they do indicate how complete our surrender is to Christ. Many people profess to be Christians, but a mere profession of faith in Christ is of no value unless it is demonstrated by loving works.

Says Sakae Kubo:

"Let us consider what it would mean if the judgment were not based on works. By what would God judge us—our skin, our race, our social class, our education, our looks, our talents, our strength, our membership in the church, our mere profession of Christ? God can judge us only by our works—good or bad."—*Your Summons to Court,* p. 20.

Good works obviously are not done by a genuine Christian to earn merit. They are the spontaneous result of a heart full of love for God and man. A love relationship with Jesus motivates His followers to behave in a manner that is pleasing to God. In His famous Sermon on the Mount, Jesus made this clear: "Let your light so shine before men, that they may see your good works and glorify your Father in heaven." Matthew 5:16.

Summing up this thought in the book of Ecclesiastes, Solomon said, "Let us hear the conclusion of the whole matter: Fear God and keep His commandments, For this is the whole duty of man. For God will bring every work into judgment." Ecclesiastes 12:13, 14.

Since our relationship to Christ is judged by our conduct, there must be some clear standard by which to measure that conduct. In our judicial procedures here on Earth, the usual standard for determining whether a crime has been committed is to determine whether or not a law has been broken. Only when a law has been violated can a man be found guilty.

In God's judgment there is also a law or standard. In the second chapter of James, we find a reference to the Ten Commandments, followed by the assertion that man shall be "judged by the law of liberty." James 2:12. God's Ten Commandment law is the standard by which the lives of men will be judged.

The purpose of the judgment is simple: Which side do we stand on in earth's great conflict? Are we with Christ? Have we let Him live out His life in us? Have we had a supreme love for His will as expressed in the Ten Commandments? Is it our joy to follow His will for us, in the strength He promised to give us? Is He writing His law in our hearts now? How would anyone know?

When Christians accept Christ as Lord and desire to become citizens of His kingdom, God asks them to pledge their love and allegiance to Him and to uphold the laws of His government. Earthly governments require their naturalized citizens to do the same. However, not all immigrants remain faithful to their solemn vows. Some outwardly seem to be loyal citizens of the land but later are found to be subversive. When this is proven, the citizenship of that person is revoked, and he or she is deported.

Likewise, not all Christians remain faithful to their vows. It is not enough to be declared righteous by our heavenly Ruler; we must allow Jesus' life of obedience and faithfulness to be lived out in us.

Jesus said, "Not everyone who says to Me, 'Lord, Lord,' shall enter the kingdom of heaven, but he who does the will of My Father in heaven." Matthew 7:21.

The whole controversy between good and evil, between Christ and Satan, is about God's character of love. God's law is a transcript of that character. No wonder it figures so prominently in the final judgment!

But a most astounding fact, little known by most Christians, is that the heavenly court is in session now! As we will learn in the next chapter, the Bible reveals that God's judgment began in the year 1844. That is why, in the closing chapters of the book of Revelation, John outlines the world's last warning and invitation by saying, "The hour of His judgment has come." Revelation 14:7.

And who is doing the judging? After portraying the dramatic picture of three angels flying in the midst of heaven, the book of Revelation depicts an angel crying out to the Son of Man, "Thrust in Your sickle and reap, for the time has come for You to reap, for the harvest of the earth is ripe." Revelation 14:15.

This same picture of the Son of Man coming at judgment time is shown in the Book of Daniel. "I was watching in the night visions, And behold, One like the Son of Man, Coming with the clouds of heaven! He came to the Ancient of Days, And they brought Him near before Him. Then to Him was given dominion and glory and a kingdom, That all peoples, nations, and languages should serve Him. His dominion is an everlasting dominion." Daniel 7:13, 14.

◆ Defense attorney and Judge

Unlike any earthly court scene, we find, then, that the one who is our Advocate is also our Judge! While the Son of Man has complete authority to judge our case, His death on Calvary provides a complete sacrificial atonement for our sins. "He is also able to save to the uttermost those who come to God through Him, since He always lives to make intercession for them." Hebrews 7:25.

We do not have to stand alone in the judgment! If we have confessed Christ as Lord and Saviour, He will confess us before His Father. "Whoever confesses Me before men, him I will also confess before My Father who is in heaven." Matthew 10:32. If we are Christ's, He is our Advocate. He has promised that in the judgment, we will appear as though we had never sinned, for we will receive credit for the perfect life of obedience He lived on Earth.

Those who love and follow Jesus with all their hearts have nothing to fear in the judgment, for Jesus will present the merits of His own shed blood to cover every confessed sin. As John writes, "The blood of Jesus Christ His Son cleanses us from all sin." 1 John 1:7.

Picture in your mind's eye the day in court for Abel—son of Adam and Eve. He chose to listen to His Lord's commands but was killed by his jealous brother. As Abel's case comes to the docket, I can imagine God and the angels reviewing Abel's life. They will see his acceptance of the death of the Lamb of God, as symbolized in the lamb's sacrifice. And all heaven nods in agreement. Jesus, Abel's Advocate, stretches out His nail-scarred hands and says: "My blood, Father, paid Abel's debt." The life of Christ is credited to Abel's account. Abel's sins are all covered by the blood of the Redeemer whom he worshiped by faith.

Abel's life is sealed, then, for all eternity, for as Scripture says, "He who overcomes shall be clothed in white garments, and I will not blot out his name from the Book of Life; but I will confess his name before My Father and before His angels." Revelation 3:5.

But not all will be clothed in white raiment and named in the Book of Life among those who will live forever. Think for a moment about Judas' day in court. Judas—one-time follower of Jesus, a prominent disciple. Judas—not an innately wicked man, not a man who couldn't have chosen to live his life in another way. Judas—the disciple who made the choice that will forever associate him with one ruthless word—betrayer. While at times this tragic figure found himself drawn to Christ, he refused to surrender completely to the Saviour's love. His human frailty won out. One weakness led to another until he sold his Lord for thirty pieces of silver. Then in anguish he hanged himself.

Jesus loved Judas. He stooped to wash his dusty feet on the night of the last supper. He gently spoke to him, hoping to touch that proud heart. Jesus looked ahead to the day of the judgment and agonized over the decisions Judas was making daily. No one could have been sadder, as Jesus watched Judas turn away from his Advocate.

So in the judgment, as Judas' name is called, angels will not hear the triumphant cry, "My blood pays the debt," but instead the final words, "He who is filthy, let him be filthy still." Revelation 22:11. Judas has only his own righteousness to bring to the judgment, and as the Bible says, "We are all like an unclean thing, And all our righteousnesses are like filthy rags." Isaiah 64:6.

Only those who have continued to make Christ first in their lives can wear Christ's robe of righteousness. Without that, no man can be vindicated in the judgment. Judas' name is wiped out of the Book of Life, not because his sins are of any greater magnitude than any other man's, but because they are not covered by the cleansing blood of Jesus.

We are living in a solemn time. Like the Israelites of old, we must take inventory of our lives. The only possible preparation for our summons to court lies in our acceptance of and our commitment to Jesus. Soon our probation will close, and the decree will go forth, "He who is unjust, let him be unjust still . . . he who is holy, let him be holy still." Revelation 22:11.

At that time, the mercy and pardon God has extended for so long will be withdrawn. Not because God's heart has hardened or His mercy has run out. But because men and women will have sealed their habits into a pattern that will never change.

◆ Lament of the lost

Thoughts lead to actions. Repeated actions become character. Our developed character settles our eternal destiny. When the mind becomes hardened because of repeated habit patterns and God's love is resisted, our eternal destiny is sealed. God has done everything He can do! There is no other way He can reach us. He has exhausted all of His possibilities. The most tragic words in the human language will be the cry of those who have put off salvation, spurning the sacrifice of Jesus on their behalf. In despair, they will declare, "The harvest is past, The summer is ended, And we are not saved!" Jeremiah 8:20.

Human beings can experience no deeper feeling of despair than knowing that the point of no return has arrived. The gospels record a parable in which only part of a wedding party is prepared for the event. Because the bridegroom tarries, ten young women fall asleep. Half have reserve oil; half have none. And then comes the inevitable shout at midnight, "Here is the bridegroom! Go out to meet him!" (See Matthew 25:6.)

Bright and glowing, five figures rush out with joy. Stumbling in confusion, five are lost in outer darkness.

God's day of judgment approaches for all of us! For many, death comes so suddenly. Many reading these pages will die before Jesus returns. Are you ready? You can be! Why not surrender your life fully to Him right now! ❏

As already noted, the investigative judgment in Heaven has been in session now for just over 150 years, having begun in the year 1844.

How do we know this? Because the Bible says so! In what is perhaps the most remarkable time prophecy in all Scripture, a 2,300-year sweep of Earth's history was previewed for the prophet Daniel.

You will be amazed as, in the upcoming chapter, you discover just how precise Bible prophecy is.

10

....

Adding Up
Daniel's Numbers

The history of the future.

Maybe you are good at math. In school, you raked in good grades in classes like Algebra, Geometry, Trigonometry, or Calculus.

Then again, maybe you're one of those who struggled valiantly just to barely pass your math courses, and math is still one of life's great mysteries to you.

In any case, you don't have to be a math whiz to understand the numbers in the great 2,300-year prophecy in the Bible's book of Daniel.

On display here is the pinpoint precision that results when a prophecy is made by Someone who knows the future better than most of us know the immediate past.

When it comes to the key events of the great controversy—the pivotal events in the War Behind All Wars—God has gone out of His way to be sure we know what is coming up and when. He knows that if we can prepare in advance, we'll be ready to play our part in this great cosmic drama.

10

．．．．．．．．．．．．．．．．．．．．．．．．．．．．．．．．．．．．．．

On May 25, 1979, John A. Spenkelink, a 30-year-old drifter convicted of murder, was put to death in the electric chair in Florida. The U.S. Supreme Court refused to delay his death. Spenkelink was the first person to be executed in the United States since Gary Gilmore demanded to face the firing squad in 1977.

It is difficult to describe the tension in a courtroom when a jury is about to announce its verdict. When all the evidence has been presented and the case has been carefully reviewed, the foreman of the jury faces a room full of people waiting for words either of hope or revenge.

The judge asks, "What is your verdict?" All creation seems to hold its breath for one eternal moment. And with two words—"not guilty"—a collective sigh of relief permeates most of the courtroom, flooding the one on trial with joy, releasing his loved ones from the clutches of despair.

In the case of John Spenkelink, no such relief ever came. "Guilty" was the only word pronounced. And with that single word, his life on earth was cut short.

One—or two words. A simple pronouncement, either way. We all face one of the two verdicts. As we learned in the last chapter, the Bible tells us that all of us will face a day in court. The ultimate pronouncement will affect us for all eternity. Every human being who

119

119

has ever lived has a case pending before the judgment bar of God, the Supreme Court of the Universe. The apostle Paul declares, "We must all appear before the judgment seat of Christ." 2 Corinthians 5:10.

The greatest issue facing mankind today is not whether we are successful at climbing the corporate ladder, not whether we have achieved worldly status and fame! It's not how many credit cards we carry in our wallets, not the amount of money we have in our bank accounts, but, as Daniel Webster once remarked, the greatest issue in our lives is our "personal accountability to God."

That accountability comes into focus at the time of God's judgment. Revelation 14:7 tells us: "Fear God and give glory to Him, for the hour of His judgment has come." Note that the text does not say "will come" at some future time, but "has come." Later, we will discover how we today are living in the time of "His judgment."

Revelation 14:6-12 clearly states that before Christ returns, a message will go to all the world announcing the judgment hour. The Bible also indicates where that judgment takes place and when it begins.

Daniel, the Old Testament book often studied together with its New Testament companion, Revelation, paints a clear picture of the great judgment. The prophet directs us to the heavenly throne room. He describes the "Ancient of Days" on His throne like "a fiery flame," with "thousand thousands" ministering to Him while "the court was seated" and "the books were opened." Daniel 7:9, 10.

The setting of the judgment, then, is heaven. The time? In Daniel 8:14, the prophet zeroes in on the timing of the judgment: "Unto two thousand and three hundred days; then shall the sanctuary be cleansed" (KJV).

◆ The desert sandbox

The cleansing of the sanctuary, as we shall see, refers to the process of the judgment. Understanding the meaning of the "sanctuary" requires a quick look at the ceremonial system of the Old Testament.

Since the time of Moses, the Jews had followed a detailed worship program centered on the earthly sanctuary service. This remarkable service was modeled after a pattern God had given to Moses (see Exodus 25:8, 9). The earthly sanctuary and the practices associated with it were to serve as an illustration of the plan of salvation. God wanted certain tremendous truths made very clear, even if He had to use a desert sandbox!

Two main services were connected with the sanctuary—the daily service and the yearly service. On a daily basis, when a man sinned, he brought a sacrifice, confessed his sin over the animal, and then killed it. A priest caught the blood in a basin, poured most of it out at the base of the altar of brass, and took the rest into the sanctuary. In this way, sin was symbolically transferred from the sinner, to the substitute, to the sanctuary. The lamb, innocent of wrong and dying for the sins of another, pointed ahead to Christ's ultimate sacrifice on man's behalf.

All year the stream of blood flowed, bringing sin into the sanctuary. And then, on the tenth day of the seventh month of the religious year—the Day of Atonement—the sanctuary was cleansed (Leviticus 16). Ten days before the Day of Atonement, silver trumpets warned the people that the Day was approaching. For ten days, the Jews searched their hearts, repented of their misdeeds, and confessed their sins in preparation of the Day of Atonement—that great day of judgment. Those who ignored the warning were shut off from the camp.

Just as the yearly cleansing of the sanctuary meant judgment to God's people in Old Testament days, so the cleansing of the sanctuary in Daniel 8:14 refers to a judgment which will take place prior to the end of Earth's history. The earthly ceremonies described in Leviticus 16 are shadows of God's judgment in the heavenly sanctuary that will take place just before Jesus appears at His second coming.

Just as a way out of man's doom was provided for men and women in Old Testament times, so God has provided a substitute in Jesus, the Lamb of God slain at Calvary. The sanctuary lamb and the Lamb of God provide the basis for reconciliation for all who claim God's promises and conditions.

During the Old Testament Day of Atonement, two goats were used—the "Lord's goat" and the scapegoat. The Lord's goat was sacrificed, and the high priest entered through the veil into the most holy place (a ceremony that happened only on the Day of Atonement), sprinkling the blood upon the mercy seat that rested on the furniture containing the original, divinely etched Ten Commandment tablets. This sacred site represented the throne of God in heaven where Jesus represents His people today.

When the high priest stood before the mercy seat, He was in the very presence of God. If he had any open, known, unconfessed sins in his life, he would be struck dead. The Old Testament foreshadowing is clear: With his role in this service, the High Priest represented Christ, our Heavenly Priest.

After the "Lord's goat" was slain and its blood used in this sacred service, the scapegoat was led out into the wilderness to wander till it died. This represented the death of Satan, the originator and accomplice of all sin. Yearly, God's people were reminded of the sacrifice of the Saviour to come and of the source of evil in the universe. Yearly, they took part in a service designed to prepare them for judgment and to make clear God's ultimate plan for the universe.

◆ 2,300 days

Thus the "cleansing of the sanctuary" in Daniel 8:14 reflects the Old Testament Day of Atonement and refers to the process of judgment in a very specific manner. But when does this process begin? What is the meaning of the numbers included in the prophet's vision: "Unto two thousand and three hundred days; then shall the sanctuary be cleansed"?

Daniel himself was perplexed as to what the dream meant! And it was just like our Lord to send an angel to explain it to him. "Gabriel, make this man to understand the vision. So he came near where I stood: and when he came, I was afraid, and fell upon my face: but he said unto me, Understand, O son of man: for at the time of the end shall be the vision." Daniel 8:16, 17.

These texts contain three points which shed light on this 2,300-day prophecy given to the prophet Daniel. First, the vision extends to the close of time. Second, the 2,300 days applies to God's heavenly sanctuary, since the earthly system of sacrifices would be done away with at the death of Christ. That is, no earthly system of sacrifices would be functioning at the end of the time prophecy. And third, the 2,300 days represent a time period couched in the symbolic language of the Bible.

Where do we find the golden key to unlock the meaning of time in Bible prophecy? In Ezekiel 4:6 (KJV) we read, "I have appointed thee each day for a year." In Bible symbolism, then, a prophetic day equals a literal year. Thus 2,300 days equals 2,300 years.

As the angel Gabriel continues his explanation to Daniel, we find that the 2,300-day/year prophecy is broken into two segments: "Seventy weeks are determined upon thy people," the angel begins, demarcating 490 (70 x 7) symbolic days, or literal years, as the time period in which the Jews must accomplish the work God gave them to do or be rejected as His people. The remaining 1,810 years lead us to the future event, called "the cleansing of sanctuary," or the time of judgment.

The master key for unlocking this entire prophecy is in Daniel 9:25. The beginning date for the 490-day/year period allocated to the Jews is given in graphic detail. "Know therefore and understand, that from the going forth of the commandment to restore and rebuild Jerusalem unto the Messiah the Prince shall be seven weeks, and threescore and two weeks." Daniel 9:25, KJV.

When this prophecy was given to Daniel, the Jews were in captivity in faraway Babylon. The city of Jerusalem lay in ruins. The angel told Daniel that the prophecy would begin when the final, imperial decree was officially passed, allowing the Jews to escape from captivity and return to rebuild the city of Jerusalem. Such a decree was given by Artaxerxes, King of Persia, in the fall of 457 B.C.

Beginning with this starting date, Daniel's amazing prophecy actually foretells, with remarkable precision, the dates of the baptism and death of Jesus, and the subsequent dates when the gospel would be rejected by the Jewish nation and proclaimed to the Gentile world.

In Daniel 9:25 we discover that 69 prophetic weeks would elapse between the time the decree would be issued to rebuild the city of

Jerusalem and the coming of the Messiah. Sixty-nine prophetic weeks (69 x 7) equal 483 literal years.

Let's go back to our starting point and apply this figure of 483 years in order to determine when and to what we are being directed. The decree to restore and rebuild Jerusalem was issued in 457 B.C. Thus, 483 minus 457 gives us 26. But since there was no zero year in history (historians recorded time from 1 B.C. to A.D. 1), we must add a year, coming up with A.D. 27. The prophecy is exact! The word Messiah means "the anointed one." Jesus was anointed by the Holy Spirit and began His ministry at His baptism in the fall of A.D. 27, during the fifteenth year of the reign of Tiberius.

The Bible says that Jesus went forth preaching, "The time is fulfilled." Mark 1:15. No doubt He referred to the time period in the pages of Daniel's prophecy that had awaited fulfillment for so many years.

◆ Prophetic precision

Thus the 69-week prophecy, given five hundred years before the Messiah, pinpointed the exact date of Christ's baptism. This amazing prediction has convinced many doubting Jews that Jesus Christ is the Messiah!

The ministry of Jesus lasted exactly three and a half years. This, too, was predicted by Daniel. "And after threescore and two weeks shall Messiah be cut off. . . And he shall confirm the covenant with many for one week: and in the midst of the week he shall cause the sacrifice and the oblation to cease." Daniel 9:26, 27, KJV.

The Bible predicted that in the midst of this last week—the seventieth prophetic week allocated to the Jewish nation—sacrifices would stop. Amazingly, at this precise time during the feast of the Passover, in the spring of A.D. 31, Jesus was crucified. The Jewish sacrificial system no longer had any meaning. Christ, our Passover Lamb, had been sacrificed.

As Daniel predicted, in A.D. 34, just three and a half years after the cross, (the remainder of the prophetic week referred to in Daniel

9:27), the Jews finally sealed their rejection by the stoning of Stephen! The gospel then went to the Gentiles. Thus, the seventy prophetic weeks (490 years) allowed to the nation of Israel were concluded.

With minute precision, centuries in advance, the prophet Daniel foretold the exact time of Christ's baptism and His crucifixion, the rejection of the gospel by the Jews, and its introduction into the Gentile world. Thus "seventy weeks" or 490 years of the 2,300–year prophecy are clearly accounted for. But what of the remainder of the prophecy? Subtracting 490 from 2,300, we find that 1,810 years remain in the prophecy. Since we left off at A.D. 34, we add 1,810 to 34 and arrive at the year 1844. And what did the Bible predict would happen at this time? "The sanctuary" would be "cleansed," or the judgment hour would begin in heaven in the great sanctuary above that provided the "pattern" given to Moses. Thus, we have been living in the judgment hour since 1844! What a solemn truth to consider!

God considers His judgment so important that He pictures an angel flying in the midst of heaven announcing it with a loud voice. "Fear God and give glory to Him, for the hour of His judgment has come." Revelation 14:7.

As the Lord looks over the books recording every transaction ever made in the history of the world, names are reviewed and cases examined. Someday, when this awesome task is completed, He will descend to earth to claim as His own those who have accepted Him as their Saviour and surrendered their lives completely to Him.

Does it really make a difference that we are living in the judgment hour today? Are there any practical lessons for our lives contained in the judgment-hour message? The first lesson is obvious: If we are really living in the judgment hour, and the judgment takes place just before the second coming of Christ, His coming must be very, very soon.

Second, if the judgment evaluates genuine Christianity, sweeping away all sham and pretense, it is impossible to play religious games with God. We are either saved or lost! We are either controlled by Christ or influenced by Satan. We are personally responsible for our actions.

The essence of humanity is freedom of choice—the ability to make moral decisions. The judgment reveals how we have used the highest freedom of all. Do you sense that you are personally accountable to God? Do you feel the nudging of His Holy Spirit to make a full surrender to Him? Are there habits in your life which would disqualify you from passing God's judgment? Are there secret sins? Do you harbor bitterness or resentment over something someone has done to you?

Why not surrender these un-Christlike attitudes and sinful habits to Jesus right now? Why not allow His grace to pardon you? Why not allow His power to change you? You will be glad that you did in the day of judgment that has been highlighted in the prophecy of Daniel 8:14. ❏

Yes, the judgment is now in session. Both God's fairness and our own life records are under review. Decisions of destiny have already been made, are being made, and will yet be made.

The basis of all these decisions? God's law—the written description of His character and the basis of all order in the universe.

Today God's law is widely ignored, even derided, in our society. And as we've drifted away from it, we've lost the love and order and fairness it provides.

We're left with chaos and crime and violence—with a society that no longer seems able to tell right from wrong. Chapter 11 explores the tragic results of abandoning the rule of law.

11

. . . .

Whatever Happened to Right and Wrong?

The war against love.

In God's universe, love is the basis of life. And the opposite of love—selfishness, or sin—is the basis of death.

Love = Life.

Selfishness = Death.

God's character is love. His law is a description of love. The foundation of His government of the universe is love.

But Lucifer came to see it otherwise. He began to see God's law as limiting life instead of promoting it. He came to see it as against him instead of being for him.

So he rebelled. He launched an attack on God's character, law, and government of love. His alternative? Selfishness.

He convinced a third of his fellow angels that selfishness was superior to love. He has sold the idea successfully to millions, perhaps billions, of human beings, beginning with Adam and Eve.

Today, we see how the world looks when it's governed by selfishness instead of love. How do you like it so far?

11

• •

Crime is skyrocketing! Lawless forces are more bold than ever. Urban streets are unsafe almost everywhere. Crime is quickly penetrating the suburbs. There seems to be no safe haven.

What's behind rising crime? Why such an explosion of lawlessness in the last few decades? What has happened to moral decency? Is it possible that no absolute moral standards exist by which nations can establish their societies?

Someone once remarked facetiously that the "nicest thing about crime is that it usually happens to someone else." But the rising statistics tell us that "someone else" is becoming more and more likely to be ourselves.

Disconcerting as the thought may be, crime is likely to touch our lives somehow, somewhere when we least expect it. No longer can we sigh apathetically and shrug our shoulders, confident that crime happens only to someone else. Statisticians claim that we stand a better than one in four chance of becoming the victim of a mugger, rapist, burglar, embezzler, or other criminal. Race riots, political assassinations, hijackings, cult murders, terrorist kidnappings, and government corruption shock the world.

The 1970s saw the illegitimate birth of "new morality" and "situation ethics." "Do your own thing" came to mean anything from smoking pot to streaking naked in public places. Or having live-in partners and aborting unwanted babies. Neon signs blatantly beckoned the man on the street into topless bars and porno movies. Gays and lesbians came out of their closets, and divorce became as casual as changing bank accounts.

◆ The results of throwing out the rules

Many authorities believe that the soaring crime rates and immorality found in society today are the ugly and predictable products of the permissive, humanistic teachings pervading in our schools. As bad, if not worse, are the adult models in government, entertainment, and—of all places—in our own homes and churches.

From our homes, a new generation of pained and confused children have emerged who are skeptical, questioning, and challenging all authority, from whatever source.

Children love to imitate, yet who are to be their ethical, moral, and spiritual role models? Fathers lie to the government, mothers seek abortions, and both parents cheat on each other. The children see it all. And the broken homes are leaving ugly scars.

Who is to instill a sense of right and wrong if parents cannot or will not? And for those families seeking to establish some type of ethical control in the home, on what basis are they to do so? Who determines what decisions are right? Is not the judgment of even good people often impaired at times? If there is no standard of right and wrong outside of ourselves, almost anything can be justified. We may steal for a "fix," commit adultery if we feel we deserve some diversion, or shoot a person with whom we may disagree.

The Bible reminds us that we are not good judges of what is right and what is wrong: "There is a way that seems right to a man, But its end is the way of death." Proverbs 16:25.

Even some churches today are teaching that God's standard of right and wrong no longer applies. His commandments, they say, have been abolished, or they are no longer relevant, or they are impossible to keep. As a result, many people are following their own desires, "doing their own thing"—and society is reaping a bumper harvest of broken homes, juvenile delinquency and violent crimes. In the words of Hosea the prophet, "They sow the wind, And reap the whirlwind." Hosea 8:7.

Society is learning the hard way that we don't find freedom by throwing out the rules. Once the standard of right and wrong is removed, chaos follows. As the apostle Paul put it in the first chapter of Romans, when man does not see fit to acknowledge God, he is given up to wallow in his own depravity. The Bible describes it so aptly: "He who trusts in his own heart is a fool." Proverbs 28:26.

But for those who will acknowledge Him, God has an answer. Many centuries ago God gave mankind a formula for a crime-free society. Had it always been followed, crime would never have existed! The morning news and the evening paper would be filled with uplifting human-interest stories, and the headlines would be devoid of shocking tragedies.

When the children of Israel camped at Mount Sinai, the Lord came down to meet them, saying, "I am the LORD your God, who brought you out of the land of Egypt, out of the house of bondage." Exodus 20:2. The Lord began this most important communication by establishing His relationship to His people, identifying Himself as their Deliverer from slavery. The One who opened up the Red Sea and rained manna from heaven, the great Protector, was saying, "I care for you. You can trust me."

With this basis of trust established, God spoke His divine law, providing us with a moral guide of conduct for all people on all continents. The Ten Commandments are the foundation for all human law. Thundering atop the mountain, God delivered these injunctions:

"Thou shalt have no other gods before Me.

"Thou shalt not make unto thee any graven image . . .

"Thou shalt not take the name of the Lord thy God in vain . . .

"Remember the Sabbath day to keep it holy. Six days shalt thou labor, and do all thy work: But the seventh day is the Sabbath of the Lord thy God . . .

"Honor thy father and thy mother . . .

"Thou shalt not kill.

"Thou shalt not commit adultery.

"Thou shalt not steal.

"Thou shalt not bear false witness against thy neighbor.

"Thou shalt not covet." Exodus 20:3-17, KJV.

As the people of Israel listened, they were greatly moved. If this were God's will, they were determined to follow it. But God knew that His spoken words were not enough, especially as He looked down the years to men and women yet unborn. So God did more than speak. He traced His standard of right-doing with His own finger, etching the words into stone slabs. No one could argue as to what was said—it was there in stone! "And when He had made an end of speaking with him on Mount Sinai, He gave Moses two tablets of the Testimony, tablets of stone, written with the finger of God." Exodus 31:18.

Although this was the first time that God had given His law in written form, it had existed from all eternity. Long before Sinai, or even Adam and Eve, the eternal, unchangeable standard of right had been the basis of God's heavenly government. Even the angels were governed by it. Some chose to follow its principles and enjoy the freedom of loving service. It is peace, whenever and wherever these principles are followed.

But Satan and his angels opted to "do their own thing" and make their own rules. This rebellion led to their expulsion from heaven (see Revelation 12:8, 9).

From the beginning of life on this earth, God's clear standard of right and wrong has been in existence. Adam and Eve, after breaking God's trust, suddenly felt the emotions of shame and guilt. They knew they had proved unfaithful. They learned immediately what every man and woman has learned since—that proving unfaithful to God's law of love and protection has consequences. Sad, bitter consequences. Instantly, their whole world began to crumble.

One generation later, only a few years from Eden, we see how quickly the human conscience can become seared and blunted. But God's law did not soften to keep pace with man's slippage. Cain, angry with God for accepting Abel's offering rather than his own, heard his Lord's counsel, "Why are you angry? And why has your countenance fallen? If you do well, will you not be accepted? And if you do not do well, sin lies at the door." Genesis 4:6, 7.

On page after page of humanity's early history as recorded in the Bible, the presence of God's law, along with its violations, is clearly established—long before it appeared in written form. The reference to Cain's "sin" implies a law, since the Bible tells us that "sin is lawlessness." 1 John 3:4.

Abraham knew and obeyed God's law long before the spoken law at Sinai. God promised to bless him, "because Abraham obeyed My voice and kept My charge, My commandments, My statutes, and My laws." Genesis 26:5.

After the Exodus, just a few weeks before the Israelites reached Sinai, the Lord rebuked Moses because the Israelites were violating His law by gathering manna on the Sabbath (Exodus 16:28). Thus the fourth commandment was recognized before Sinai.

◆ Order—or chaos?

God's law is the eternal standard of right for the universe. Since, as Paul states, God is "not the author of confusion" (1 Corinthians 14:33), should it come as a surprise that an orderly God operates on the basis of rules of order? No orderly government can exist without laws. No harmonious, happy, safe society can exist without rules. Nature itself has laws. Even children cannot play games without rules.

In the chambers of the Supreme Court of the United States, towering above the heads of the justices, two great figures are carved in stone. One represents Majesty of Government, and the other, Majesty of Law. Between the two appear the two tables of the Ten Commandments.

Impressive as this may be, commandments etched in stone or attached to chamber walls are not enough. "For not the hearers of the law are just in the sight of God, but the doers of the law will be justified." Romans 2:13.

Not only is it important to know the commands of God, we must also respond and comply. Jesus said, "If you love Me, keep My commandments." John 14:15. Quoting from the Old Testament, He pointed out that love is the basis for keeping all the commandments: "'You shall love the LORD your God with all your heart, with all your soul, and with all your mind.' This is the first and great commandment. And the second is like it: 'You shall love your neighbor as yourself.' On these two commandments hang all the Law and the Prophets." Matthew 22:37-40.

If we really love God with all our heart, mind, and soul, a logical response will be the expression of that love by keeping the commandments. Loving a person—either God or another human being—involves a relationship of trust, of choosing to prove faithful to the expectations of that other person. If we choose not to live up to expectations, we are also saying that we do not think highly of that other person, that we do not value that person's expectations, that we consider ourselves wiser than that other person. We cannot have a relationship without fidelity to each other's expectations.

It has been estimated that more than thirty-five million laws have been drafted by men and women to control behavior. But, in less than three hundred words, God drafted a code of conduct that covers all human behavior. But unlike the defective or unwise laws that men make and remake, "The law of the LORD is perfect." Psalm 19:7.

Theologian Augustus Strong wrote, "Law is only the transcript of God's nature." The Ten Commandments are but a reflection, a profile, of God's character—a character that is unchangeable! "I am the LORD, I do not change." Malachi 3:6.

Any change made by men and women in the law of God would make it less than perfect. Being a perfect law, it can never be altered. That is the truth Jesus spoke when He said, "It is easier for heaven and earth to disappear than for the least stroke of a pen to drop out of the Law." Luke 16:17, NIV.

God never meant His law to be a burden on man or for it to restrict his happiness. On the contrary, God intended His commandments to be a wall of protection, shielding us from sorrow and guilt, insuring freedom and safety, giving us restful nights and peaceful days. His wish for His children was "that their hearts would be inclined to fear me and keep all my commands always, so that it might go well with them and their children forever!" Deuteronomy 5:29.

Just as we build guardrails on bridges and mountain roads to keep us from plunging off, God gave us His law to protect and guard us on the road of life.

Another important function of the law is to reveal sin to us. Through an understanding of God's standard, we have a clear sense of right and wrong. Paul makes two statements clarifying the relationship between sin and the law: "Through the law we become conscious of sin." Romans 3:20. And "I would not have known what sin was except through the law." Romans 7:7.

◆ Smashing the mirror

Dr. Arthur Bietz tells of an African princess whose subjects extolled her great beauty and comeliness. However, her self-esteem was shattered one day when a trader passing through her village sold her a mirror. Horrified by the reflection of her own ugliness, she smashed the mirror!

Like a mirror, God's law reveals exactly who we are. As we peer into the reflective glass, we may be horrified, like the African princess, with what we see. Destroying the law, or ignoring it, will not change our condition. The imperfections will remain.

"Anyone who listens to the word but does not do what it says is like a man who looks at his face in a mirror and, after looking at himself, goes away and immediately forgets what he looks like. But the man who looks intently into the perfect law that gives freedom, and continues to do this, not forgetting what he has heard, but doing it—he will be blessed in what he does." James 1:23-25.

The law points out sin. But the law can no more remove the sin than a mirror can wash one's face. We need something more than the law to make our lives right again. The law cannot remove the guilt of sins past. The law cannot provide power to overcome sin's temptations in the future. The sinner needs help that the law cannot provide. Its function is to point out the right way to live—it points out where we fail. But law can never be our Saviour. "If a law had been given that could impart life, then righteousness would certainly have come by the law." Galatians 3:21.

But for all, the goodness of God provides us all with hope—the hope of forgiveness and power to live changed lives. We call that goodness "grace." Grace is the gift of God, made possible through the life and death of our Lord Jesus Christ. Through this unspeakable gift of God to this world, we all may receive eternal life (Romans 3:23). Even if we were to keep the law perfectly from this day forward, the sins we have already committed would condemn us to eternal death. But Jesus paid the price for our sins on Calvary's cross, and only by His grace can our sins be forgiven.

Willing obedience, and gratitude for the opportunity to give God full access to assist our thoughts and actions, are the natural expressions that spring forth when we accept Christ's sacrifice on our behalf. Obviously, willing obedience is not the means by which we earn God's favor, but rather the result of our accepting it. As such, obedience is an indication of whether our plea for forgiveness is genuine and whether our heart is changed—whether we are born again.

Although we cannot be saved by our obedience (because it takes more than our best efforts to comply with God's law of love), our willing obedience (coupled with the empowering of the Holy Spirit) reveals the fruit of our new relationship with God. We call that relationship "salvation." Salvation always has been and always will be the result of God's grace working in our lives. Men and women have, in all ages, been saved by God's grace through faith—the trusting response of grateful men and women.

Being saved by grace does not lead to an apathetic or careless response to the law, but rather to a renewed determination to keep it. Imagine the response of a young man, apprehended for murder, taken to prison, and sentenced to die. If by some law of the land, his own father were able to step in before the execution and offer his own life in exchange for his son's, what would be the obligation of this freed prisoner? Would this young man, pardoned by the grace of his own father, be inclined to spurn the sacrifice and continue in a life of crime? To live a lawless life? To do his own thing?

Not at all! Pardoned by the blood of his own father, the young man should feel more than ever his obligation to uphold the laws of the land. At the top of all his reasons to be law-abiding would be his gratitude for his father's sacrifice!

With far greater consequences for all of eternity, Christ has lived and died in order that we might be saved from the consequences of our sinful choices. Our grateful response seems obvious: a forgiven man or woman responds with an increased commitment to follow that law which His Lord has upheld through His eternal sacrifice. Accepting Christ as our Saviour means accepting His forgiveness and His power to keep His commandments, permitting His laws to be etched in our minds as they once were on tables of stone (see Hebrews 8:10).

Once His law becomes the focus of our desire, our choices, and our habits, we are freed from a sense of restriction. For those who married their sweethearts, responding to each other's expectations becomes each partner's chief delight. We call it commitment.

But loving commitment is not an emotion for easy times only. At times, loyal commitment leads to hard decisions—such as when the relationship between two lovers may call for turning away from all other desires or goals one has held dear.

◆ The cost of commitment

The world's greatest demonstration of the cost of loyal commitment to the will of God was vividly seen on a cold, dark night under an old olive tree in a garden called Gethsemane. With drops of blood seeping through His pores, the faithful Lord prayed, "My Father, if it is possible, may this cup be taken from me. Yet not as I will, but as you will." Matthew 26:39.

The fate of the human race hung in the balance—a guilty world was to be saved or lost. Would this young Galilean put all desire for life and human fulfillment aside and die at Calvary? Without guilt, wiping the sweat from His brow, He could have said: "Let the sinner suffer the consequence of his own sins."

Or, He could let wicked men nail Him to a cross so man could be pardoned. In that awful crisis when everything was at stake, Jesus dipped His pen of love into the crimson ink drained from His own veins and wrote "pardoned" across your record and mine.

The old rugged cross on a hill called Calvary is one eternal reminder of the price God was willing to pay to satisfy the claims of the broken law and to save guilty man. If the law could have been abolished or changed, Jesus' death on Calvary would have been unnecessary. But Christ's death was very much a reality: "By his own blood he . . . obtained eternal redemption for us." Hebrews 9:12, KJV.

Christ stands with His arms outstretched to all of us today, telling us to "Come." Come to Him for peace and pardon and power. Words that have cheered men and women for centuries are still fresh. They still call: "Let him who thirsts come. Whoever desires, let him take the water of life freely." Revelation 22:17.

Salvation can be yours today, friend. When Adam sinned, the door was open for the whole human race to do likewise. With Adam, we all have sinned. When Jesus died, the entire human race died with Him. We are one with Jesus. If we accept the fact that He has already paid the price for our sins, we may receive the freedom from guilt He offers. Motivated by His love, we follow Him on this earth wherever He leads—and then, in the earth made new, we follow Him "wherever He goes" (Revelation 14:4).

We are never without the ability to do what He asks (and whatever He asks is the only way for us to find lasting happiness). He supplies both the desire and the power for whatever He wants us to think or do. Let us reach out to Him today—and receive the freshness of new hope and power in our lives. His hand is never withdrawn. He still is able "to save to the uttermost those who come to God through Him, since He always lives to make intercession for them." Hebrews 7:25. ❑

If God's law is a description of love, why did perfect Lucifer come to hate it so?

The reasons may not ever be fully known—how, after all, can the origin of evil ever be adequately explained? But we do know that Lucifer came to desire for himself things that were out of harmony with love. He wanted to receive the worship that belonged only to God. He wanted the power and authority of God.

Whatever his reasons, Lucifer, now Satan, has spent thousands of years now attacking the law. And of these Ten Commandments, he has leveled perhaps his most savage attacks against the Fourth—the Sabbath commandment.

12

....

The Memory Lapse That Spawned Evolution

The Sabbath under seige.

"Remember the Sabbath day . . ." the fourth commandment begins.

The Sabbath, as the Bible reveals it, is a weekly celebration of God's power as our Creator.

If we should ever forget the Sabbath, God knew that in time we would also forget Him as the Creator.

And in fact, that is exactly what has happened. The world has almost universally forgotten the Sabbath as explored in the chapter just ahead.

The result? Most of us no longer even believe in a Creator. Against all logic and reason, we prefer to believe that human beings are descended from apes or salamanders—or even from floating bits of protoplasm in a primordial sea, ignited into life by the chance strike of a passing lightning bolt.

Which do we do first when confronted with such nonsense— laugh, or cry? For such a theory is at once both laughable and sad.

Can you begin to see why Satan attacks the Sabbath so aggressively? After all, it keeps people focused clearly on the power of his greatest enemy.

No wonder one of the greatest battles in the War Behind All Wars is the battle over the Sabbath!

12

Have you ever created something you were especially proud of? Working into the early hours of the morning, fired by a vision of the final product, have you ever shaped wood, fired pottery, crafted words, stitched a tapestry? Something inside all of us responds pleasurably to the process of creating, the energy of the doing, the satisfaction of the finished product. That something is modeled after the divine. God created you and me in His image (Genesis 1:26, 27).

The Bible tells us that God experienced that creative satisfaction when He created the universe. Beginning with the earth, which was without form and void of life, He added new touches each day, sitting back each evening and saying, "It's good!" (Genesis 1.)

One of the most amazing truths of the New Testament is that Jesus, who existed from all eternity as a member of the Godhead, held the primary role in creating the universe. The Bible's message is consistent on this point:

"In the beginning was the Word, and the Word was with God, and the Word was God. He was in the beginning with God. All things were made through Him, and without Him nothing was made that was made. . . . And the Word became flesh and dwelt among us, and we beheld His glory, the glory as of the only begotten of the Father, full of grace and truth." John 1:1-3, 14.

Paul, the apostle, clearly shows how God the Father and His Son worked together in the creation of this world: "God . . . created all things through Jesus Christ." Ephesians 3:9.

The third person of the Godhead, the Holy Spirit, was also involved in the creation of Planet Earth. The Bible (Genesis 1) says that the earth was without shape and that total darkness covered it. Then the Spirit of God moved upon the waters.

The amazingly intricate world as we know it today was created in six literal days. Starting with a shapeless mass of darkness, God dazzled it with light, enveloped it with atmosphere, salted it with seas, brightened it with plants, graced it with stars, enlivened it with wild things—day by day looking upon his handiwork and saying, "It's good!"

And then came the crowning act of creation. Turning to the Father, the Creator said, "Let Us make man in Our image, . . . in the image of God He created him; male and female He created them." Genesis 1:26, 27.

Man could receive no greater honor! God could have shown no greater love! The human race is God's masterpiece of creation—the object of His supreme love! And this love was meant to be shared, for God said, "Be fruitful and multiply; fill the earth and subdue it; have dominion over . . . every living thing that moves on the earth." Genesis 1:28.

After the creation of Adam and Eve on the sixth day, the Bible says, "Thus the heavens and the earth, and all the host of them, were finished." Genesis 2:1. Just six days of work, and creation was done. Such a short time! But not for God! The Bible says, "For He spoke, and it was done; He commanded, and it stood fast." Psalm 33:9.

Adam and Eve must have gazed in wide-eyed wonder as the blazing sun, in all its glory, began to slip over the western horizon, ending the sixth day of creation.

But the Genesis account of creation does not end there. The Bible record continues: "On the seventh day God ended His work which He had done, and He rested on the seventh day from all His work which He had done." Genesis 2:2.

God rested! Why? Not because He was weary, for the prophet Isaiah tells us that God never gets weary (Isaiah 40:28). The Creator of the Universe permitted Himself the satisfaction of enjoying His completed creation. And then, pleased with His accomplishments over Earth's first six days, God did something especially significant. "Then God blessed the seventh day and sanctified it, because in it He rested from all His work which God had created and made." Genesis 2:3.

◆ A reminder of our roots

God blessed the seventh day! He made the seventh day an object of divine favor, a day that would contain an endless fountain of spiritual refreshing for His people, for all time to come.

Next, He sanctified the seventh day! He set it apart as a holy day, a special time every seven days to continually remind us of our beginnings—our roots!

As long as you and I set aside the seventh day to worship our Creator, we will never lose sight of who we are, where we came from, or what our eternal destiny may be. Every seventh day, we are forever linked with our Creator.

God knew that it was essential for men and women, even in Eden, to set aside the seventh day as a day of rest and worship. He appointed this special segment of time for fellowship with His creatures. At the end of each week, Adam and Eve celebrated the birthday of the world with their Creator.

The creation of the world, and man's recognition of God's creative powers through Sabbath-keeping, is outlined not only in Genesis, the first book of the Bible, but also in Revelation, the last. The great message in Revelation which prepares the last generation to be ready for Christ's second coming echoes the story of creation found in Genesis:

"Then I saw another angel flying in the midst of heaven, having the everlasting gospel to preach to those who dwell on the earth—to every nation, tribe, tongue, and people—saying with a loud voice, 'Fear God and give glory to Him, for the hour of His judgment has come; and worship Him who made heaven and earth, the sea and springs of water.'" Revelation 14:6, 7.

We in our day are called to worship the Judge of all mankind—God the Creator. Just before the Creator Himself returns to the earth to reclaim it as His own, His final message is to go forth with full force! Fear God. Honor Him. Acknowledge His Creative powers.

Could it be that God, looking down through the centuries, saw that mankind would forget its roots? Could it be that God perceived the great gulf that sin would create as it broke communion between creatures and Creator, obliterating the truth of man's divine creation?

Bible history reveals the sad truth that by the time of Moses, God's people, who were in Egyptian bondage, had forgotten their roots and God's special day of fellowship. But God had a plan to remind His people of His special day. As Moses led the Israelites from Egypt to Palestine, the promised land, food rations ran out in the Sinai wilderness. Here, God miraculously provided bread from heaven, called "manna," for forty years.

But the story is about more than receiving a daily bread supply for forty years! The manna appeared on the ground only six days a week—Sunday through Friday! But on Friday, the sixth day, the Israelites were instructed to gather up enough manna for the seventh day! The manna never fell on the seventh day, and if extra was gathered in advance on any day other than the sixth, it would spoil.

Why? God wanted His people to know that the One who had led them out of Egypt was also their Creator. God wanted to point His creatures back to their creation. Signifying the importance of the seventh day through the way He supplied the manna, God wanted His people to know that His day was very special—that it had in no way faded in significance with the passing of time.

God's instruction regarding the manna was, "Six days you shall gather it, but on the seventh day, which is the Sabbath, there will be none." Exodus 16:26. Some of the people, refusing to follow God's advice and gather an extra portion on the sixth day, went out on the Sabbath to gather manna. But they did not find any. And our patient Lord asked, "How long do you refuse to keep My commandments and My laws?" Exodus 16:28.

From Genesis to Revelation, the Bible speaks with one voice regarding the importance of the seventh day, the weekly Sabbath. Several weeks after the beginning of the manna experience, God again came close to men and women when He etched on tablets of stone, with His own finger, the great truths He had spoken in the Garden of Eden.

The Israelites were emphatically reminded of how God felt about the seventh day—the Sabbath—when Moses came down from Mount Sinai carrying God's handwritten message:

"Remember the Sabbath day, to keep it holy. Six days shalt thou labour, and do all thy work: But the seventh day is the Sabbath of the Lord thy God: in it thou shalt not do any work, . . . for in six days the Lord made heaven and earth, the sea and all that in them is, and rested the seventh day: wherefore the Lord blessed the Sabbath day, and hallowed it." Exodus 20:8-11, KJV.

In these immortal words, God asks men and women to remember the weekly memorial of creation—the seventh-day Sabbath. And He promises His people many blessings in connection with this special day:

"If you turn away your foot from the Sabbath, From doing your pleasure on My holy day, And call the Sabbath a delight, The holy day of the LORD honorable, And shall honor Him, not doing your own ways, Nor finding your own pleasure, Nor speaking your own words, Then you shall delight yourself in the LORD." Isaiah 58:13, 14.

◆ The high cost of forgetting

Had men and women always remembered this memorial of God's creation, the problems so prevalent today—lack of meaning in life, identity crises, loss of self-esteem—would never have arisen. There would be no evolutionists, no skeptics, no agnostics!

The prophet Isaiah, a thousand years after Moses, emphasized a point that should never have been forgotten: The Sabbath was never intended to be confined to Israel; it was not a Jewish holy day or even a Jewish holiday. Far from it! God gave the Sabbath to men and women thousands of years before there was a Jew.

God did not restrict such a blessing to one race only. He invited all people to remember and keep the Sabbath with Him: "Everyone who keeps from defiling the Sabbath, . . . I will bring to My holy mountain, And make them joyful in My house of prayer. . . For My house shall be called a house of prayer for all nations." Isaiah 56:6, 7.

Nowhere in the Bible is the Sabbath called "the Sabbath of the Jews." Jesus made it clear that it was a day for all mankind when He said, "The Sabbath was made for man, and not man for the Sabbath." Mark 2:27. And Jesus also said that He is "Lord even of the Sabbath." Matthew 12:8.

The Sabbath is more than a memorial of creation. It is a weekly reminder of the profound relationship between God and man, an acknowledgement of God's divinity, "that you may know that I am the LORD your God." Ezekiel 20:20.

The creative power used in sanctifying the Sabbath is the same power God uses today in sanctifying sinful men and women. That promise means that our Creator is also our Saviour. "Moreover I also gave them My Sabbaths, to be a sign between them and Me, that they might know that I am the LORD who sanctifies them." Ezekiel 20:12. To observe the Sabbath is to recognize and receive God's creative, sanctifying power in our lives today.

The Sabbath was instituted and celebrated before sin reared its head on Planet Earth, and the Sabbath will also be celebrated after sin is forever banished from Earth:

"'For as the new heavens and the new earth Which I will make shall remain before Me,' says the LORD, 'So shall your descendants and your name remain. And it shall come to pass That from one New Moon to another, And from one Sabbath to another, All flesh shall come to worship before Me,' says the LORD." Isaiah 66:22, 23.

Imagine this: Throughout all eternity God's people will celebrate the Sabbath to honor their Creator and Redeemer. Does it not seem reasonable that if the Sabbath was celebrated before sin came to Earth, and if it will be celebrated when the Earth is made new, God's people should celebrate it now?

Throughout the New Testament we find that our friendly example, Jesus Christ, did not forget this special memorial of creation while

He was on this earth. Luke tells us, "So He came to Nazareth, where He had been brought up. And as His custom was, He went into the synagogue on the Sabbath day, and stood up to read." Luke 4:16.

Jesus' custom, then, was to go to the synagogue on Sabbath. But, you might ask, which day is the Sabbath? How can we be certain on which day Jesus worshiped? How do we know that somewhere between the time of Moses and Jesus, God might have changed the day?

Think about it for a moment. If the day had been changed or forgotten between Adam's time and Moses' time, God would have rectified it when He wrote the Ten Commandments at Sinai. If the Sabbath day had been lost between Moses' time and Jesus' time, Christ would surely have set the record straight.

If God were to make such a major change involving one of His finger-etched commandments, surely somewhere in the Bible we would find a record of it! The issue of which day was the Sabbath never arose while Jesus was on Earth. The only controversy arose over how He kept it.

◆ Piling on the rules

Ever since their return from captivity in Babylon, Jewish leaders were determined that never again would their nation forget their Lord. Never again would they forget the importance of the weekly Sabbath. In this dedication to "remembering" the Sabbath day to "keep it holy," Jewish leaders, in spite of their good intentions, made the Sabbath a cruel burden. They distorted Sabbath observance by heaping upon it austere, cumbersome regulations. For example, they would not allow a man to spit on the Sabbath, for fear he would irrigate the grass! A man could not travel more than a certain number of miles from his home on the Sabbath. If he had plans to do so, he could travel part way the day before and leave some token—a handkerchief, a piece of cloth—to set up a temporary "home" and thus justify the additional miles.

Jesus tried to eliminate such meaningless man-made requirements and show the true beauty and significance of Sabbath observance. When He was accused of breaking the Sabbath because He healed people on that day, He answered, "It is lawful to do good on the Sabbath." Matthew 12:12.

As we look at Calvary, the true meaning of Sabbath observance is demonstrated by the devoted followers of Jesus. On Friday, the day before the Sabbath, the disciples' hopes in Jesus had been crushed. They witnessed Him dying a cruel death on the cross. Their dreams and hopes lay in a darkened tomb. As a last act of devotion, they wanted to anoint His dead body. But first they paused to give honor and glory to God during the Sabbath hours.

Under the shadow of the world's greatest crisis, Jesus' friends rested according to God's command. Note carefully the sequence of events in these texts:

"That day was the Preparation, and the Sabbath drew near. And the women who had come with Him from Galilee followed after, and they observed the tomb and how His body was laid. Then they returned and prepared spices and fragrant oils. And they rested on the Sabbath according to the commandment. Now on the first day of the week, very early in the morning, they, and certain other women with them, came to the tomb bringing the spices which they had prepared." Luke 23:54-24:1.

Let us review the order of events. On the preparation day (now called Friday), Jesus died, and the women prepared spices and ointments. On the Sabbath day (now called Saturday), the women rested according to the commandment (the fourth commandment of the Ten), and Jesus rested in the tomb. On the first day of the week (now called Sunday), the women came to anoint Jesus, but found the tomb empty because Christ had risen!

Here, three consecutive days are mentioned in the Bible. The preparation day, or Good Friday; the first day of the week, or Easter Sunday; and the day in between, or Saturday, which the Bible calls the Sabbath.

There is no possible doubt as to which day was the Sabbath at the time of Jesus' death. Jesus hung on the cross on Friday and cried, "It is finished." His work of redemption completed, He rested in the tomb over the Sabbath and arose on Sunday, the first day of the week. Even in death, Jesus kept the Sabbath!

And the closer we get to the cross today, the more we realize that just any day in seven will not do! To tamper with the Sabbath is to tamper with creation, Sinai, and Calvary itself!

Our Creator asks us to "remember!" Yet so many have forgotten! This blurring of God's special memorial also blurs our relationship with our Creator.

Jesus expected that Christians would keep the Sabbath for all time. Note His words of instruction given on an earlier occasion, referring to events yet to come to the Jewish people: "And pray that your flight may not be in winter or on the Sabbath." Matthew 24:20. Jesus expected that about forty years after His death, when Jerusalem was destroyed, Christians would still be keeping the Sabbath.

The New Testament reveals that Jesus' followers did keep the Sabbath after the resurrection. In fact, the book of Acts records eighty-four meetings that Paul held on the Sabbath. For example: "They came to Thessalonica, where there was a synagogue of the Jews. Then Paul, as his custom was, went in to them, and for three Sabbaths reasoned with them from the Scriptures." Acts 17:1, 2.

On another occasion, as Paul preached in the synagogue, a group of visitors approached him and requested that he speak the following Sabbath. "The Gentiles begged that these words might be preached to them the next Sabbath. . . . On the next Sabbath almost the whole city came together to hear the word of God." Acts 13:42, 44.

◆ A golden thread

Yes, the Sabbath runs like a golden thread from Genesis to Revelation. The Book of Revelation describes those who are prepared to meet Jesus when He comes: "Here is the patience of the saints; here are those who keep the commandments of God and the faith of Jesus." Revelation 14:12.

Jesus said, "If you love Me, keep My commandments." John 14:15.

And one of those commandments tells us to "remember" the Sabbath day—a sign between God and man forever!

This biblical truth about the Sabbath may be new to you. You may never have realized before that God's Sabbath is for all mankind. You may never have considered the towering importance of the Bible teaching on this subject.

We all have an appointment with God each Sabbath day, every week. Established at creation, given in the heart of the Ten Commandments, kept by Jesus, and honored by the disciples, the Sabbath is God's sign of eternal loyalty. He personally invites you to experience the rewards of Sabbath-keeping.

The Sabbath provides rich opportunities for spiritual renewal, physical rejuvenation, and mental relaxation. It's a time of family fellowship and social interaction. Why not experience the overwhelming joy of Sabbath-keeping for yourself? Why not begin this week a wonderful habit of celebrating God's goodness each Sabbath? ❏

First, Satan attacked the Sabbath by helping God's people forget it. After all, when you become a nation of slaves, your time is no longer your own—especially your weekly day of worship.

Then the devil attacked the Sabbath by loading it down with so many rules that people dreaded to see the Sabbath coming.

Finally, he attacked the Sabbath by changing it from the day of the week God had chosen to another day entirely.

How did he pull this off? Find out in Chapter 13.

13

• •

Assault on Heaven's Constitution

The Ten Suggestions?

The great enemy in this cosmic war would like nothing better than to convince us that God's Ten Commandments are really just His Ten Suggestions.

He prefers, of course, that we simply believe that the Ten Commandments have been abolished—that they no longer apply. But if we don't buy that, then at the very least he wants us to view them as optional.

Consider the Sabbath, for example. Did God say that He had set aside the seventh day of the week as holy? What He really had in mind, the devil argues, is that we observe one day out of every seven.

And to underscore his point, the devil took matters into his own hands and "moved" the Sabbath to another day.

He couldn't get this done without some human assistance, however. So he enlisted the help of an apostate Christian church and a pagan empire. Soon the job was done.

Through His prophet Daniel, God warned His people ahead of time that Satan would try to tamper with the Fourth Commandment. Here in this chapter is what Daniel had to say.

13

During the days of Imperial Russia, the czar was walking through one of the beautiful parks connected with his palace one afternoon, when he came upon a sentry standing guard near a patch of weeds. Surprised to find a guard in that place, he inquired, "What are you doing?"

"I don't exactly know," answered the sentry. "I am simply following the captain's orders."

The czar then asked the captain, "Why do you have a sentry standing guard over some weeds?"

"Regulations have always been that way," the captain responded. "But I don't know why."

After a thorough investigation, the czar discovered that nobody in his court could remember a time when a guard had not been commissioned to pace back and forth in that very spot. As far back as anyone could remember, it had always been that way.

The czar turned to the archives containing the ancient records and the story of Catherine the Great's once-beautiful rose garden. One hundred years before, on this guarded spot, Catherine had planted a special rose bush. Then she stationed a sentry to guard it. The plant had long since died. For years, guards continued to protect they knew not what!

In a similar way, scores of people in the Christian church today are

155

defending a doctrine that has slipped into the church by tradition and not as a commandment of God. The prophet Daniel clearly predicted that this would happen. In his book, Daniel outlines four great lines of prophecy in chapters 2, 7, 8, and 11. Each of these chapters, covering the same time period, contributes its own unique details, some of which apply with special force to the last days.

◆ Four beasts from the sea

In chapter seven, Daniel describes a vision of four great beasts that arise, in succession, from the sea. The first, a lion-like beast, has eagles' wings, which are plucked, forcing the beast "to stand on two feet like a man, and a man's heart was given to it." Daniel 7:4.

The second beast is like a bear, raised up on one side, with three ribs in its mouth, devouring "much flesh" (verse 5).

The third beast is like a leopard, with four wings on its back and four heads. And if this is not frightening enough, the prophet says of the next beast, "Behold, a fourth beast, dreadful and terrible, exceedingly strong" (verse 7). This creature has great iron teeth, which it uses to devour the vulnerable, breaking them into pieces and stamping what's left of them with its feet. This ten-headed beast is different from all the others.

A vast seascape on a stormy day provides the setting for this unusual vision. Strong winds whip the waves into fury while the four curious-looking beasts march up, in order, out of the surf.

Winds, waters, and beasts are commonly-used symbols in Scripture. Where do we find the keys to unlock these prophetic symbols? Three Bible texts unlock the meaning.

In Revelation, the meaning of "water" is revealed: "The waters which you saw . . . are peoples, multitudes, nations, and tongues." Revelation 17:15.

Jeremiah tells us what "winds" mean: "I will bring the four winds From the four quarters of heaven, And scatter them toward all those winds." Jeremiah 49:36. Since God scattered Israel with the winds of war, the connotation here is that of battle.

An angel tells Daniel the meaning of the beasts. "Those great beasts, which are four, are four kings which arise out of the earth." Daniel 7:17.

As a result of wars among the nations, four great kingdoms would rise and fall. The four metals in the image of Daniel 2—gold, silver, brass, and iron—also represent these four powers. History reveals only four universal kingdoms since Daniel's day (see Chapter 5).

The first beast which appeared—the lion with eagle's wings—paralleled the head of gold in Nebuchadnezzar's image, representing the kingdom of Babylon. Depicted by the finest of metals and the king of beasts, ancient Babylon was truly a mighty empire!

But in the year 539 B.C., Medo-Persia, represented in the prophecy by a bear with three ribs in its mouth, overthrew Babylon. The ribs, no doubt, stand for the three conquests that brought the Persians to power. Egypt, Lydia, and Babylon were successively subdued.

A leopard with four wings on its back represents the third world empire. The Grecians, under Alexander the Great, literally flew from conquest to conquest to dominate the world. The leopard had four heads, symbolizing the fourfold partition of the empire after Alexander's death.

The dreadful, indescribable fourth beast represents the cruel, crushing power of the Rome Empire. She ruled the world for six centuries, beginning in 168 B.C. In the great image of Daniel 2, the kingdom of the Caesars is likened to iron that "breaks in pieces and shatters everything; and like iron that crushes, that kingdom will break in pieces and crush all the others." Daniel 2:40. The "iron monarchy" of the world did just that!

◆ Ten horns, three horns, one horn

This terrifying beast of iron was distinguished from the others by ten horns, with another little horn that came up among them, uprooting three in the process. Daniel explained, "The ten horns are ten kings Who shall arise." Daniel 7:24. No animal in nature has ten horns. Those of this symbolic beast were placed there one thousand years ahead of time to accurately forecast the breakup of Rome into ten parts. These divisions of the Roman Empire laid the foundations of the modern European nations.

The significance of the little horn which comes up from the ten horns, uprooting three, is not to be underestimated. Daniel reveals several identifying characteristics to clearly show its true face.

The first fact we are given is that the little horn comes up from among the ten horns. That is, it arises from the head of the fourth beast, which is undoubtedly the Roman Empire.

Next, it emerges with significant power after the ten horns arise. Third, it is diverse from the first ten kingdoms, being different in character. As the ten horns represented political organizations, this little horn would draw his authority from a different source—as the texts indicate, a religious power. And three of the ten kingdoms would be displaced in its rise to power!

As Daniel continues to draw his graphic picture, we find that this horn has "eyes," not of God but of man. It is guided by human intelligence, human leadership, and human authority, with a single man as a leader. It usurps God's authority!

Given these facts, we are led to these questions: What power rose to prominence in Western Europe, as the Roman Empire was disintegrating, by subduing three nations? How was this power different from the four succeeding kingdoms?

History provides an answer, and only one answer, to the identity of the little horn power. Just after the ten kingdoms had brought down the Roman Empire, a Christian church-state was established. The papacy steadily expanded its influence in the next several centuries, rising to prominence in Western Europe.

Its rise to power was highlighted by a destruction of three kingdoms—the Heruli, Ostrogoths, and Vandals. These three tribes were plucked up by the roots as the prophecy describes. Seven of these ten tribal-kingdoms can be found in Europe today. But these three—the Heruli, the Ostrogoths, and the Vandals—were completely destroyed by the rise of the little horn power.

This power gained authority at the exact time the prophecy foretold, in the location the prophecy predicted, and in the way the prophecy indicated. Different from any power ever to rule before, it was a religio-political power, as the prophecy so clearly states, "diverse," or different, from the other kingdoms.

Throughout the New Testament, we find that early church leaders were already looking ahead to a time when apostasy would enter the church—an apostasy already predicted in Daniel's prophecies. Concerned for the future of the church, Paul wrote to the elders of Ephesus, "For I know this, that after my departure savage wolves will come in among you, not sparing the flock. Also from among yourselves men will rise up, speaking perverse things, to draw away the disciples after themselves." Acts 20:29, 30.

Speaking to the Thessalonians, he said, "For the mystery of lawlessness is already at work." 2 Thessalonians 2:7.

◆ Attacked from outside—and inside

Three things troubled Paul about the future: First, opposition would come from without, which he compared to the damage wolves do among a flock of sheep. This envisioned the savage persecution by which Satan would try to destroy the church by outside political pressures.

The second problem would be more serious—apostasy from within. Church leaders would arise, speaking perverse things.

The third problem would be the quick appearance of the apostasy. "From among yourselves men will rise up." Paul pleaded with tears for the preservation of the purity of the faith, but he knew apostasy would soon come. And it did.

Paul warned of a "falling away" or a departure from truth. To the Thessalonians, he wrote, "Let no one deceive you by any means; for that Day will not come unless the falling away comes first, and the man of sin is revealed, the son of perdition." 2 Thessalonians 2:3.

This term "son of perdition" is used in only one other place in Scripture—to describe Judas Iscariot. This description of Judas gives us a picture of betrayal by one who outwardly acted the part of a friend.

Paul predicted that popular Christianity would be caught up in a landslide that would betray the essentials of the gospel while maintaining all the outward forms and professions of fidelity. It would be led by a "man of sin," professing himself to be a man of God while transgressing His very law.

The picture of this growing apostasy became clearer as the years went by. The great struggle of the centuries would not be the battle between religion and atheism, but between truth and error. Opposition from without would only purify and strengthen the church. The enemy against pure doctrine would work most effectively from within. Christian leaders, often without clear knowledge of what they were doing, overthrew the truth and used the church itself to spread falsehoods about God's character—as well as to develop counterfeit doctrines about how God plans to redeem men and women from sin.

In Daniel 8, we find the same appalling prediction: The little horn grows and becomes "exceedingly great," actually casting down the truth to the ground! "He shall speak pompous words against the Most High, Shall persecute the saints of the Most High, And shall intend to change times and law. Then the saints shall be given into his hand For a time and times and half a time." Daniel 7:25.

Over a specified period of time, the apostasy in the Christian church would in some way undermine the authority of God, subvert His law, and change His " times." This subversion was not accepted by all Christians; always, groups existed that would not conform to these theological changes.

But trouble and persecution awaited those who resisted the trends. "He [the little horn] . . . Shall persecute the saints of the Most High." This can only refer to religious persecution, which the annals of history all too graphically record.

In what way would the little horn power challenge the authority of God? Scripture makes it clear that God's authority is based on His position as Creator and Sustainer of the universe—and of our world in particular. The Bible continually appeals to creation as the basis of God's authority. The angel, flying in the midst of heaven, warns, "Fear God and give glory to Him, for the hour of His judgment has come;

and worship Him who made heaven and earth, the sea and springs of water." Revelation 14:7.

God's right to be worshiped, and the authority of His law, is built on the fact that He created this world and its inhabitants.

◆ Tampering with heaven's Constitution

The prophecy regarding the attributes of the little horn power focuses on its usurping of God's authority. How could that be? That a Christian church would usurp God's authority and "think to change times and laws" (Daniel 7:25, KJV)! The thought is almost unbelievable!

The "laws" referred to here cannot be mere human laws, since such changes in a nation's laws occur automatically when one kingdom overthrows another. The reference was obviously to the laws of God. To meddle with these would, in a very real sense, be speaking great words against Him!

But while the church would presume to attempt changes, God says, "My covenant I will not break, Nor alter the word that has gone out of My lips." Psalm 89:34. God spoke his ten laws on Mount Sinai, and He declares, "I will not change them!"

Has the Roman church—that power that arose from the head of the fourth beast—ever tried to change God's holy Ten Commandment law, specifically, the "times" included in that law? The only specific reference to time in the commandments is found in the fourth commandment. God said, "Remember the sabbath day, to keep it holy. Six days shalt thou labour, and do all thy work: but the seventh day is the sabbath of the Lord thy God: . . . for in six days the Lord made heaven and earth, the sea, and all that in them is, and rested the seventh day: wherefore the Lord blessed the sabbath day, and hallowed it." Exodus 20:8-11, KJV.

The Sabbath was given to humanity as a perpetual memorial of creation. Genesis declares, "Thus the heavens and the earth, and all the host of them, were finished. And on the seventh day God ended His work which He had done, and He rested on the seventh day from all His work which He had done. Then God blessed the seventh day and sanctified it, because in it He rested from all His work which God had created and made." Genesis 2:1-3.

God did three things upon the seventh-day Sabbath: He rested upon it; He blessed it; and He sanctified it. The Sabbath was established in the Garden of Eden and will be kept in Eden restored, for Isaiah 66:23 says, "And it shall come to pass That from one New Moon to another, And from one Sabbath to another, All flesh shall come to worship before Me,' says the LORD."

Christ and His disciples kept the Sabbath, and throughout the book of Acts the Sabbath day was remembered and kept by early Christians as their weekly day of rest and worship. In no place does the Bible state that Christ or the disciples ever kept any other day than the seventh-day Sabbath. When we look about through most of Christianity today, something obvious has happened. The day of worship is usually Sunday. Somehow, the biblical Sabbath was changed by someone, somewhere—but by whom, and when?

Early in the second century, some Christians began to celebrate the first day of the week. What was behind their new emphasis? The reason is not wrapped in a mystery. Christians suffered much from the fact that many of them had converted from Judaism to Christianity, and Jewish people were an irritant to the Roman leaders. Anything that reminded gentiles of the Jewish religion and other practices aroused their hatred. The commemoration of the weekly Sabbath became a highly visible link to Judaism, and all the hostility directed against Jews was also—by confusion, of course—directed against Christians. Consequently, some Christian leaders, deciding that prudence was more important than loyalty, proposed a change in the day of worship.

Sixtus, the bishop, or "papa," of the church in Rome, began the process that ended in a transference of the day of worship for regions beyond Rome. Early in the process of change, church leaders came up with theological reasons to celebrate our Lord's resurrection. Part of the actual changeover from Sabbath to Sunday occurred with the first step Sixtus initiated: To make Sunday worship an annual observance.

The Christians in the city of Rome, especially, dreaded being confused with the Jews, who had become extremely unpopular because of a series of Jewish revolts against Roman rule. By gradually changing the weekly holy day to Sunday (using the resurrection theme as the higher reason), they hoped to avoid being thought Jewish.

Further, as one compromise followed another, the Christians in Rome saw the "missionary advantage" in worshiping their Lord on the same day set aside by pagan Romans to honor the sun. The baptized sun-worshiper would feel very much at home in the Christian spring festival, held on the sun's day, to honor the resurrection of the Lord.

The next important act in the drama came around A.D. 200, when Pope Victor sought to enforce the annual observance of resurrection Sunday, ordering the excommunication of all bishops who would not follow the plan of celebrating the resurrection festival. Sunday observance was the vehicle the bishop of Rome used in his attempt to gain control of the church.

The next leap in the changing of the "times and laws" of Christian worship occurred when Emperor Constantine, in March of A.D. 321, issued the first law for Sunday observance: "On the venerable Day of the Sun let the magistrates and people residing in cities rest, and let all workshops be closed."—Codex Justinianus, lib. 3, tit. 12, 3; trans. in Philip Schaff, *History of the Christian Church*, vol. 3, 5th ed. (New York: Scribner, 1902), p. 380.

◆ Accelerating apostasy

As the landslide into apostasy predicted by Paul and Daniel gained momentum, so did the process of changing the times of Christian worship. In the year A.D. 386, Theodosius I forbade litigation on Sunday and originated a practice still widespread in the western world: "No person shall demand payment of either a public or private debt [on Sunday]."—*Seventh-day Adventist Source Book*, pp. 1001, 1002. Theodosius II, in A.D. 425, turned his attention to the sporting activities of his people and forbade all amusements, both circuses and theaters, on Sundays. The increasing emphasis on Sunday as the

Christian's day of worship and the deliberate deemphasis of the seventh-day Sabbath is well-documented in the history of Christianity.

The Roman Catholic Church sees in the change a sign of the power of the church, rather than a fulfillment of Daniel's prophecy. They do not quarrel about the change from Saturday to Sunday, emphasizing that the change was a gradual process over several centuries, based on church authority only.

Examples of this official position are found in the following statements taken from Catholic writings.

"Have you any other way of proving that the church has power to institute festivals of precept?"

"Had she not such power, she could not have done that in which all modern religionists agree with her;—she could not have substituted the observance of Sunday the first day of the week, for the observance of Saturday the seventh day, a change for which there is no Scriptural authority."—Stephen Keenan, *A Doctrinal Catechism*, p. 174.

The Roman Catholic position is entirely clear. Daniel predicted the change, and the church admits that the change is a sign of its religious authority.

The issue is much more than a matter of a day. It is a matter of which master we plan to obey.

"Do you not know that to whom you present yourselves slaves to obey, you are that one's slaves whom you obey, whether of sin leading to death, or of obedience leading to righteousness?" Romans 6:16.

God has sent a message in these last days to prepare men and women for His soon return. The issue in this final conflict is loyalty; the choice, the commandments of God or the traditions of men.

In the words of Joshua, "Choose for yourselves this day whom you will serve." Joshua 24:15. The question is extended to each of us daily—who is the master of our lives? Will we be among the number in the last days who are described in Revelation 14:12: "Here is the patience of the saints; here are those who keep the commandments of God and the faith of Jesus"? ❏

If there is anything at all to admire about Satan, it is his consistency.

Without fail, as we've already noted, every time God acts or speaks, Satan meets the truth with a lie, the genuine with a counterfeit.

Did God say the seventh-day Sabbath was holy? Then count on Satan to come along with a counterfeit Sabbath on the first day of the week.

Is Jesus planning soon to return in power and glory to Earth? Then count on Satan to try preempting the King by staging his own counterfeit second coming.

Has God shared with us the truth about what happens when we die? Then count on Satan to meet this truth with a lie. In fact, it's the first lie he ever told ("You will not surely die!").

In Chapter 14, we contrast the devil's great lie about death with God's truth.

14

....

Where Do We Go
When We Die?

The first great lie
is still going strong.

Someday, of course, the Great War will be over. Prince Michael will win. Love will triumph, and selfishness—along with its author Satan—will cease to exist.

What must God do to ensure that sin never rises up again to plague His universe? He must convince us all beyond any possible doubt that sin hurts—that ultimately, sin kills! If we truly become convinced of that, we'll want nothing further to do with sin—ever!

Before sinless Adam and Eve ever sinned by eating the forbidden fruit, God warned them that if they did, they would die.

When Eve repeated God's warning to Satan, he laughed it off with "You will not surely die!"

And ever since, he's convinced the majority of each generation that death is a lie—that we all have immortal souls that live on after the body gives out.

Sin is the cause. Death is the effect.

Death is the inevitable consequence of sin.

If Jesus proved anything at the cross, He proved that.

Satan is desperate to keep us from connecting sin with death. If we don't believe that sin kills, what's the big problem with sin?

So he trots out his psychics and channelers and astrologers and best-selling authors and even mistaken preachers to echo his first lie: No one ever dies.

The truth is far more satisfying. Read on.

14

. . . .

The allure of the supernatural! The mystifying, the unknown, the frightening—all this seems to captivate the American public.

Movie marquees scream terror mixed with sex, often connected with aliens from another world. Titles laden with ESP, spiritualism, occultism, Satanism, and witchcraft line the shelves of mall bookstores. Television interviewers feature popular figures claiming to have had contact with their dead loved ones now living in the spirit world, or with those who lived in previous generations.

Yet despite its popularity and macabre fascination, the idea of death is not a pleasant thought. Death, like the chill of an Arctic night, is an unwelcome, depressing fact of life. No sooner are we born than we begin to die. Whether we like it or not, sooner or later, death is an uninvited, unwanted guest that inevitably knocks at everyone's door.

But where does man go at death, if anywhere? Isn't it a little frightening to take a journey, not knowing what the destination may be— or whether we will ever come back?

When Henry Ward Beecher, a famous minister of the last century, was dying, he said, "Now comes the mystery." And as Socrates prepared to drink a cup of hemlock poison, he exclaimed: "Farewell, I go the way of all flesh, but whether to life or oblivion, I know not."

What a sad, uncertain way to end one's life! The most frightening thing about death is the unknown—the uncertainty about what lies beyond.

An epitaph on a tombstone in Richmond, Virginia, reads:

Stranger that is passing by,
As you are now, so once was I.
As I am now, so shall you be.
Prepare for death and follow me.

After reading the inscription, a schoolboy took a crayon and added these lines:

To follow you I'm not content,
Until I know just where you went.

The line is witty, but it is more than a clever piece of poetry. The basic question is at the heart of our deepest wonderings. Where do we go when we die? Heaven? Hell? Purgatory? Oblivion?

Is death a great new adventure, or just endless silence? Are our goodbyes the final act, or is death just a pause between two eternities? Where are our beloved dead?

Centuries ago, Job asked the question that every person asks himself at sometime in his life: "If a man dies, shall he live again?" Job 14:14.

The modern religious world offers an array of answers. Muslims believe man's ultimate destination is either heaven, a paradise—or hell, a fiery and horrible place. Buddhists believe in several levels of existence, with a series of heavens and a series of hells! Hindus believe in reincarnations and Nirvana, with an ultimate goal of becoming part of the cosmos.

Some tribes of African peoples view the soul as separate from the body, traveling to distant places after death and eventually entering an invisible spirit world.

Even within Christianity itself, interpretations vary. Some would have us believe that immediately after death a person must "face the music"—and either go "up" or "down!" Others believe that those who have died have entered into a sleep, resting in the grave until the return of Jesus to this earth.

But how can we know the real truth about death? The answer to life's deepest question becomes even more important to those whose families have been touched by the cold finger of death.

◆ A bishop deceived

In 1966, the son of the noted Episcopal Bishop James A. Pike committed suicide by shooting himself in his New York City apartment. Two weeks after his son's death, the Bishop noticed that all the clocks in the young man's apartment had stopped at precisely 8:19 p.m.—the exact time of his son's death.

Taking this as a sign that his son was attempting to contact him, Bishop Pike sought out a spiritualist medium. The lights were dimmed, the candles lit, and Pike waited. Reportedly, a presence came into the room, identifying itself as the spirit of his departed son. Pike later related the conversation he had in the room that night. Asking his son what "life is like" on the other side, Pike claims to have heard the response, "Life is wonderful here." And the questions went on. "What about Jesus," Pike queried. "Oh, Jesus is here, but he is just a good man. Just one of the prophets, not divine, but human."

From that night on, the Bishop was committed to spiritualism and psychic phenomena. Leaning on feeling, trusting his unreliable senses of sight and sound over the ultimate authority of the Bible, he was left to founder like a ship without compass or map.

Had he thought for a moment to turn to the words of Isaiah the prophet, Bishop Pike could have been spared his delusion: "And when they say to you, 'Seek those who are mediums and wizards, who whisper and mutter,' should not a people seek their God? Should they seek the dead on behalf of the living?" Isaiah 8:19.

In the frightening grip of questions we cannot answer, fears that haunt us, confusion that cripples, God asks us to listen carefully to the simple instruction of scripture and to put all our trust in Him and His word. Isaiah wrote, "To the law and to the testimony! If they do not speak according to this word, it is because there is no light in them." Isaiah 8:20.

So where shall we turn to find answers about death? To 800 or 900 numbers and spiritualist mediums and "psychic friends"? To parapsychology books and horoscopes? God tells us there is only one safe route to go. And that is to open the pages of that ancient book, the Holy Bible, and investigate its pages thoroughly.

We find again, in the book of Isaiah, a helpful statement: "Your dead shall live; Together with my dead body they shall arise. Awake and sing, you who dwell in dust." Isaiah 26:19.

Yes, the Bible promises that there is a life beyond death! Our beloved dead will live again! But when? At the moment of death—or at some later time? What, exactly, happens when a person dies?

The Bible's teaching on death is consistent, not confusing. There may be some surprises, but its answers are both reasonable and satisfying—and best of all, comforting.

One of the most-quoted passages of Scripture concerning the dead is found in Ecclesiastes 12, which describes what happens to a man when he dies: "Then the dust will return to the earth as it was, And the spirit will return to God who gave it." Ecclesiastes 12:7.

In other words, when we die, our bodies, made up of the basic minerals of the earth, returns to dust, and our spirits return to God. In order to fully understand what the Bible writer means by the term "spirit," let's take a look at the very first book of the Bible and watch as God creates mankind: "And the Lord God formed man of the dust of the ground, and breathed into his nostrils the breath of life; and man became a living soul." Genesis 2:7, KJV.

God takes the elements of the earth: carbon, hydrogen, oxygen, nitrogen, calcium, iron, phosphorous, sodium, and other, and forms the body.

Adam now has a brain, but he is not yet thinking. He has a heart in his chest, but it is not yet beating. He has blood in his arteries and veins, but it is not yet circulating.

He is ready to live, but life has not yet entered his body. But watch! Now God tenderly bends over him and breathes into his nostrils the breath of life, and a miraculous process occurs which no modern scientist has ever been able to duplicate—man becomes a living soul!

Or, as the New King James Version of the Bible puts it, "Man became a living being."

Thus the breath, or the spirit, is life's spark—the spirit, or breath, distinguishes a live person from a dead one! Says Job, "All the while my breath is in me, and the spirit of God is in my nostrils." Job 27:3, KJV.

James also refers to this life force as the "spirit": "The body without the spirit is dead." James 2:26, KJV.

◆ Equations of life and death

Simply put, the Bible equation is: DUST + SPIRIT = A LIVING SOUL. Or to put it even more clearly: THE ELEMENTS OF EARTH + BREATH = A LIVING BEING.

If this is the process of life, then, what happens at death? Just the reverse: DUST - SPIRIT = A CORPSE. Or, more simply: ELEMENTS OF EARTH - BREATH = A CORPSE.

We can best understand this truth by the following illustration. When you connect a light bulb to electricity, what happens? You get light! No one "puts" the light in the bulb. The light comes on by the uniting of the two components: bulb + electricity. When you disconnect the electricity, the light goes out. Just so at death. When the breath, or spark of life, goes back to the Creator, man dies. All that is left is the body, composed of the elements of Earth, which returns to dust. The living soul, or living being, simply ceases to exist.

The word *soul* is mentioned sixteen hundred times in the King James Version of the Bible. Never once is it linked with the word *immortal*. The expression "immortal soul" used so freely by many Christians is not found in the Bible. Job cries out, "Shall mortal man be more just than God? shall a man be more pure than his maker?" Job 4:17. In our present state we are mortal—subject to deterioration and death.

According to the apostle, we seek for immortality (Romans 2:7). Only God has it (1 Timothy 6:16). But we shall receive everlasting life when Jesus returns and resurrects the righteous (John 5:28, 29).

At death, the Bible tells us, we lay down to sleep; we no longer are aware of what happens on earth.

The Bible states: "Do not put your trust in princes, Nor in a son of man, in whom there is no help. His spirit departs, he returns to his earth; In that very day his plans perish." Psalm 146:3, 4.

But where do the dead spend their time between death and the resurrection? Job tells us, "If I wait, the grave is mine house." Job 17:13, KJV.

According to the Bible, when a man dies, he does not go to heaven. He does not go to hell. He does not go to purgatory. In fact, he does not live at all, anywhere! Death is a cessation of life until the resurrection morning, when body and breath are united again. "For the living know that they will die; But the dead know nothing." Ecclesiastes 9:5.

However comforting it may have been to Bishop Pike to believe that he was talking with his loved one, God says, "The dead know nothing." Nothing! Zero! Clearly, the dead do not know what the living are doing, for the Bible says of the man who has died: "His sons come to honor, and he does not know it; They are brought low, and he does not perceive it." Job 14:21.

◆ Heaven would be hell

Isn't that the best way, after all? Think for a moment. Imagine a young mother dying and going directly to heaven, leaving behind a husband and several small children. From her place in glory, the young woman looks down and sees all that is happening on earth. Let's suppose her husband begins to drink heavily and beats the children; further, he has a live-in mistress who cruelly neglects them. Day after day, the young woman watches the scene below, appalled at the situation but helpless to do anything about it. How would you describe the daily horror that young woman would feel? No relief, day or night! Would heaven be hell for her? Or what about parents who would see their children blown apart in the ravages of war?

One of the most comforting truths in God's Word is that when a person dies, he or she rests quietly, undisturbed by the problems of life or by concern for loved ones, until the call of the Lifegiver. Is it any wonder that the Bible likens death to a sleep?

The prophet Nathan told King David, "When your days are fulfilled [you will] . . . rest with your fathers." 2 Samuel 7:12.

The story of Lazarus reveals many insights into the biblical view of death. In speaking of the demise of His dear friend, Jesus Himself called death a "sleep." He told His disciples, "Our friend Lazarus sleeps, but I go that I may wake him up." John 11:11.

The disciples, knowing that Lazarus had been ill for some time, replied, "'Lord, if he sleeps he will get well.' However, Jesus spoke of his death, but they thought that He was speaking about taking rest in sleep. Then Jesus said to them plainly, 'Lazarus is dead.'" John 11:12-14.

As Jesus and the disciples made their way to Bethany, Martha, the sister of Lazarus, rushed out to meet Jesus, crying, "Lord, if You had been here, my brother would not have died." John 11:21. No doubt she was right!

Confidently, Jesus answered Martha, "Your brother will rise again" (verse 23). Notice carefully Martha's response: "I know that he will rise again in the resurrection at the last day" (verse 24).

Martha was a close friend and follower of Jesus. Often she had pressed close to her Saviour, listening to His words of hope and courage. Possibly, she had been in the crowd when Jesus said, "Do not marvel at this; for the hour is coming in which all who are in the graves will hear His voice and come forth." John 5:28, 29.

Assuming, then, that Jesus was referring to His second coming, Martha expressed her assurance in the events that would transpire at the end of the world. Little did she realize that Jesus was about to give a dramatic preview of that event! Coming to the cave where Lazarus' tomb had been sealed, Jesus asked that the stone over the entrance be taken away. Concerned by such a request, Martha objected, "Lord, by this time there is a stench, for he has been dead four days." John 11:39.

But the stone was rolled away, and Jesus cried out (verse 43) in a loud voice, "Lazarus, come forth!"

Imagine the electrifying impact on the crowd as Lazarus did indeed come forth, wrapped in the same grave clothes with which he was buried. Although he had been dead for four days, the Bible gives no record of Lazarus recounting experiences of his four days of death. How could he, if the "dead know nothing"? Jesus had simply called him forth from the sleep of death—a sleep that can only be broken by the call of the Lifegiver Himself!

This is the call that Job anticipated: "You shall call, and I will answer You." Job 14:15.

Martin Luther said the same thing in the sixteenth century:

> "We shall sleep until he comes and knocks on the little grave and says, Doctor Martin, get up! Then I shall rise in a moment and be happy with Him forever."—*The Christian Hope*, p. 37.

What a wonderful hope Christians have of a life beyond the grave! In the tombs of the catacombs of Rome are the inscriptions of those who died in pagan hopelessness. Over and over again are inscribed these words of sorrow and finality: "Goodbye for all eternity. Goodbye forever."

Yet, on the tombs of those early Christians are found these words of hope and courage: "Goodbye until we meet again." "Goodnight until the morning."

◆ No final goodbyes

Don't you like that? Isn't it comforting to have the Christian hope— to know that our goodbyes are not final? That's the promise—that a great resurrection morning will come after the dark night of death! Christ will call, and our beloved dead will answer!

No! Christians need not sorrow and grieve in utter despair like those who have no hope of being reunited with their loved ones! This is the comforting message the apostle Paul shared with the early Christians. "But I do not want you to be ignorant, brethren, concerning those who have fallen asleep, lest you sorrow as others who have no hope." 1 Thessalonians 4:13.

The real hope, the real comfort, for sorrowing, grieving hearts, is not in the seance chamber or in the confused messages of a New Age channeler. Real hope is in the Lord Jesus Christ!

An essential part of the Christian message that shook the pagan Roman Empire was the good news of the resurrection. Pagans had lost confidence in their religion. Death seemed like a dark pit from which no one returned. Paul and the early Christians pointed to the resurrection as God's answer to death—the grim enemy of all mankind.

Through Christ's death on the cross, His burial in the tomb, and His glorious resurrection, we have victory not only over sin, but over death itself! Jesus proclaimed triumphantly, "I am the resurrection and the life. He who believes in Me, though he may die, he shall live." John 11:25.

What a comforting message! After death, we rest until that wonderful day when Jesus will return to take us home to live with Him forever. ❏

If our bodies are just going to wear out and be buried at death anyway, what each of us does with our body doesn't really matter much, right?

Well, as it turns out, there are some excellent reasons for taking good care of our physical bodies. Reasons God shares with us in His Word. Reasons you can read about in the next chapter.

15

. . . .

It Pays to Read the Owner's Manual

Four good reasons
to pursue good health.

■ *Because the old cliché—"a sound mind in a sound body"—is true. Science continues to confirm the strong link between mind and body. When the body is fit, the mind benefits. And faced as we are in this Great War with daily decisions that determine destiny, we need our minds to be as sharp and clear as possible.*

■ *Because part of our role in this Great War is to fill our lives with doing good. The longer we live, and the more energy we have, the more good we can do.*

■ *Because God tells us that our bodies—amazingly enough—are His own temple. In some mysterious way, He lives in us through His Spirit. If our body is God's home, don't we want it to be clean and in good repair?*

■ *Because we want to demonstrate to the universe that when we follow the Manufacturer's instructions, we are at our happiest and healthiest. Why become a walking advertisement for the sickly results of living Satan's way?*

15

Have you noticed how sudden illness puts our lives into quick perspective? When we are in good health, we often take it for granted. When all is well, we tend to agonize over minor decisions, often presenting our petitions before the Lord in over-exaggerated earnestness. If only we could have a new car, or that new promotion, or a house by the sea.

But when illness strikes, all those "important needs" shrink into insignificance. The new car, the promotion, and beach house—all would be gratefully cast aside if we could face each day knowing that it would be free of pain and the worry of feeling our physical strength spiral downward.

Good health. When we have it, we forget about it. When we lose it, we forget about everything else. How much is it worth to be well? What would you give? Ask the terminal cancer or emphysema patient. Ask the parents of children dying from leukemia or grandparents deformed by arthritis.

The Bible tells us that God is concerned about our health and happiness here and now. In the book of John we read, "Beloved, I pray that you may prosper in all things and be in health." 3 John 2.

In fact, Jesus said, "I have come that they may have life, and that they may have it more abundantly." John 10:10. Not a ho-hum, dull existence! Jesus wants us to have a happy, joyous, exuberant life. To live life to its fullest, with every day more exciting than yesterday!

When God brought the Israelites out of Egypt, He reminded them of some definite rules and regulations concerning healthful living. After outlining His plan for good health, He gave a most remarkable promise to them if they would follow His instructions: "If you diligently heed the voice of the LORD your God and do what is right in His sight, give ear to His commandments and keep all His statutes, I will put none of the diseases on you which I have brought on the Egyptians." Exodus 15:26.

What an amazing promise! Commenting on the fulfillment of this promise, David tells us that "there was not one feeble person among their tribes." Psalm 105:37, KJV.

But was disease less prevalent during the time of the Exodus? Was it somehow not as easy for the Egyptians to stay well?

◆ Learning from the mummies

A team of specialists from around the world gathered at the Manchester Medical School in England in 1975 for the specific purpose of performing autopsies on Egyptian mummies dating back to 1900 B.C. The findings were remarkable. The ancient Egyptians suffered from many illnesses common to us today: heart disease, cancer, vascular diseases, arthritis, hepatitis, tetanus, trichinosis, and others.

Although Egypt was the educational and cultural center of the world during Moses' lifetime, medical knowledge and remedies were saturated with superstition and folklore. Yet God's people stood radically apart, following the principles of public health given by God and taught by Moses—principles that later brought the plagues of black death and leprosy under control during the Middle Ages.

Referring to the millions of lives saved as scientists turned to church leaders for help in the Middle Ages, George Rosen wrote:

> "Leadership was taken by the church, as the physicians had nothing to offer. The church took as its guiding principle the concept of contagion as embodied in the Old Testament; . . . This idea and its practical consequences are de-

fined with great clarity in the book of Leviticus."—*History of Public Health,* pp. 63-65.

What a shame that sixty million people died from these plagues, when the Bible's concept of isolation was there all the time! Is it not logical to assume that if God designed our bodies, He knows exactly how they function and how they can be kept in optimal condition?

When you buy a new car you receive an owner's manual. It tells you what type of fuel to use. It specifies the type of oil and when it should be changed. It suggests how often to service the car and how to maintain it to secure optimum performance.

Why do manufacturers issue an owner's manual? Because those who create something know best how to keep it functioning smoothly. Wise consumers heed such advice to avoid unwanted and unneeded trouble.

Think of our bodies. God gave men and women wonderful bodies, with almost unlimited possibilities. But such potential is only realized as this marvelous machine is treated with the care necessary for peak efficiency.

Let's go back to the garden of Eden and notice some of the things God shared with Adam and Eve which would promote good health. The Bible says that after God created this first couple, He gave them some work to do—some useful activity and exercise: "Then the LORD God took the man and put him in the garden of Eden to tend and keep it." Genesis 2:15.

After Adam sinned, God increased his work: "In the sweat of your face you shall eat bread Till you return to the ground." Genesis 3:19.

God intended work to be much more than a dreadful curse. It was also to be a blessing. God knew that an inactive body deteriorates. Because of His great love for Adam and Eve, He instructed them in the benefits of useful exercise.

The benefits of exercise are promoted today by health enthusiasts and physicians worldwide. The principles are basic: Exercise improves the tone of muscles and blood vessels. The lungs become more efficient, able to process more air with less effort. The heart is more efficient, pumping more blood with each beat. Energy-producing oxygen is carried to the tissues, which improves the overall condition of the body. As a result, exercise protects the body from many diseases and slows down the aging process.

In addition to offering the principles of aerobics to the first couple on this Earth, God gave Adam and Eve a perfect diet to sustain and promote their health. The Bible tells us, "And God said, 'See, I have given you every herb that yields seed which is on the face of all the earth, and every tree whose fruit yields seed; to you it shall be for food.'" Genesis 1:29.

Thus man's original diet was quite simple, consisting of fruits, grains, and nuts. God also gave Adam and Eve the right to eat of the tree of life in the center of the garden of Eden. This fruit supplied their diet with a special life-giving substance which would insure eternal youth and health.

After Adam and Eve sinned, God separated them from the tree of life and added vegetables to their diet: "And you shall eat the herb of the field." Genesis 3:18.

◆ The first is still the best

Fruits, grains, nuts, vegetables. It's interesting to note that man's early diet, as prescribed by God, is being heralded in medical circles today as the answer to many of our twentieth-century health problems.

A national newsmagazine recently carried an article in which dietitians stated that the four food groups ought to be changed from the standard quad of meat, dairy, grains, and fruits/vegetables to legumes, fruit, vegetables, and grains. Man's Genesis diet! Such a diet makes sense, when you look at the fact that the people before the flood lived to be more than nine hundred years old!

After the flood, men and women began to eat meat, and their lifespans decreased markedly. Compared to Methusaleh's 969 years (before the flood), Noah's son Shem lived 600 years. His grandson, 239 years. His great grandson, 175 years. By the time of King David, man's life span had decreased to 70 years.

Since the flood destroyed plant life on Earth, and since Noah's supply of food was exhausted after he and his family had been confined in the ark for a year and ten days, God allowed the consumption of animals as an emergency measure.

Yet not all plants and animals were good for food. When God directed Noah in selecting animals for the ark, he made a distinction between animals which were clean and those which were not. "You shall take with you seven each of every clean animal, a male and his female; two each of animals that are unclean, a male and his female." Genesis 7:2. Although God did not spell out specific differences at this point, we know that Noah must have been previously aware of the distinction, otherwise he would not have been able to comply.

God detailed such dietary principles more clearly shortly after the Israelites were delivered from the bondage of Egypt. Wishing to preserve the health of His people and promote their longevity, God gave Moses dietary principles and regulations. In Deuteronomy, we find a classification of the animals, fowl, and fish which God said were clean to use for food: "These are the animals which you may eat: the ox, the sheep, the goat, the deer, the gazelle, the roe deer, the wild goat, the mountain goat, the antelope, and the mountain sheep." Deuteronomy 14:4, 5.

The next text gives the basic rule of thumb for identifying clean and unclean food sources from the animal kingdom. "And you may eat every animal with cloven hooves, having the hoof split into two parts, and that chews the cud, among the animals." Deuteronomy 14:6.

Note that God said the animal must both chew the cud and part the hoof to be safe for food. The following texts clarify the point: "Nevertheless, of those that chew the cud or have cloven hooves, you shall not eat, such as these: the camel, the hare, and the rock hyrax; for they chew the cud but do not have cloven hooves; they are unclean for you. Also the swine is unclean for you, because it has cloven hooves, yet does not chew the cud; you shall not eat their flesh or touch their dead carcasses." Deuteronomy 14:7, 8.

God's dietary rules are not arbitrary. He designed our bodies. He knows what will best keep us functioning at peak efficiency. The Bible tells us, "No good thing will He withhold From those who walk uprightly." Psalm 84:11. The animals which He cautions us against eating, are, in general, scavengers—the garbage collectors of the earth!

For some, bacon may be tempting when looked at in the midst of a sizzling, spicy bacon cheeseburger. Yet if we could see the life history of most of these butchered animals before taking that first bite, our appetites might not be so keen!

A scavenger, the hog routs around for anything which appears to be edible. Garbage eaten by the hog is digested and converted into food in a matter of hours. The cow, on the other hand, has a complex digestive system. It takes forty-eight hours for the food it eats to be converted into flesh. It also has a more complex elimination system.

Pork is often infected with trichina larvae, or worms. When a person eats infected pork, the hard cyst surrounding the larva is dissolved. The worm then burrows into the intestinal wall and multiplies. These worms enter the bloodstream and are carried to other parts of the body.

Trichinosis can be a fatal disease, depending on the number of larva eaten. Often the disease is wrongly diagnosed as arthritis or food poisoning. Not just a modern illness, trichinosis has been a threat for many centuries. Autopsies have revealed that many Egyptian mummies were infected with trichina worms! Apparently God knew what He was doing when He warned His people to stay away from the flesh of swine.

God gave specific instructions about which sea creatures were good for food and which should be avoided: "These you may eat of all that are in the water: whatever in the water has fins and scales, whether in the seas or in the rivers—that you may eat. But all in the seas or in the rivers that do not have fins and scales, all that move in the water or any living thing which is in the water, they are an abomination to you." Leviticus 11:9, 10.

God's Word bears up under the investigation of modern research. Dr. Bruce Halsted spent years doing research for the United States Army and Navy health services to determine which fish were safe for human consumption. If servicemen were shipwrecked or stranded, the Navy wanted to know which fish they could eat for survival.

After all the research was completed, Dr. Halsted felt the "rule of thumb" for the Army and Navy men to follow would be the one set forth in Deuteronomy 14:9: "These you may eat of all that are in the waters: you may eat all that have fins and scales." A few short words of instruction given by God to man so long ago! Still a safe guide.

God placed one more restriction on man's diet: "This shall be a perpetual statute throughout your generations in all your dwellings: you shall eat neither fat nor blood." Leviticus 3:17. For years people thought this command forbidding the eating of fat and blood was merely a ceremonial restriction. Modern research confirms the wisdom of God's command.

We now know that blood carries impurities, germs, viruses, and wastes of the body. Many diseases are passed on through the blood.

We also know that highly saturated fats as found in meats and dairy products cause a rise in the cholesterol level of the blood—an important factor in vascular and heart diseases. Cholesterol is not found in grains, fruits, nuts and vegetables—only in animal products.

The importance of caring for our bodies can only be understood when we know what God has said in the Bible. The apostle Paul—in discussing the importance of sexual propriety as it relates to caring for our bodies—made this inspired statement: "Do you not know that your body is the temple of the Holy Spirit who is in you, whom you have from God, and you are not your own?" 1 Corinthians 6:19.

God dwells in a Christian through the presence of the Holy Spirit. As the apostle Paul states further, we are not our own, for we are bought with a price (verse 20). The damaging of our "earthen vessels" (our bodies—see 2 Corinthians 4:7) is an offense God considers serious. "If anyone defiles the temple of God, God will destroy him. For the temple of God is holy, which temple you are." 1 Corinthians 3:17.

◆ Sting of the viper

The defilement of the human body can take many forms. In his Corinthian letter, Paul lists fornicators, idolaters, adulterers, and drunkards as among those breaking the commandments of God. Solomon—the wisest man that ever lived—speaks of the consequences of alcohol abuse. "Wine is a mocker, Strong drink is a brawler, And whoever is led astray by it is not wise." Proverbs 20:1.

In a later verse he says of wine that "At the last it bites like a serpent, And stings like a viper." Proverbs 23:32. The danger of alcohol has increased enormously as modern technology makes more demands for alert minds—for workers in complete control of their faculties.

Today, alcoholism is one of the world's greatest health problems. More than half of all automobile accidents can be traced directly to a driver or pedestrian "under the influence." In more than half of all murders, either the killer or the victim—or both—have been drinking!

Alcohol impairs the body's utilization of vitamins, and sugar in alcoholic drinks lessens the body's ability to fight infection. Inevitably, the alcoholic develops a fatty liver, and his chances of dying from cirrhosis of the liver are great. Statistically, his lifespan is shortened by at least twelve years. And according to the latest figures, two out of every five who take the first drink proceed to experiencing serious problems with alcohol; one in ten becomes a full-blown alcoholic.

For a Christian, drinking alcoholic beverages has even greater consequences. Every Christian needs full use of his or her mind to avoid the temptations of Satan. A Christian cannot afford impaired judgment or a diminished ability to distinguish right from wrong.

On the cross, our Lord refused the stupefying potion offered Him by the soldiers to deaden the sense of pain. Even though Jesus suffered excruciating pain, He would receive nothing that would becloud His mind at the moment of death.

◆ Coffin nails, indeed

Alcohol is not the only culprit today which not only weakens our ability to use our minds to full capacity but breaks down our health. If you smoke, your chances of dying prematurely with lung cancer are 1,000 percent greater than those who have never smoked. And cancer is not the Marlboro Man's only killer. A smoker's chances of dying from heart disease are 103 percent greater than those who have never smoked on a regular basis. Emphysema claims many thousands of lives each year. And research has shown that nicotine increases the buildup of cholesterol along the inner walls of the arteries.

Smoking mothers bequeath to their children a full range of detrimental effects, from restricted fetal movement, to growth retardation, to increased respiratory illness later in life. All these are due to a diminished oxygen supply and the effects of nicotine. Newborn deaths are up to 27 percent higher in infants of smoking mothers.

The late Dr. Linus Pauling, a Nobel Prize-winning scientist, said: "Every cigarette a person smokes takes fourteen and a half minutes off his life."

Many of us are taking poisonous drugs into our bodies daily: "The average cup of coffee contains from two to four grains of caffeine, depending on the strength of the coffee. Caffeine, the drug contained in coffee, is classed in textbooks as both a stimulant and a poison. The fatal dose is listed as one-third ounce (10 grams). It would require the amount of caffeine contained in 80 to 100 ordinary cups of coffee, then, to prove fatal if taken in a single dose by mouth."—*You and Your Health*, vol. 1, p. 413.

Tea and cola drinks also contain caffeine. All of these beverages are now being linked with heart disease, neurological disorders, and cancer of the bladder.

In what other ways can we injure our health? With health clubs springing up all over the country, more and more people are realizing the dangers of ignoring the condition of their bodies. "Someone has estimated that every pound of body fat calls for another two-thirds of a mile of new blood vessels. And the heart must pump blood through this extra system of vessels."—*You and Your Health*, vol. 1, p. 395.

Not only does the heart have to work harder when we are overweight, but the kidneys, liver, and lungs also are overworked.

Overweight persons suffer from sixteen diseases not common to their thinner friends. The large amount of refined sugar and fat consumed today contributes to a national weight problem, as well as to several lifestyle-related diseases. In addition, sugar makes it difficult for those who are ill to throw off an infection, since it lowers the natural immune system's ability to destroy bacteria.

Tobacco. Alcohol. Caffeine. Sugar. Fat. Swine. All are enemies of the abundant life God has so graciously promised us. Our Creator wants us to take good care of our bodies so we can enjoy life at its best here and now. He wants us to be responsible, moral, joyous people. He wants us to have an abundant life—life in all its fullness.

God's blueprint for our well-being includes moderation in not only the good food we eat or drink, but also in lifestyle—balancing work with rest and relaxation. The weekly Sabbath gives us a much-needed opportunity to lay aside our problems, deepen family relationships, reconnect with our Creator, and rejuvenate for the week ahead.

God wants us to have a little bit of heaven here and now—a foretaste of the Earth made new, where all the diseases and illnesses that plague mankind will be forever banished. As we attempt to shake off those habits which now tighten their grip on our lives after endless poor choices, we can be confident that Jesus offers the strength to make our new hopes a reality. Like the apostle Paul, we can claim the victory: "I can do all things through Christ who strengthens me." Philippians 4:13.

◆ More than a match for any addiction

We can be confident that we can have no bodily craving greater than His power. No temptation is too great for Him, as He helps us overcome. Our urge for cigarettes or alcohol, our aversion to exercise and a nutrition-driven diet, are not as powerful as His grace. Our appetites may be out of control until we meet Him—then miraculously, He enables us to do what all the self-help courses in the world are powerless to do.

John had a problem with alcohol. On Friday afternoons he often began drinking and continued through the rest of the weekend. Under the influence of alcohol, he became one of Moscow's infamous criminals. In and out of prison seventeen times by the age of 32, his life had no purpose. One day he wandered into our Kremlin evangelistic meetings being held in the center of Russian atheism.

For the first time in his life, he felt a love that would not let him go. He came face to face with a Person whose power was greater than alcohol. Today he rejoices in the new life Christ has given him. He is no longer under the control of alcohol. He has a new direction, a new hope, in his life.

You, too, can have a new Person in your life, providing power to control your appetites. You can experience the thrill of knowing you are no longer dominated by bodily urges and physical habits you can't control. Right now, you can experience Christ's power in your life. Ask Him to take complete control of you. A new beginning awaits you. ❑

Once we've chosen which side we want to be on in this Great War, we then have the opportunity of promoting the values and agenda of the leader we have chosen.

By caring for our physical health, we demonstrate the superiority of God's way. The results are energy, longevity, and freedom from disease.

Likewise, we are privileged to demonstrate the superiority of God's principles of management. And as you will find in the next chapter, this has to do with a lot more than just business and finances.

16

· ·

Secrets
Wall Street
Doesn't Know

Business partners.

Before the war between Michael and Lucifer moved from somewhere out there beyond Orion to turn Earth itself into a war zone, God went into business with Adam and Eve.

God was the Owner of everything, of course. But He invited the human beings He had created to become His partners—His managers.

Following His principles of love-based management, they would make of Earth an ever-more-wondrous paradise. He taught them how to manage their environment, their time, their resources, their very lives.

The fallen Lucifer, now Satan, changed all that. He introduced force, fear, greed, theft, oppression, cheating, fraud, guilt, and a raft of other dark realities into his self-centered approach to management.

Today our world operates almost universally on the basis of Satan's school of management.

But thanks to God, throughout this long war, our power of choice has been preserved intact. We can still choose the better, higher way.

This chapter is your invitation to once again go into business with your Creator.

16

Planet Earth had just come from the Creator's hands in all its splendor and perfection, glorious beyond description. The stroke of the Master Artist greeted the eye at every turn. Magnificent sunrises were rivaled only by breathtaking sunsets. Peaceful lakes nestled between the hills. Gorgeous flowers of every hue and blossoming vines delighted the senses. Majestic trees swayed in the gentle breeze, and tree branches drooped under their load of tempting fruit. Birds of every description filled the air with their clear tunes. Streams and lakes teemed with multicolored fish. Animals roamed unafraid in the lush meadows.

What a paradise Adam and Eve enjoyed! But God wanted to demonstrate His love in another special way for this first couple.

"The LORD God planted a garden . . . and there He put the man whom He had formed." Genesis 2:8.

Just think! Somewhere amid the wonder and beauty of the newborn world, God designed a garden home for Adam and Eve. The most lavish home on Earth cannot begin to compare with the world's original garden home. No supermarkets or waiting lines were necessary in Eden, for God supplied the food. Indicating the vastness of the storehouse all around, He said to Adam and Eve, "I have given you every herb that yields seed which is on the face of all the earth, and every tree whose fruit yields seed; to you it shall be for food." Genesis 1:29.

Adam and Eve had no rent or taxes, no locks or keys, no threat of vandals or burglars, no hospitals or drugstores. They enjoyed perfect health and endless youth, undying commitment to one another, and a boundless love for God. And God wanted them to share all these blessings, for He said, "Be fruitful, and multiply, and replenish the earth." Genesis 1:28, KJV.

◆ Managing the environment

It was God's design that Planet Earth be inhabited by one big, happy, healthy family. Master of the science of happiness, God realized that His subjects' continued happiness would not spring from a laissez faire attitude toward their surroundings, lying on their backs while He maintained the environment. For inherent in all human beings is a Godlike quest for a challenge, a searching for responsibility and accomplishment, a pleasure in doing and in having done something well. So God entrusted Earth's first couple with the management of His world, saying, "Have dominion over the fish of the sea, over the birds of the air, and over every living thing that moves on the earth." Genesis 1:28.

While the extravagant bounty of this world is God's and His alone, He has entrusted mankind, from the time of Adam and Eve to the present, with stewardship of the earth. Scripture is replete with references to God's ownership. We find that "The earth is the LORD's," (Psalm 24:1); that "the silver . . . and the gold" belong to Him (Haggai 2:8); and that "every beast of the forest . . . And the cattle on a thousand hills" (Psalm 50:10) are His.

As stewards, men and women today have been given the sacred trust of managing God's property. In essence, every cent we earn comes as a result of the blessings of health and strength God gives us as His subjects. To put it simply, we really do not own anything! As Creator, God has a prior claim on us and our possessions. "And you shall remember the LORD your God, for it is He who gives you power to get wealth, that He may establish His covenant which He swore to your fathers, as it is this day." Deuteronomy 8:18.

The *Concise Oxford Dictionary* defines *steward* as "a person entrusted with the management of another's property." Today when a person enters into a stewardship relationship, he wants to know what the owner expects of him. God had just such an understanding with Adam, for the Bible states, "Of every tree of the garden you may freely eat; but of the tree of the knowledge of good and evil you shall not eat, for in the day that you eat of it you shall surely die." Genesis 2:16, 17.

God tested man's love and loyalty through this one restriction. Adam and Eve could eat from all the other trees in the garden, but they were not to eat the fruit of this specific tree. By obeying God they would show their recognition of His ownership. If they were faithful stewards and chose to maintain their allegiance to God, they would live forever in a world that was paradise from pole to pole!

But that is only the beginning of the story. Eve listened to the serpent and ate the forbidden fruit. Then, "She also gave to her husband with her, and he ate." Genesis 3:6.

This couple, with the hope of the whole world before them, failed the one simple test God required of them. They were unfaithful stewards, and they lost everything: happiness, undying love, the lushness of a garden, the security of home, the dominion of the Earth. From heirs to slaves, they became chained to an Earth cursed by sin.

And watching in sadistic satisfaction behind it all was Satan, that fallen angel who resented God's authority. Usurping the dominion enjoyed by Adam and Eve, he hoped to have control of the world forever. His assumption was shattered by Christ's entrance into the world centuries later. Presuming to deceive the Divine Son of God as easily as he had tricked the first couple, Satan waited until Jesus had not eaten for forty days. Then he took Him up to an "exceedingly high mountain" (Matthew 4:8) and showed Him all the kingdoms of the world, saying, "All these things I will give You if You will fall down and worship me" (verse 9).

But the deception did not go over as it had in the Eden garden. The things Satan promised to give Christ were not really his to give; they had been obtained by fraud and deceit. Ultimately, Satan's fate was sealed forever at Calvary. By His life and death, Christ proved Satan wrong about his lying charges against God and made possible the return of man to his original dominion.

Thus everything we are or have comes stamped with the cross, made possible by Christ's eternal gift to human beings. Whether we love and serve Him or not, our very lives and all our possessions are His property. He is our Creator and our Redeemer! Just like Adam and Eve, we are stewards of what God entrusts to us, and as such, are "required" to "be found faithful." 1 Corinthians 4:2.

As God's stewards, we will be held accountable for how we use our time, abilities, talents, and possessions. In the final analysis, God will want to know if we have used His unique blessings to enrich ourselves and satisfy our whims and pleasures, or if we have used them to bless others.

◆ Managing life

The greatest of all God's gifts is one we often take for granted—the very life that surges through our bodies. Writes Paul, "God, who made the world and everything in it . . . gives to all life, breath, and all things." Acts 17:24, 25.

Our life originates with God, and He sustains it. Every heartbeat, every breath of air, every pulse of our bodies is a gift from God. Paul urges us to "present . . . [our] bodies a living sacrifice, holy, acceptable to God." Romans 12:1.

A "living sacrifice" means unreserved commitment, or submission to Christ and His leadership in our lives. He is our example; we are to follow His example of unselfish service, going "about doing good." Acts 10:38.

◆ Managing time

Every man is also a steward of time—that elusive dimension we all flow through. Benjamin Franklin once remarked that "time is the stuff life is made of." The psalmist requested of God, "So teach us to number our days, That we may gain a heart of wisdom." Psalm 90:12.

To waste time is to waste life—to squander that talent God Himself has given to each man and woman. Every person has the same number of hours in a day, the same number of minutes in those hours, and will be held accountable for the choices made to fill them.

And while God expects that each of us will use our time wisely in a general sense, He also expects us to set aside a specific time period, the Sabbath, as a means of expressing our belief in Him as our Creator. God asks that one-seventh of our time be devoted to fellowship with Him, resting in His word, drawing refreshment from His promises, putting aside the weekly pressures of work and shopping and worldly pursuits.

◆ Managing money

As we "Seek first the kingdom of God and His righteousness" (Matthew 6:33), we discover that all of God's blessings are showered upon us. In addition to giving of our time, we find in Scripture that dedication to God means giving also of our means, acknowledging the Source of our material blessings by returning to God His portion.

When the Elamites invaded and overthrew Sodom, Abraham's nephew, Lot, was taken captive. When the news reached Abraham, he determined to rescue Lot, praying for God to be with him and give him success.

Not only did God give him the release of Lot and his family, but He also delivered over to him the captors along with their treasures. When Abraham returned, the King of Sodom came out to meet him and urged him to keep the treasures he had recovered, but to return the captives. But Abraham refused to take the gain for himself.

Melchizedek, a priest of God, brought Abraham a meal and blessed him. Then, as the Bible says, Abraham "gave him a tithe of all." Genesis 14:20.

Abraham wanted to express his appreciation for God's help in securing the release of Lot, acknowledging God's ownership and blessings. One hundred and fifty-three years later, Abraham's grandson expressed his gratitude to God in the same way. While fleeing from his angry brother, Jacob felt utterly alone and afraid. He wanted so much the protection of his God, but he felt so guilty for robbing his brother Esau that he feared God had forsaken him and would not forgive him. With a great sense of remorse, Jacob confessed his wrongs to God and then wearily lay down on the ground and slept.

"Then he dreamed, and behold, a ladder was set up on the earth, and its top reached to heaven; and there the angels of God were ascending and descending on it." Genesis 28:12.

In this dream, Jacob saw the Lord standing above the ladder and heard God say, "I am with you and will keep you wherever you go, and will bring you back to this land" (verse 15).

When Jacob awakened, he knew God had spoken, promising guidance and protection. Deeply touched, he gratefully promised, "Of all that You give me I will surely give a tenth to You" (verse 22).

David felt the same way when he asked, "What shall I render to the LORD For all His benefits toward me?" Psalm 116:12. David longed to show his appreciation to God for all the blessings He had given him.

Have you ever wondered how to thank God for His incredible goodness to you—for the gifts of life, family, health, material blessings? Do you sometimes wonder if "thank you" is enough? The Bible principle of stewardship provides a tangible way of expressing our appreciation to God for all His benefits. Jacob said he would return to God a tenth, or tithe, of all he received, just as his grandfather, Abraham, had done.

The first written instruction regarding tithing, or returning a tenth to the Lord, is recorded in the Book of Leviticus. "And all the tithe of the land, whether of the seed of the land or of the fruit of the tree, is the LORD's. It is holy to the LORD." Leviticus 27:30.

As we return a tenth of all we earn, we are continually impressed with the truth that God is the Creator and the Source of every blessing. And how is the tithe to be used? The book of Numbers gives a clear explanation: "I have given the children of Levi all the tithes in Israel as an inheritance in return for the work which they perform, the work of the tabernacle of meeting." Numbers 18:21.

Throughout the scriptural record we find that the tithe always supported the work of God. In the New Testament, Paul explains, "Do you not know that those who minister the holy things eat of the things of the temple, and those who serve at the altar partake of the offerings of the altar? Even so the Lord has commanded that those who preach the gospel should live from the gospel." 1 Corinthians 9:13, 14.

Jesus commended the tithing system when He rebuked the scribes and Pharisees with these words: "For you pay tithe of mint and anise and cummin, and have neglected the weightier matters of the law: justice and mercy and faith. These you ought to have done, without leaving the others undone." Matthew 23:23.

◆ God's strange math

Throughout the years of my ministry, I have seen a simple principle at work over and over again in the lives of people I have encountered. Strange as it may seem, it is easier to live on nine-tenths of your income than on ten tenths! How many times have I sat in the living rooms of men and women who have agonized over the area of personal finances, struggling to take that leap of faith. We are barely making it now, they tell me over and over again—how can we possibly give a tenth of our income to the Lord? And then, somehow, the decision is made to trust in God's guidance and wisdom in instituting the tithing system. Weeks later, these same ones enthusiastically testify, "Oh, Pastor, we tried it, and what a miracle has happened in our lives! Somehow, nine-tenths of our income stretches farther than ten tenths ever did!" Here is a secret to financial security that even Wall Street doesn't know!

There are some who ask, "Isn't tithing only for the Jews?" To such I would ask in return, "Are the blessings of heaven only for Jews?" I think of Jim, who squeezed an honest tithe out of a scant paycheck, later to be blessed with his own business, which flourished and brought him financial security. Or Ed, who took a leap of faith by closing his Christmas tree farm on Sabbaths—the busiest days of the season— only to be rewarded by increased business on the other six days of the week.

Such Christians have discovered firsthand the blessing promised in Malachi: "'Bring all the tithes into the storehouse, That there may be food in My house, And try Me now in this,' Says the LORD of hosts, 'If I will not open for you the windows of heaven And pour out for you such blessing That there will not be room enough to receive it.'" Malachi 3:10.

The Lord says that a tenth of everything is holy to Him. The tithe is not a gift to God, for it already belongs to Him. He gives us the privilege of returning it to Him in order to test our stewardship, to see if we will honor and acknowledge His ownership. If we refuse to do that, we are actually robbing God, according to Scripture. "But you say, 'In what way have we robbed You?' In tithes and offerings." Malachi 3:8.

While the tithe, or tenth part of our income, belongs to God, we are invited to give abundantly, even beyond that portion which is already rightfully God's. With offerings, it is left up to each of us to decide how far we will extend ourselves. However, there are some guidelines in the Bible. Jesus said, "Give, and it will be given to you: good measure, pressed down, shaken together, and running over." Luke 6:38.

The image is a rich one. One pictures a basket of apples, shaken down to fit in one more apple, then brimming over with additional apples rolling off the basket onto the ground. The unselfish, giving heart is prepared to be continually filled to overflowing with God's richest blessings. God's plan for financing His work on Earth is simple and beautiful. He asks His people to give from their hearts, never fearing for their own needs, which will ultimately be met far beyond expectation. But again, Wall Street knows nothing of this amazing divine economy.

◆ A foolish farmer

Jesus once told of a rich farmer who had a tremendous crop. The harvest was so great that his barns could not contain it. Finally, the man made a decision. "I will do this: I will pull down my barns and build greater, and there I will store all my crops and my goods. And I will say to my soul, 'Soul, you have many goods laid up for many years; take your ease; eat, drink, and be merry.'" Luke 12:18. 19.

This wealthy man did not acknowledge where his blessings came from. He did not recognize his Creator or his obligation as a steward. He utterly forgot the poor, the orphans, the widows. He thought only of himself. Yet he was pulled up short by a sobering reality. "Fool! This night your soul will be required of you; then whose will those things be which you have provided?" Luke 12:20.

Matthew wrote, "For what profit is it to a man if he gains the whole world, and loses his own soul?" Matthew 16:26.

God wants us to give to Him because we love Him. He does not want our gifts if they are given merely out of a sense of duty.

"He who sows sparingly will also reap sparingly, and he who sows bountifully will also reap bountifully. So let each one give as he purposes in his heart, not grudgingly or of necessity; for God loves a cheerful giver." 2 Corinthians 9:6, 7.

God says that our money and our hearts are closely associated, telling us that where our treasures are, there our hearts will be also. In this day and age of rapid transit, exploding information, beating the clock, and corporate ladders, it is easy to forget where all of our blessings come from. It seems so natural to fall into apathy and passivity in our relationship toward God—the Giver of our talents, time, and treasures.

Faithfulness in tithing is one way of tangibly acknowledging how much we appreciate His goodness to us. It is our statement of "thanks" for His overwhelming mercy. It is our testimony of His love and grace. Sacrificial giving from a loving heart acknowledges our daily dependence on Him. It starves selfishness. It strangles pride. It speaks eloquently of a God who is worthy of our highest praise and deepest allegiance.

This week, why not enjoy the satisfaction of financing the spread of the gospel around the world and paying tribute to your loving Lord in your tithes and offerings? ❏

Once committed to God's side in the great controversy, it becomes our ever-increasing joy to make Him look good—to expose the devil's lies about Him for what they are.

And every day we have opportunities to demonstrate before the whole universe the superiority of His laws, His ways, His values.

His suggested lifestyle produces superior health. His suggested principles of management lead to stability and even prosperity.

But soon the side we've chosen in the war will be even more apparent. The final showdown looms. All neutral ground is about to vanish.

Because soon, every person on earth will be sealed by God or marked by the beast.

What is this seal? What is this mark? The next chapter seeks answers to these questions.

17

....

Far More Than a
Bar Code

Your military I.D.

Some of us are already battle-weary. We've seen enough of life on this planet to know that there's just too much misery, too much pain, too much sorrow here.

We watch the daily network or cable news, and by turns, we're horrified, sickened, or heartbroken.

The conviction deepens: This can't possibly be the way life was meant to be!

And how true that is.

But according to the book of Revelation, before the long war is finally over, things will first get even worse than they are now.

Our land of freedom will turn into a land of force and oppression for those who stand with God in the conflict. Those loyal to the King of the Universe will be intimidated, threatened, persecuted.

But God will be their Strength and Protector. And before the whole world and the universe itself, the seal of God will testify of their loyalty to the King.

Those aligned with Satan will also show their loyalty to him by receiving the mark of the beast.

The seal. The mark.

Can it really be true that each of these has to do with something as simple as a day on a calendar?

T he Mark of the Beast! This chilling, mystifying phrase has captured the imagination of millions through the years, but never more than today. We see the phrase and the mysterious number 666 displayed everywhere, from movie marquees to paperback book covers. The idea of a mark in the right hand or in the forehead, as the Bible describes it in Revelation 13:16, presents a graphic visual image, calling forth all manner of interpretations and explanations.

Revelation 14 issues a terrifying warning, declaring that those who worship the "beast and his image" (Revelation 14:9) and receive his mark will be the objects of "the wine of the wrath of God, which is poured out full strength into the cup of His indignation" (verse 10).

According to Bible prophecy, the inhabitants of Planet Earth will be divided into two groups as earth's last great religious crisis races to a climax. The two groups: Those loyal to God who obey His commandments—and those who worship the beast and receive his mark! The second group also receive the seven last plagues!

If receiving the "mark" has such dire consequences, what exactly is this mark, and how can we avoid receiving it? God never leaves us unprepared. Not only does He give us a clear warning message in Revelation, but He also gives us the key to unlocking the prophecy that reveals the identity of the beast and the source of the fated mark.

207

The beast, as described in Revelation 13, rises up "out of the sea" and has "seven heads and ten horns, and on his horns ten crowns, and on his heads a blasphemous name" (verse 1).

Several biblical symbols are woven into this prophecy. The beast in Bible prophecy, as explained in Daniel 7:24, represents an earthly power or kingdom. Water, as revealed in Revelation 17:15, denotes people.

The beast of Revelation 13, then, is a power or kingdom, rising up from among a multitude of people. This beast has seven heads and ten crowns, covering seven historic periods with ten kingdoms supporting it. Since it is speaking blasphemy, or words against God, it is apparently a religious power.

The description goes on: "Now the beast which I saw was like a leopard, his feet were like the feet of a bear, and his mouth like the mouth of a lion. The dragon gave him his power, his throne, and great authority." Revelation 13:2. Here is pictured a composite beast. John employs the same symbols as those used by Daniel in describing the great world powers (Daniel 7). You will recall that the lion represented Babylon; the bear, Medo-Persia; the leopard, Greece; and the ferocious dragon-like beast, the Roman Empire.

The beast of Revelation 13 succeeds these four great world empires. In this chapter we are given seven characteristics which clearly identify this beast power. Only one power on earth has all the characteristics found in this prophecy. Scripture and secular history make identification certain.

◆ Clue One

In Revelation 13:2, God gives us the first clue to its identity. Speaking of the beast, John wrote: "The dragon gave him his power, his throne, and great authority."

Did the dragon power—the Roman Empire—ever give its seat of authority to any succeeding power? The answer is yes! What power received it? In A.D. 350, Constantine, the Emperor of Rome, decided to move the seat of his empire from Rome to Byzantium. He named the new capital after himself—Constantinople. Not wanting to leave Rome in a political vacuum, yet unwilling to turn it over to a national political leader who might be a future threat to his power, he gave control of the city to its religious leader. History books contain the record of Constantine, the Emperor of pagan Rome, donating his capital—the city of Rome—along with a treasury and an army, to the Bishop of Rome.

> "It was a sad blow to the prestige of Rome, and at the time one might have predicted her speedy decline. But the development of the church and the growing authority of the Bishop of Rome, or the Pope, gave her a new lease on life and made her again the capital. This time the religious capital of the civilized world."—Abbot's *History of Rome,* p. 236.

Another prominent historian, Arthur P. Stanley, describes the shift from a political power to a religious hierarchy in these words:

> "The popes filled the place of the vacant emperors of Rome, inheriting their power, prestige, and titles from paganism. . . . Constantine left all to the Bishop of Rome. . . . The papacy is but the ghost of the deceased Roman Empire, sitting crowned upon its grave."—*Stanley's History,* p. 40.

Pagan Rome gave its authority over to papal Rome. Here is the first clue to the identity of the beast. Is it possible that papal Rome fits the other identifying characteristics given in Revelation?

◆ Clue Two

John's second clue: The beast power of Revelation 13 would be primarily religious and would demand worship. "They worshiped the dragon who gave authority to the beast; and they worshiped the beast, saying, 'Who is like the beast? Who is able to make war with him?'" Revelation 13:4.

This second characteristic emphasizes how different this beast-power is compared to the other world empires. Its influence would extend far beyond geographical boundaries, not primarily in the realm of politics, but in the arena of religion, holding power over the souls of men, not simply their bodies. This power dares to command worship! In verse 7 we read, "And authority was given him over every tribe, tongue, and nation." The worship described here is a universal system, not simply a localized power, confined by geographical borders.

◆ Clue Three

The third characteristic of the beast that John points to: "He was given a mouth speaking great things and blasphemies." Revelation 13:5. Blasphemy is a biblical term, not one used by civil governments.

However, in the Bible, blasphemy is not defined merely as taking God's name in vain. Christ Himself was accused of blasphemy. Why? And by whom?

"For a good work we do not stone You, but for blasphemy, and because You, being a Man, make Yourself God." John 10:33.

If Jesus had not been God, it would have been blasphemy for Him to make such a claim. Here we see that any claim on the part of mere man to be God represents blasphemy. A power impersonating God, assuming His titles of office or His authority, and presuming to exercise the special privileges belonging to Him alone, is a blasphemous power. Does the papacy claim any of these powers or privileges of God? Let's turn the pages of history again.

From the *Prompta Bibliotheca*, we read, "The Pope is of so great dignity and so exalted that he is not a mere man, but as it were God, and the vicar of God."—Extracts from Lucius Ferraris, "Papa II" (art.), *Prompta Bibliotheca*, vol. 6, pp. 25-29.

We read from Pope Leo XIII, in an encyclical letter dated June 29, 1894: "We hold upon this earth the place of God Almighty."—*Encyclical Letters of Leo XIII*, p. 304.

◆ Clue Four

Not only does the papal power claim the titles of Christ, but also the privileges of God, by claiming it has the power to forgive sins.

Ask our Roman Catholic friends about the purpose of the confessional.

When Jesus said He forgave a certain man's sins, the Jews were furious, claiming Christ had blasphemed: "Why doth this man thus speak blasphemies? who can forgive sins but God only?" (Mark 2:7) they ranted.

Christ did not commit blasphemy—He was God! The Bible tells us in 1 Timothy 2:5 that there is "one God, and one mediator between God and men, the man Christ Jesus."

But listen to the claims of the Roman church:

"Seek where you will, through Heaven and earth, and you will find but one created being who can forgive the sinner. . . . That extraordinary being is the priest, the Catholic Priest."—*The Catholic Priest*, pp. 78, 79.

From *Dignity and Duties of the Priest*:

"God Himself is obliged to abide by the judgment of His priest, and either not to pardon or to pardon, according as they refuse or give absolution . . . . The sentence of the priest precedes, and God subscribes to it" (vol. 12, p. 2).

The church claims that its leader has the privilege and prerogatives of God. Yet only God is worthy to be worshiped. Only God can forgive sins. Only He is worthy of our deepest allegiance and fondest obedience. No earthy religious leader has the right to interpose himself between our souls and God.

◆ Clue Five

The next identifying characteristic of the beast-power is provided in Revelation 13:7: "And it was given unto him to make war with the saints, and to overcome them."

Has the Roman Church ever persecuted dissenters? Conservative estimates place the number of Christians martyred by the state church during the Dark Ages at over 30 million. Whole communities were wiped out for no other crime than that of "heresy"—that is, daring to believe or teach something contrary to the doctrines of the Church.

One has only to read the history of the Dark Ages—including the account of the Spanish Inquisition, the history of the Waldenses, and the story of Huss and Jerome—to discover that this power fulfills the prophecy of a persecuting power.

The interesting fact here is that the Roman Church admits to the persecution it has inflicted. "The Church has persecuted. Only a tyro in church history will deny that."—*Western Watchman,* December 23, 1908.

A Catholic textbook observes:

> "The church may by divine right confiscate the property of heretics, imprison their persons and condemn them to the flames. . . . In our age the right to inflict the severest penalties, even death, belongs to the church. . . . There is no graver offense than heresy . . . therefore it must be rooted out."— *Public Ecclesiastical Law,* vol. 2, p. 142.

Is it possible to believe with all our hearts that we are right—and yet be wrong? The apostle Paul had that very experience! He persecuted Christians and participated in the stoning of Stephen. But when the error of his ways was revealed and he saw the light of truth, he reversed himself and joined the church he had formerly persecuted.

The Bible says, "There is a way that seems right to a man, But its end is the way of death." Proverbs 16:25.

Let's examine some biblical mathematics as we note the next characteristic of the beast-power. Math is an exact science, and it gives convincing evidence that the papal system is the beast power! In Revelation 13:5, we discovered that power was given to the beast "to continue for forty-two months." Since a day stands for a year in Bible prophecy (Ezekiel 4:6), the beast's power was to last for 1,260 years.

Did this happen? Does this part of the description fit this power? Opening our history books again, we note that, by A.D. 538, the last of the three powers in conflict with the papacy was conquered, and the pope had secured his religio-political throne. This marked the beginning of papal Rome's rule over Europe. Adding 1,260 years to A.D. 538, we arrive at A.D. 1798.

At this point, as described by John, one of the heads of the beast appeared "as if it had been mortally wounded." Revelation 12:3.

Did something happen to "wound" papal power in 1798? Indeed it did!

In the year 1798, Napoleon sent the French general, Berthier, to Rome to take the pope captive. Notice the historical account of this event.

> "The murder of a Frenchman in Rome in 1798 gave the French an excuse for occupying the Eternal City and putting an end to the Papal temporal power. The aged Pontiff himself was carried off into exile to Valence. . . . The enemies of the Church rejoiced. The last Pope, they declared, had reigned."— *Church History*, p. 24. (See also Richard Duppa, *A Brief Account of the Subversion of the Papal Government*, 2nd ed., pp. 46, 47.)

Had Napoleon and "the enemies of the church" consulted scripture, they would have realized that the papal system was not finished, only "wounded": "And his deadly wound was healed. And all the world marveled and followed the beast." Revelation 13:3.

One day the deadly wound inflicted in 1798 would heal, opening the way for the papacy to regain its universal influence! This recovery from its "wound" will set the stage for its dramatic role in the last days.

◆ Clue Six

The sixth identifying characteristic of the beast is found in the 18th verse of Revelation 13: "Here is wisdom. Let him who has understanding calculate the number of the beast, for it is the number of a man: His number is 666."

In the Bible, the number seven represents perfection, completeness, or fullness. On the other hand, six is a symbol of imperfection.

It represents humanness and incompleteness. The number six stands for rebellion rather than obedience. A triple six, therefore, symbolizes the triple union of error—the union of the dragon, beast, and false prophet. A powerful confederacy under the pope of Rome!

◆ Clue Seven

After revealing these six identifying characteristics of the beast, the prophet John foretells how the beast will use his power to force mankind to comply with its demands in the last days. "He causes all, both small and great, rich and poor, free and slave, to receive a mark on their right hand or on their foreheads, and that no one may buy or sell except one who has the mark or the name of the beast, or the number of his name." Revelation 13:16, 17.

This mark has been the focus of unique interpretations. Some interpret it literally, relating it to everything from bar codes on store packaging to high-powered computer chips imprinted on driver's licenses or even implanted under the skin of everyone's forehead! But according to the Bible's description of those who will not receive the beast's mark, the "mark" is actually a symbol of rebellion or disloyalty to the government of God. The Bible says, of those who do not receive it, "Here is the patience of the saints; here are those who keep the commandments of God and the faith of Jesus." Revelation 14:12.

Revelation 13 and 14 make it clear that one group of people will receive "the mark of the beast," while the other will also receive a mark—but it will not come from the beast! "I saw another angel ascending from the east, having the seal of the living God. And he cried with a loud voice to the four angels to whom it was granted to harm the earth and the sea, saying, 'Do not harm the earth, the sea, or the trees till we have sealed the servants of our God on their foreheads.'" Revelation 7:2, 3.

The seal of God, as noted in Isaiah, is contained in His law: "Seal the law among my disciples." Isaiah 8:16. Thus the focus of the controversy in the last hours of this earth's history will center on man's response to God's commands. Earth's final issue will be over the seal of God and the mark of beast—between God's true sign of authority and Satan's counterfeit.

Government seals usually contain three essentials—name, title, and territory of ruler and government. The seal of the president of the United States of America, for example, looks like this:

- Great Seal of the President of the United States of America (president's name)
- Title—President
- Territory—United States of America

The seals of the presidents or kings of most governments read in a similar manner. The crucial components of God's seal, too, are name, title and territory—as found in His Holy Law.

In the very heart of God's Ten Commandment law we discover God's Holy Sabbath, which contains the seal of His authority. God's name, title, and territory are all revealed in the Sabbath command:

"Remember the Sabbath day, to keep it holy. Six days shalt thou labour, and do all thy work: But the seventh day is the Sabbath of the Lord thy God:. . . for in six days the Lord made heaven and earth, the sea, and all that in them is, and rested the seventh day; wherefore the Lord blessed the Sabbath day, and hallowed it." Exodus 20:8-11, KJV.

Here in the heart of God's Ten Commandments, we find his name ("the Lord thy God"), title (Creator), and territory (heaven and earth). In this way, the Sabbath can be considered God's seal!

The final controversy between Christ and Satan will center on God's creatorship and His rulership. Satan has refused to acknowledge God as divine Sovereign and Creator, ever since he began his war in heaven (Revelation 12). This hostility against his Maker has extended to this earth, as Satan has induced men and women to reject God's rulership in their lives.

With this background of rebellion, we can now see how the Sabbath becomes the central issue in the last days. In a very practical way, the beast power has forced the whole world to a test, a test of who has ultimate authority—the traditions of the Church or the commandments of God.

From the beginning of time, the Sabbath has been a special sign between God and man. "Hallow My Sabbaths, and they will be a sign between Me and you, that you may know that I am the LORD your God." Ezekiel 20:20.

God calls the Sabbath His sign, or mark of authority. What does the beast power claim as its mark of authority? Reading from Catholic publications, we find the answer to this crucial question—a question that involves tampering with one of God's commandments:

> "Sunday is our mark of authority. . . . The Church is above the Bible, and this transference of Sabbath observance is proof of that fact."—*Catholic Record*, Sept. 1, 1923.

And from Father Enright, former President of Redemptorist College:

> "The Bible says, remember that thou keep holy the Sabbath day. The Catholic Church says, No! By my divine power I abolish the Sabbath day, and command you to keep holy the first day of the week. And, lo! The entire civilized world bows down in reverent obedience to the command of the holy Catholic Church."

◆ The challenge to Protestants

The Catholic Church claims Sunday as the mark of its religious supremacy. Implicit in this declaration is the challenge to Protestants to show why they worship on Sunday. If Protestants are "protesting" against the errors of Catholicism, why don't they reject the Sunday-Sabbath—the proud mark of the Catholic Church's authority?

From a study of the prophecies in God's Word, we can see that the time is not far distant when everyone, under threat of boycott and death, will be required to keep holy the first day of the week in direct violation of the command of God.

But not a single person has the mark of the beast yet, in terms of its Revelation 13 setting! God has true followers in every church. When Sunday-keeping is enforced by civil law, the issue will then be clear. Decisions will become unavoidable. Those who have not been aware of the eternal issues involved in loyalty to God will see their relationship to God in a new light. Then every person must choose either the seal of God (revealed in observing His seventh-day Sabbath)—or the mark of the beast (as manifested in the man-made, counterfeit day of worship on the first day of the week).

And to those who commit themselves without reservation to follow God comes this beautiful promise: "And I saw something like a sea of glass mingled with fire, and those who have the victory over the beast, over his image and over his mark and over the number of his name, standing on the sea of glass, having harps of God." Revelation 15:2.

Even now God is pleading with His true followers to step out of the counterfeit religious systems to follow Him completely.

The issues are serious: The mark of the beast—or the seal of God! Taking a stand on God's side—or giving allegiance to the beast power! Obedience—or disobedience! Loyalty—or rebellion!

How do you stand, friend? Have you made that commitment to Jesus Christ? Are you willing to place Him first in your life? Will you lay aside all your human opinions to serve Him? Jesus Himself invites you to do it! Don't turn the Saviour down. Right now, bow your head and open your heart to Jesus by saying, "Yes, Jesus, I love you enough to be completely loyal to You from this moment on, and by Your grace keep Your commandments, now and forever." ❏

You hear it all the time. A sickening crime is committed in some sheltered little rural town. The TV news nearly always features a disbelieving local citizen repeating in a daze, "We never thought it could happen here."

Do you think freedom-loving America could ever turn against its own citizens with deadly force? Can't happen here?

Before you answer, read the next chapter.

18

. . . .

The Clock Runs Out on America's Freedom

Storm warning.

Already, we've traced the Great War from its beginnings in Heaven through its long history on Earth.

We've seen right and wrong, good and evil, locked in mortal combat on many battlefields through the centuries.

You and I were born late in the war. But we can't escape it. It is the backdrop against which we live out our lives. It enters into every detail of our existence.

Soon the war will take what to most will be a completely unexpected turn. According to Bible prophecy, the primary battlefield of the war is soon to become the United States of America.

And when that happens, the Bible says, freedom will turn to force.

Inconceivable? Impossible?

But remember. This isn't a tabloid prediction. It is the prediction of a book filled with prophecies that have never missed.

Remember too that Satan doesn't have much time left, and he knows it. He's about to take off the gloves and pound away at truth and right with every fury-driven ounce of his strength.

The stage is already being set for a radical change in America's traditions of freedom and democracy.

Will you be ready when the storm breaks?

18

. . . .

The Bible is a record of God's dealings with His people; it is not primarily a history book. But when nations relate to the destiny of God's people, they are highlighted in Bible prophecy. Babylon, for example, attacked and overthrew Jerusalem around six hundred years before Christ.

Most of the Israelite nation were taken into captivity and marched hundreds of miles east, to Babylon on the Euphrates. Thus the Bible foretells the length of their captivity in Babylon.

In the first century, pagan Rome, through its authority in Palestine, attempted to kill Christ and place itself in direct opposition to the plans and purposes of God. Stories of Christians being thrown to the lions and burned at the stake are common from those early days of Christianity. But God encouraged His people by predicting the final end of pagan Rome's tyranny.

However, Satan eventually changed his tactics by introducing pagan practices into the Christian church through a substitute system of religious worship. As we studied in our last chapter, the leopard beast of Revelation 13 clearly represents papal Rome. The evidence is unmistakable.

Let's review these identifying characteristics:

■ It receives its power, seat, and great authority from pagan Rome (Revelation 13:1, 2).

■ It has power to demand worship. Thus it is a religious power with world-wide influence (Revelation 13:3, 4).

■ It is a blasphemous power (Revelation 13:5, 6), claiming (a) to forgive sins (Luke 5:21) and (b) to be equal with God (John 10:33).

■ It reigns for 42 months, or 1,260 literal years (30 days x 42 months = 1,260 years—see Revelation 13:5). In A.D. 538, Justinian, in close cooperation with the papacy, defeated the last of the Roman foes within the Empire. For the next 1,260 years, the papacy reigned supreme until 1798, when Napoleon's general, Berthier, took the pope captive.

■ It has the number of a man—666 (Revelation 13:18). In the book of Revelation, 7 signifies perfection, or completeness. There are the 7 churches, 7 seals, 7 trumpets, the 7 spirits before the throne, the 7-branched candlestick. A triple 7 indicates perfection of the Godhead. Thus, many Bible scholars believe that 666 indicates imperfection of human origin, not divinity.

The above evidence that the leopard beast represents the papal system seems convincing. You will recall that thousands fled from papal persecution and death on the European continent. Many went to England to escape religious oppression. But as the tentacles of papal supremacy reached throughout Europe and into England, scores of Puritans set sail to discover a new country in which they could establish a government founded upon the principles of religious freedom. They desired a state without a king and a church without a pope.

Thus, the United States was founded upon two fundamental principles of Protestantism and republicanism.

During the infant years of this nation while it struggled for independence, these two principles were sometimes lost sight of. But by the mid-1700s, a strong, new nation emerged.

On July 4, 1776, the Declaration of Independence was adopted by the unanimous decision of the Continental Congress. During the Congress, Patrick Henry gave a moving speech summarizing the great principles of the new nation and urged each delegate to sign this monumental document. In part, he said:

"That parchment [the Declaration of Independence] will speak to kings in language sad and terrible as the trumpet of the archangel. You have trampled on the rights of mankind long enough.

"Methinks I see the recording angel speak his dreadful message, 'Father, the Old World is baptized in blood. Father, it is drenched with the blood of millions who have been executed in slow and grinding oppression. Father, look with one glance of Thine eternal eye over Europe, Asia, and Africa and behold everywhere a terrible sight—man trodden down between the oppressor's feet, nations lost in blood, murder and superstition walking hand in hand over the graves of their victims, and not a single voice to speak hope to man . . .

"Let there be light again. Let there be a new world.

"Tell My people, the poor, downtrodden millions, to go out from the old world."

Under the inspiration of this moving appeal, the delegates unanimously adopted the Declaration of Independence. Eleven years later, in 1787, the first states ratified the Constitution.

◆ The United States in Bible prophecy

The First Amendment reads: "Congress shall make no law respecting an establishment of religion, or prohibiting the free exercise thereof."

For the first time in history, a nation was established without the power of kingly authority and without a state church. Under the circumstances, would it not be surprising indeed if the United States were not mentioned in prophecy? Would God leave one of the most significant developments in the religious history of the world out of Bible prophecy? Note the accuracy of detail with which the United States is described.

After discussing the papal power in Revelation 13, John introduces another beast. Verse 11 reads: "Then I saw another beast coming up out of the earth, and he had two horns like a lamb." You will recall that in Bible prophecy a beast represents a kingdom or ruling power (Daniel 7:17). We notice three things about this power:

◆ The lamb and the lamp

1. Its location. The Bible says, "I saw another beast coming up out of the earth." All of the other beasts (that is, nations) that we have studied have come up out of the sea. According to Revelation 17:15, the sea represents "peoples, multitudes, nations, and tongues." The previous empires have risen from among the populated areas of the world.

Here is a beast or power that rises in a sparsely populated area. The earth is the opposite of the sea, so it must represent an unsettled wilderness area.

A prominent writer, describing the rise of the United States, speaks of "the mystery of her coming forth from vacancy. . . . Like a silent seed we grew into an empire."—G. A. Townsend, *The New World Compared With the Old*, p. 635).

A European journal in 1850 spoke of the United States as a wonderful empire that was "emerging . . . amid the silence of the earth, daily adding to its power and strength,"—Quoted in Uriah Smith, *Daniel and the Revelation*, p. 578.

2. The time of its rise. The second beast rises at the same time the first beast is going into captivity (Revelation 13:10, 11). Papal supremacy was broken by the French in 1798; thus, the second beast must rise to prominence in the late 1700s.

3. The manner of its rise. Revelation 13:11 says, "And he had two horns like a lamb." The ancient Chinese philosopher Confucius said, "A picture is worth a thousand words." Certainly this is true in this case. What does a lamb represent? Youthfulness. This is not an old beast—it is pictured as a baby lamb. Here is described a new power among the older nations.

This lamb has two horns—horns being symbols of power. But these horns are uncrowned, indicating no king. The lamb is also a symbol of freedom and innocence. The expression "free as a lamb" suggests a joyful, carefree existence—the opposite of the Old World's tyranny. It speaks not of bondage but of liberty; not of chains but of freedom; not of oppression but of tolerance.

Further, throughout the Scriptures, the lamb is a symbol of Christ. John declared, "Behold! The Lamb of God who takes away the sin of the world!" John 1:29. Jesus invited men and women to find freedom from bondage in Him. "Come to Me, all you who labor and are heavy laden, and I will give you rest." Matthew 11:28.

The words inscribed at the base of the Statue of Liberty, penned by Emma Lazarus, express the same sentiment that Christ expressed almost 2,000 years ago:

> *Not like the brazen giant of Greek fame,*
> *With conquering limbs astride from land to land;*
> *Here at our sea-washed, sunset gates shall stand*
> *A mighty woman with a torch, whose flame*
> *Is the imprisoned lightning, and her name*
> *Mother of Exiles. From her beacon-hand*
> *Glows world-wide welcome; her mild eyes command*
> *The air-bridged harbor that twin cities frame.*
> *'Keep ancient lands, your storied pomp!' cries she*
> *With silent lips. "Give me your tired, your poor,*
> *Your huddled masses yearning to breathe free,*
> *The wretched refuse of your teeming shore.*
> *Send these, the homeless, tempest-tossed to me,*
> *I lift my lamp beside the golden door!"*

A lamp. What a fitting symbol of the United States!

So then, here is a new nation, a republic, rising into prominence without a king around 1798, in a sparsely populated area, with the lamb-like qualities of innocence and freedom. What country in the world could John be describing, except the United States? Our nation exactly fits the prophecy. Oh, friend, what a thrill it is to know that this nation is a nation of destiny! It has been ordained of God to champion religious and civil liberty.

How thankful we should be to live in this land of freedom, to live in a land where freedom reigns and the harsh despotism of the Old World is dead! Would to God that it would remain that way as long as time lasts.

Unfortunately, the prophetic picture changes. "And he . . . spoke like a dragon." Revelation 13:10. Obviously, sometime in the life of this nation a serious, sad change takes place. No longer will the United States speak with the gentle tones of a lamb; it is pictured as speaking with the dictatorial demands of a dragon!

But the picture gets even darker. Verse 12 contains this amazing declaration: "And he exercises all the authority of the first beast in his presence, and causes the earth and those who dwell in it to worship the first beast, whose deadly wound was healed." According to this prophecy, the United States will cause all within its territory to worship some aspect of the papacy. Church and state will cooperate in this country. The strong arm of the state will be used to enforce the sign of papal power—Sunday worship!

You ask, How is this going to come about? The prophecy does not indicate that some dictator will take over and subvert our liberties. Rather, it suggests that the people will desire legislation governing worship, and they shall seek to put pressure on their legislators regarding it. Revelation 13:13, 14 (KJV) reveals the amazing way this will take place and the events that will cause multitudes to unite with the beast power in the enforcement of his mark:

"And he doeth great wonders, so that he maketh fire come down from heaven on the earth in the sight of men, And deceiveth them that dwell on the earth by the means of those miracles which he had power to do in the sight of the beast."

How are those on earth deceived? What is it that leads the United States to give its allegiance to the beast of Revelation 13? "Those miracles which he had power to do."

Many people believe that if a miracle occurs, God's power caused it. Here is a young man struggling with a drug habit; then, miraculously, he is delivered. Here is a woman afflicted with cancer. She is told she has six months to live. Then, instantly, at a faith-healing meeting, she is cured. "These signs are undeniable evidence of the power of God," thousands will proclaim.

But are these "miracles" from God? Are miracles always evidence of God's favor and power?

God can and will work miracles as He thinks best. But because miracles happen does not mean they are always the result of God's power. Satan, too, can work miracles.

Jesus warned His followers concerning the last days with these words found in Matthew 24:24: "For false christs and false prophets will rise and show great signs and wonders to deceive, if possible, even the elect." Jesus here warns us all: Beware, spectacular signs and wonders are not necessarily a sign of divine favor.

◆ A dazzling deception

The devil knows how to work miracles and perform sensational signs and wonders. Since most people would rather have some sensational sign than the simple, straightforward truth of God's Word, they will be deceived. Revelation 16:14 says, "For they are spirits of demons, performing signs, which go out to the kings of the earth and of the whole world, to gather them to the battle of that great day of God Almighty."

Kings are going to be deceived—great men, politicians, statesmen— by the wonder-working power of the enemy. This work of dazzling deception will lead men and women to unite around the beast's sign of authority and enforce Sunday worship.

You can see how this may easily take place. Our nation has been racked by war, ripped apart by crime, and riddled with lawlessness in the last few years. Our large cities have become unsafe after dark. The mugger, the rapist, and the thief stalk our streets. Scores of honest people, from the man on the street to our ablest politicians, cry out, "What is the answer?"

In a society confused and groping for answers, looking for a solution to its problems, the stage is set. The answer will be found in a revival of religion in America, of all places! A mighty false revival will sweep America—a revival marked by undeniable signs and wonders.

Miracles will be wrought; the sick will be healed. A spirit of unity and fellowship will prevail. It will be declared, "If we unite and worship on Sunday, God will be pleased, our nation will be blessed, and all will be well on the home front again."

Some religious leaders have even boldly suggested that a common day of worship may be a partial solution to our recurring energy crises. They have suggested that by forbidding all driving on Sunday, except to church, we may save up to 15 percent of our gasoline supply.

◆ Forced Sunday observance

For example, in the May 7, 1976, issue of *Christianity Today*, then editor Harold Lindsell entitled an article, "The Lord's Day and Natural Resources." He proposed, for the purpose of conserving energy, that "all businesses, including gasoline stations and restaurants, should close every Sunday." Lindsell expressed his conviction that such a move would accord both with the natural laws that govern man's well-being and with the "will of God for all men." Sensing that people are "highly unlikely" to observe Sunday as a rest day through voluntary action alone, he further suggested that the only way to accomplish the dual objectives of Sunday observance and the conservation of energy would be "by force of legislative fiat through the duly elected officials of the people."

Some time ago, the U.S. Supreme Court ruled that is some instances, Sunday laws may be enforced, not on the basis of religious considerations, but in the interests of safeguarding the health and welfare of the American people. The late Justice William O. Douglas disagreed and stated the following in his dissenting opinion to the majority decision of the court:

"It seems to be plain that by these laws, the states compel one, under the sanction of law, to refrain from work or recreation on Sunday because of the majority's views on that day. The state by law makes Sunday a symbol of respect or adherence."

The miracles described earlier will lead our national legislators to accept those proposals that will attempt to unify this country at a time of great moral twilight and probably economic stress. In the enforcement of a national Sunday law, the mark of the beast will be enacted. Not long afterward, an economic boycott will be enforced on those who refuse to yield—exactly as predicted.

Revelation 19:20 puts it clearly: "Then the beast was captured, and with him the false prophet who worked signs in his presence, by which he deceived those who received the mark of the beast and those who worshiped his image. These two were cast alive into the lake of fire burning with brimstone." But another point of deception is predicted in Revelation 13. Note the 13th verse: "He performs great signs, so that he even makes fire come down from heaven on the earth in the sight of men."

Fire coming down from heaven? What does fire represent in the Bible? Fire has always been a symbol of the presence of God. Moses entered the presence of God at the burning bush. Fire in the sanctuary was a symbol of God's presence. In the New Testament, fire is a symbol of the energizing presence and power of God, manifest in the work of the Holy Spirit.

In the last days, fire—a symbol of the Spirit's power—will be counterfeited. This strange fire will be one of the signs and wonders that deceives multitudes! What is this strange fire? Referring to the work of Jesus, John the Baptist said, "He will baptize you with the Holy Spirit and fire." Luke 3:16. This promise was fulfilled on the day of Pentecost.

In Acts 2:2-4, we read: "And suddenly there came a sound from heaven, as of a rushing mighty wind, and it filled the whole house where they were sitting. Then there appeared to them divided tongues, as of fire, and one sat upon each of them. And they were all filled with the Holy Spirit and began to speak with other tongues, as the Spirit gave them utterance."

Fire from heaven! What better description could God give John the Revelator of a false revival that would put great emphasis on speaking in tongues and unity among all churches?

I should insert here a point so no one will misunderstand: The Bible teaches that there is a genuine gift of tongues. Note these important points about it.

1. The gift of tongues, throughout the book of Acts, referred to a real language understood by those who heard it, directly or through an interpreter, for the purpose of spreading the gospel (see Acts 2, 10, 19).

2. This gift was regarded by the early church as one of the least of the gifts and never regarded as an absolute necessity for every believer. Jesus never spoke in tongues or commanded His followers to do so.

3. In his Corinthian letters, Paul cautions against undue emphasis on tongues and speaks out against incoherent babbling. He said, "I had rather speak five words with my understanding . . . than ten thousand words in an unknown tongue. . . . Let all things be done decently and in order." 1 Corinthians 14:19, 40, KJV.

◆ Rattling the gates

Thus, in the United States of America, a counterfeit religious revival will arise, emphasizing the gift of tongues and miracles. The manifestation of "tongues" and miracles will be used to prove the genuineness of the revival.

But this will be a counterfeit revival. Those involved in it will not accept biblical truth regarding the Lord's description of His people (Revelation 14:12) but will instead appeal to the evidence of the miracles done in their midst and the presence of the gift of tongues as fire from heaven. This great revival, with its signs, wonders, and counterfeit tongues and miracles, will lead to unity among the churches for the enforcement of the mark of the beast.

One of the surest signs that the mark of the beast will soon be enforced is this: The counterfeit signs and miracles that deceive the inhabitants of the United States (and other lands), leading them to enforce the mark of the beast, are now taking place.

In a most remarkable fashion, Neo-Pentecostalism has grown in numbers and in influence during the past several decades. It has gained a foothold in more than forty denominations in this country. More than two thousand ministers of churches affiliated with the National

Council of Churches speak in tongues and are actively promoting charismatic gifts.

This force is "rattling the gate of every major denomination," as millionaire industrialist George Otis put it.

Neo-Pentecostals look on the movement as a miracle-working force to bring Protestantism, Catholicism, and, ultimately, the whole religious world, under the mantle of the Holy Spirit.

David J. DePlessis, for ten years one of the leaders of the Pentecostal World Conference, describes the movement as a "spiritual ecumenicity" in contrast to the "institutional ecumenicity" represented by the World Council of Churches. This is exactly the path the Bible predicted the last-day, false revival would take.

We must look at this unfolding picture as our Lord does. He knows that many sincere and honest people are involved in this false revival—people whose regular churches have become cold and formal. In their desire to satisfy their souls' longing, these people have been understandably misled by the warm fellowship and compelling manifestations they experience in "tongues" and "miracles."

Many have brought this convincing experience back to their once formal and largely dead mainline churches. From all outward appearances, Neo–Pentecostalism has brought new life to churches of most all denominations by the infusion of these manifestations. But when the truth becomes better known, these sincere worshipers within Neo-Pentecostalism will respond to the last-day invitation: "Come out of her, my people." Revelation 18:4.

Where is all this leading? What will be the outcome of this unity brought about by a false revival and counterfeit miracles?

Revelation 13:16, 17 graphically outlines the future: "He causes all, both small and great, rich and poor, free and slave, to receive a mark on their right hand or on their foreheads, and that no one may buy or sell except one who has the mark or the name of the beast, or the number of his name."

This false revival, uniting widely differing religious groups, will give life to the legislative movements that will usher in a union of church and state. When individuals accept the spectacular and the apparently miraculous as truth, they often become unreasonable. They will argue that their "supernatural" experience proves their movement must be of God. This kind of thinking and feeling will lead to a Sunday law.

What then is the safeguard against this false revival? Certainly God can and does work miracles for His people! Certainly God often provides special power to His people on earth. In the last days, He has promised special intervention.

Revelation 18:1 describes the genuine revival in the last days in these words: "After these things I saw another angel coming down from heaven, having great authority, and the earth was illuminated with his glory." The earth, illuminated with God's glory! A genuine revival! How can one tell the difference between the true and the false? What is the distinguishing characteristic between the genuine and the counterfeit?

Take your Bibles and look at Acts 5:39: "If it is of God, you cannot overthrow it." The true ministry of the Holy Spirit is to lead each believer into a knowledge of the truth. The genuine gift of miracles, in addition to tongues (breaking the language barrier to communicate the gospel), will be given to God's church, enabling it to accomplish its mission of proclaiming the gospel to the ends of the earth.

The Bible says, "We are His witnesses to these things, and so also is the Holy Spirit whom God has given to those who obey Him." Acts 5:32. To whom is the Holy Ghost given? To those who obey Him. In these last days, two uniting movements will draw the line, each moving in opposite directions, each compelled by different leaders. Both emphasize doctrinal unity, but the counterfeit movement will increase in influence and power until compelling pressure will be brought upon lawmakers to enforce a Sunday law.

The second group throughout the world love truth and read carefully those divine predictions which portray religious conditions in the last days. Deep within their hearts, they say, "God, we love our brothers and sisters in all religious groups; at the same time, we want to obey the civil law. No one wants unity more than we do. But, Lord, the Bible says, 'Buy the truth, and sell it not.' Unity is too high a price to pay for compromising truth. Truth is more precious than unity."

They remember their Lord's prayer in John 17:21: "That they all may be one, as You, Father, are in Me, and I in You; that they also may be one in Us, that the world may believe that You sent Me." But this unity that Jesus prayed for was a unity in truth—a unity through truth and unity with truth.

Jesus prayed, "Father, that they may be one," three times. Then He said, "Sanctify them by Your truth. Your word is truth." John 17:17.

In the last days of earth's history, Jesus will have a unity movement. His Spirit will lead men and women from varying faiths and creeds to unite on the truth of His Word. And His Spirit is at work. What He is doing is absolutely amazing!

◆ Swept away by the sensational

A young woman brought up in the State of Maine was telling me that when she was nine years old, a man sold Christian literature to her mother. This little girl began to read the books. As she read, she thought, "This indeed is Bible truth." As she listened to Bible studies that were being given to her mother, she thought, "This is truth." She accepted the fact that Jesus was coming very, very soon. She accepted the fact that when He came, men and women would be in one of two classes—either saved or lost. She gave her heart to her Lord to be in the class that He could save.

She continued to study. She learned the wonderful truth of the Bible Sabbath. She rejoiced in that truth and began keeping the true Sabbath, the seventh day of the week—Saturday. She learned that it was Jesus who made the Sabbath, that He was the Creator. She kept the Sabbath, not as a legalistic requirement, but in love for Jesus Christ as she honored Him as her Lord.

So, at only nine years of age, she stepped out to follow Jesus wherever His truth would lead her.

In a few months, her family moved from that community to one without a Sabbath-keeping church. In that community was a wonderful minister—a very loving man—and he visited this new family. He charmed this girl's home with his caring spirit. Soon, the young Bible student and her sister began attending his church. It was a church that emphasized miracles, especially what appeared to be healings, and "tongues." The girl was caught up in that movement. For three years she turned her back on the true Bible Sabbath. She brushed aside the things she had learned. She was so caught up in what was taking place around her—the healings, the tongues, and other "miracles"—that she now thought, "This must indeed be of God."

One Sunday morning the pastor made an appeal for the young people to give their lives to Jesus and move ahead in baptism. Although she had been baptized previously in a Sabbath-keeping church, the young lady, now thirteen, said, "I'm going to lead the way." She stood to her feet. As she stood, many other young people stood as well. The baptismal service was scheduled for the next Sunday.

Before she went to sleep the Saturday night before the baptism, she struggled with her decision. A text in her mind kept returning: "To the law and to the testimony! If they do not speak according to this word, it is because there is no light in them." Isaiah 8:20. To the law of God, the Ten-Commandment law, and to the testimony of Scripture—if they do not speak according to this Word, there is no light in them.

Notice, Isaiah doesn't say there is no truth in them. Satan delights in mingling truth with error. It says there is no "light" in them. The light is what we follow! Light is what we long for!

As she went off to sleep that night, with thoughts troubling her about her baptism into this miracle-working, tongues-speaking movement, she had a dream. In her dream, the world came to an end. She dreamed about those two classes—the saved and the lost, those who received the mark of the beast and those who received God's special seal. In her dream, she saw herself among the lost—among those destroyed when Jesus came. The dream was so dramatic that she awoke and couldn't sleep.

When she woke up, the Lord impressed her that He had a day of rest and worship—which He indeed wanted her to observe. The dream confirmed what she had already studied in the Scriptures. She went to her Bible and began to study again. She reviewed those Bible texts that indicate the place of God's day of rest and worship in the last days. In that last-day picture, God is calling a people to stand for Him alone, at any cost and at any price.

◆ "I have been misled."

In those early Sunday-morning hours, after studying those Bible passages, she said, "I cannot join this church. This has not been the truth of God. I have been misled."

So to church she went, with her encyclopedia and Bible. During Sunday school, she stood up and said, "I have to be honest with my convictions." She began to share the convictions that God had given her regarding the true Bible Sabbath. As she stood alone, she was ridiculed by her friends. "Oh, they're just a little group that keep the Bible Sabbath. They're a sect. You don't have to do that."

But as she read the Bible texts, she said, "Here I stand. I can do no other."

The church service that morning was used as an attempt to convince her she was wrong. Still, she remained loyal to her convictions. As she stood on the shore of a lake, she watched as one after another of her young friends was baptized. She stood there alone and said to herself, "I just can't do it. God is leading me to His true movement. I believe in the message of the Bible. I believe in the true Bible Sabbath. Yes, I want unity in love, but I cannot do it without truth. I must not do it."

Within a very short time, God arranged for her family to move to a city that had a Seventh-day Adventist church—a Sabbath-keeping church. She began attending an Adventist school. After high school, she attended a Seventh-day Adventist college, where she met an Adventist ministerial student. Today she is assisting him in conducting Bible lectures for hundreds throughout the United States.

You see, at a critical moment in her life, God miraculously intervened. Although she went through a terrible struggle, she asked only, "God, what do You want me to do?" God confirmed the truth with a dream just before she was to make a decision that would have changed the whole course of her life.

Friends, in the last days of earth's history, men and women who are honest in heart, who love and honor Jesus Christ, are being touched by the true ministry of the Holy Spirit. God's genuine unity movement—in which Protestants and Catholics alike are being guided back to the teachings of the Word of God—is encircling the world. The Bible says, "To the law"—the Ten Commandment law that includes the Sabbath commandment—"To the law and to the testimony! If they do not speak according to this word, it is because there is no light in them."

◆ Power and light

Isaiah doesn't say, "There's no power in them." Counterfeit religion surely has power—power, in fact, is their chief attraction!

The issue is light. Which teaching regarding the seventh-day Sabbath, for example, can pass the "light" test?

Friend, what church, in its teachings, can pass the "light" test? If we ignore the Law of God, if we do not take seriously the Bible's focus on the Sabbath as a major issue of loyalty to God in the last days, by what test can we evaluate which church is teaching the truth about salvation?

Many wonder, Is this church true? Is that church true? Is this movement true? Is that movement true? You will always be perplexed unless you accept the sure light test God has given.

He's given a simple test: "To the law and to the testimony." If they don't speak according to this word, God says, there is no light in them.

You ask, "Where are the true people of God today?" Revelation 14:12 says, "Here is the patience of the saints; here are those who keep the commandments of God and the faith of Jesus." The true people of God in these last days of earth's history will be a people who love and honor the Lord with all their hearts. They will be Christ-centered people, a people who exalt Jesus, yet a people who lead men and women to obedience to the law that Jesus etched with His own finger on tablets of stone.

Our Lord has His hands outstretched, inviting you to join this people who best represent His gracious message to all, everywhere on this planet today. ❏

At times, it has appeared that Satan could declare victory in the war. The whole world seemed to be on his side.

But God has always had His loyal followers on Earth. So it is today. And so it will be in the days just ahead when the battle intensifies.

At the end, two characteristics will clearly identify God's true followers, the Bible says.

Learn what these two marks are in the chapter coming up.

19

. . . .

Survivors of
the War Behind
All Wars

A passion to make God look good.

As fiercely as Satan attacks God's loyal followers—especially at the end—it's a wonder any of them are left standing.

But stand they will. Boldly. Firmly. Without compromise.

They are the final survivors of the Great War. The unconquerable Remnant of God.

Who are these people? Are they already somewhere to be found? If so, how can they be identified? Can any of us join this band of remnant survivors?

The book of Revelation answers all of these questions.

It brings to view a group so loyal to God that they would sooner die than dishonor Him. A group prepared to make any sacrifice to defend God's good name. A group ready to accept whatever God offers, do whatever God asks, and trust whatever God says.

They may not have been around when the war began. But they will play a pivotal role in helping to end it.

19

We seem to be born with inexpressible cravings for something we do not have. Subconsciously, we seem to seek and grope for something we cannot even describe—but something we know we want and need. Carl Jung once said that man was created with a "God-shaped vacuum" inside.

Augustine said much earlier: "Thou has made us for Thyself, O God, and our hearts are restless till they find their rest in thee."

Seeking to calm this restlessness, even modern, sophisticated man finds himself drawn to religion. A recent poll indicated that sales of Bibles and books on spiritual themes remain brisk even when retailers in other markets fear that an economic downturn may ruin their business. New churches are rapidly springing up across the country.

Large numbers of young adherents, often in distinctive garb, are selling flowers, candles, or ginseng tea in airports. Others congregate on street corners chanting to the rhythm of tinkling bells and monotonous drumbeats. Preachers from storefront churches—as well as those on coast-to-coast TV and radio—claim to be teaching the one true faith.

Catholicism has found a new vitality from the days of charismatic Pope John XXII to the present pope, John Paul II. As he makes his way around the world, millions jam the streets to see him. In the Middle East, Ayatollah Khomeini sparked a remarkable Islamic revival. Mormons, Jehovah's Witnesses, Pentecostals and Seventh-day Adventists are multiplying at record rates.

Each of these religions claims to present God's truth for today. Yet the briefest consideration of their conflicting messages reveals obvious differences. Although all these groups want to be known as Bible-based, they are in conflict.

How can the average person ever sort out all the claims and counterclaims of these religious organizations and know for certain what is the real gospel? Does God actually have a special group that faithfully sets forth God's truth for these last days? What was the apostle Paul referring to when he wrote of "the church of the living God, the pillar and ground of the truth"? 1 Timothy 3:15.

John Milner sums up our dilemma in these words:

"There is but one inquiry to be made, namely, which is the true church . . . By solving this one question . . . you will at once solve every question of religious controversy that has ever been or that ever can be agitated."—*The End of Religious Controversy*, p. 95.

But where does one start in this quest for truth? Wherever we look, we find so many denominations, so much controversy, especially in the religious community. Why doesn't God make it easier to sort it all out so we can clearly identify His last-day church?

◆ Why so many churches?

According to scripture, Jesus never intended that there should be such confusion, such a profusion of denominations. Just before His crucifixion, He prayed that "they all may be one, as You, Father, are in Me, and I in You." John 17:21.

Christ did not want divisions in His church. In fact, Paul pled that "there should be no schism in the body." 1 Corinthians 12:25.

But realist that he was, Paul added that division would come. Using the analogy of wolves among a flock of sheep, Paul spoke of men arising, speaking "perverse things" and drawing disciples away (Acts 20:30).

As we turn the pages of church history, we discover that this is exactly what happened. Following the establishment of the New Testament Church, false teachers arose.

Some members accepted their heresies and left. Others became confused. Disciples were drawn away, forming divisions within Christianity, even within the first one hundred years! But through it all, God has had a church which remained faithful to the teachings of Christ.

In the book of Revelation, God revealed to His prophet John the apostasy and religious confusion that would exist in earth's last days. In chapter 12, John was given a panoramic view of the history of the church from the time of Christ's birth to the end of the world.

The chapter is written in symbolic language, picturing a woman in white, clothed with the sun, standing on the moon with a crown of twelve stars on her head, crying out to be delivered in childbirth. The woman, in Bible symbolism, represents God's people—His church (Jeremiah 6:2).

The apostle Paul uses the same terminology in describing the Corinthian church. "I have betrothed you to one husband, that I may present you as a chaste virgin to Christ." 2 Corinthians 11:2.

As Revelation's prophecy continues, we find that this pure woman, or God's true church, has an evil enemy lying in wait to destroy her child at birth: "And the dragon stood before the woman who was ready to give birth, to devour her Child as soon as it was born." Revelation 12:4.

The identity of this dragon is unmistakable. He is none other than the same dragon that made war in heaven, "that serpent of old, called the Devil and Satan." Revelation 12:9.

As the symbolic picture of Revelation continues, we read that the woman gave birth to "a male Child who was to rule all nations with a rod of iron. And her Child was caught up to God and His throne." Revelation 12:5.

This part of the prophecy, too, is not difficult to unravel, as it uses the same words employed later in Revelation—words that clearly refer to Christ Himself. "Now out of His mouth goes a sharp sword, that with it He should strike the nations. And He Himself will rule them with a rod of iron." Revelation 19:15.

Thus we see in Revelation a vision of the great controversy between good and evil, the powerful struggle between Satan and God and later His church, the conflict between truth and error. The battle originated in heaven, where Satan, desiring to be like the Most High, stirred up one-third of the angels to attempt to overthrow God's kingdom. The evil angel was thrown to earth, where the battle continued with renewed vigor. The devil gained confidence as he succeeded in tempting the Eden couple.

Centuries later, he tried to take the life of Jesus, the man child of Revelation, as soon as He was born. Herod, the local Roman ruler, hearing talk that the Messiah might have been recently born, ordered that all male children two years old and under be murdered. But Mary and Joseph, with angel guidance, were able to escape with Jesus into Egypt. (See Matthew 2:16-23.)

Throughout the ministry of Jesus, the devil dogged His footsteps, hoping to block God's plan to save the fallen world.

As Christ's body hung on the cross, Satan thought he had won the battle. But the empty tomb proved all his efforts to be in vain. Christ arose and returned to His heavenly Father. The prophecy was on schedule, just as John the Revelator had been shown.

Having failed in his attempt to destroy God's Son, Satan then turned his wrath on the woman—the Christian church. All but one of Christ's disciples died a martyr's death. The apostle Paul was beheaded outside the walls of Rome. Christians were tortured and thrown into dungeons; many sealed their loyalty with their blood.

As long as the apostles were alive, the church stood firm and true. But with succeeding generations, commitments began to waver, compromise and apostasy became common.

In the fourth century, Emperor Constantine tried to hold the Roman Empire together by uniting pagans and Christians in one great system of religion. As a result, Christianity lost much of its old stigma as it gained popularity by incorporating pagan beliefs and practices.

◆ Compromise and commitment

During this time of galloping compromise, many Christians remained faithful to God's truths and protested the changes, refusing to compromise their position. Soon, the Roman emperors issued edicts making the rejection of these false practices of the state church a crime punishable by death. Historian Archibald Bauer writes,

> "Great numbers were driven from their habitations with their wives and children, stripped and naked . . . many of them inhumanly massacred."—*The History of the Popes*, vol. 2, p. 334.

Thus began the bitter persecution of God's people spoken of in the book of Revelation: "Then the woman fled into the wilderness, where she has a place prepared by God, that they should feed her there one thousand two hundred and sixty days." Revelation 12:6.

John prophesied that the persecution was to last 1,260 days, or, according to the biblical value of symbolic time, 1,260 years.

How accurately history confirms this Bible prophecy! The reign of intolerance against those who protested the errors in the state church began in A.D. 538, when the Roman emperor Justinian declared the bishop to be "the head of the church, the true and effectual corrector of heretics." Such a decree came shortly after Justinian had ordered the Roman general, Belisarius, to destroy the three Arian powers that opposed the church in Rome. Interpretations of Bible truth were to be viewed only in one way, and that way was determined by the church of Rome. All other viewpoints would be considered heretical and cause for persecution.

Faithful Christians who continued to cherish the truths revealed in God's Word found only one way to preserve their faith and existence. Just as God had prophesied, "The woman fled into the wilderness."

The Waldenses, Albigenses, Huguenots, and other faithful Christians fled to the Alps in northern Italy and southern France, hiding in secluded valleys, remote caves, and high mountains. They were hunted down as common criminals, and many were slain. Their crime? They would not give up the teachings of Jesus.

Millions of Christians suffered death during this time of terrible persecution during the Dark Ages rather than compromise their faith. Some historians estimate the figure ran as high as fifty million.

It is tragic that many who died were martyred by other professed Christians, who mistakenly believed they were doing the will of God.

Long centuries of persecution followed, but finally God's truth was again to triumph. The Bible, long chained to monastery walls and cathedral pulpits, was translated into the common language of the masses and secretly scattered throughout the world. No longer was God's truth hidden. Light broke through the darkness.

Courageous reformers boldly proclaimed God's Word. Many, like Huss and Jerome, were burned at the stake. Others, like Luther, Wycliffe, and Tyndale, were hunted and persecuted.

But the fires of the Protestant Reformation would not be put out. Other reformers arose, and Bible truths, long obscured by man-made traditions, surfaced. With such religious awakening came the increased wrath and fury of Satan.

During this time, America was discovered, offering new freedom and a refuge for the persecuted of Europe. Here on the shores of a newborn nation was laid the foundation of civil and religious liberty.

The era of compromise and persecution prophesied in Revelation 12 finally came to an end in 1798 when the atheistic government of Napoleon sent General Berthier to take the pope captive. As Revelation's prophecy had so clearly predicted, the reign of persecution lasted exactly 1,260 years, spanning the years from A.D. 538 to 1798.

At the end of the eighteenth century, as this prophetic time period came to a close, God still had a group of faithful believers who clung to the Bible and its teachings. This small group—or the "remnant," as described in Revelation—became the focus of the "dragon's" wrath.

◆ The remnant

Just as a fabric remnant represents the last part of the original, so God's remnant is the last true body of believers on earth—God's last-day church—the final survivors of the war behind all wars—the faithful children of the dragon-beseiged woman. John describes two characteristics that identify this group. God's followers at the end of time, he says, will "keep the commandments of God and have the testimony of Jesus Christ." Revelation 12:17.

The description sounds quite basic, and a cursory look at the array of Christian religions today might indicate fairly widespread compliance in both respects. Yet do all religions today really "keep the commandments of God"—or do many only claim to promote God's requirements while ignoring the specifics of His commands?

The second commandment states, "Thou shalt not make unto thee any graven images," yet many congregations are accustomed to bowing before icons of wood and glass. "Thou shalt not take the name of the Lord thy God in vain," states the third, while many ignore the sacredness of God's name. And most of the religious world has lost sight of the memorial of creation described in the fourth commandment: "Remember the sabbath day, to keep it holy. Six days shalt thou labour, and do all thy work: But the seventh day is the sabbath of the Lord thy God." Exodus 20:8-11, KJV.

The seventh day. A glance at the calendar reveals that the seventh day of the week is Saturday, not Sunday. But a stroll through the middle of town on a Saturday morning in America would reveal most churches to be closed, their parking lots vacant, their doors locked. Yet one of the distinguishing characteristics of God's true church is an obedience to His commandments—all ten of them, including the fourth, which instructs us to labor on six days and keep the seventh holy.

Christian churches generally agree upon nine of the commandments. The difference of opinion and practice is over the fourth. But a church which keeps only nine of the ten cannot be characterized as a commandment-keeping church; rather, it is a commandment-breaking church, for James wrote: "For whoever shall keep the whole law, and yet stumble in one point, he is guilty of all." James 2:10.

Thus a church that does not keep all ten of the commandments can be eliminated as a candidate for God's last-day church. So we are limited, in looking for God's body of believers on earth, to those that keep all ten of the commandments.

But we can refine our search process even further. The text in Revelation 12 mentions that God's church will also have the "testimony of Jesus." A later text explains that "the testimony of Jesus is the spirit of prophecy." Revelation 19:10. God's last-day church will have the gifts of the Spirit, including the spirit of prophecy.

Other characteristics are also given in scripture to help us in our search for God's special last-day church. His people will be engaged in the mission of reaching the world with the Gospel, for Jesus commissioned His church: "Go therefore and make disciples of all the nations, baptizing them in the name of the Father and of the Son and of the Holy Spirit, teaching them to observe all things that I have commanded you; and lo, I am with you always, even to the end of the age." Matthew 28:19, 20.

◆ The remnant's message

The three angels of Revelation seen "flying in the midst of heaven" further clarify the role of God's last-day church. Described in Revelation 14, the angels bear a message which God's last-day church is to present to the world. The first part of this threefold message emphasizes two great truths to be shared with every person. "Fear God and give glory to Him, for the hour of His judgment has come; and worship Him who made heaven and earth." Revelation 14:7.

Judgment and worship. Two crucial components of the message of God's last-day church. God's remnant will be calling men and women to recognize God's creative power and to worship Him on that great memorial of creation, the seventh day. And they will be teaching that the judgment hour has come.

God has an urgent message for today, proclaiming His soon return. God's true church pulsates with an advent consciousness. It believes and preaches with power that Jesus is coming soon. In all of its teachings, it places emphasis on the second coming of Christ.

◆ Called out of confusion

The second part of the threefold message borne by the angels flying in the midst of heaven is found in verse 8: "And another angel followed, saying, 'Babylon is fallen, is fallen, that great city, because she has made all nations drink of the wine of the wrath of her fornication.'" Revelation 14:8.

This message calls for God's true people to separate themselves from the confused religious world, to recognize the apostasy in religion today, and to have no part of the counterfeit. It calls them from law breaking to law keeping. It appeals to them to leave every commandment-breaking church and unite with God's commandment-keeping church.

The last and most solemn appeal is found in the third portion of this prophecy. The third angel follows the first two and calls in a loud voice, "If anyone worships the beast and his image, and receives his mark on his forehead or on his hand, he himself shall also drink of the wine of the wrath of God." Revelation 14:9, 10.

God's remnant church has this added responsibility: One of its major tasks is to warn the world regarding the dire effects of worshiping the beast or his image, or receiving the beast's mark. Any of these will result in receiving the seven last plagues, as described in Revelation 18.

Thus God's last-day church will not be the most popular religious body on earth. You will not find God's people attracting millions, offering light-hearted platitudes to people who want their religion more to care for their anxieties than to reinforce their loyalties to truth. God's last-day church will be a bold movement, calling for commitment, crying out for change, pointing to the Bible, warning of judgment, upholding the commandments.

While a commitment to such a body of Christians is not one to be taken lightly, it leads directly to something that no other commitment could ever begin to touch—a peace of mind and heart that comes only from following God wherever the light of truth leads. As Jesus said, "If ye know these things, happy are ye if ye do them." John 13:17, KJV. ❏

250 • BEYOND ORION'S GATES

The Remnant is no exclusive club. It is a worldwide movement at the end of time that issues an urgent final call to God's true followers everywhere to come out of their comfortable but confused and error-plagued churches to help tell the world the truth about God.

Next: Evacuating a dangerous city.

20

. . . .

A City Called Confusion

A stunning discovery.

What do you do when—in the midst of battle—you discover that you are not where you thought you were? That instead of being safe in your own barracks, you're really in the camp of the enemy—and that you've been there all along?

As we close in on the final days of this universal war, a lot of us are going to make that very shocking discovery!

We will find that what we have sincerely been following as truth turns out to be error. We will find that—like a boat that pulls loose from its moorings—the church we've always called our spiritual home has drifted away from truth without our even realizing it.

God knew that at the end, His enemy would stir up so much confusion in the churches that many would despair of ever really knowing where to find the truth.

So in His Word, He first told us where to find the truth. Then He sounded the alarm to come out of the foggy confusion of error and stand with Him under the banner of truth.

If you discover that despite your sincerity and loyalty, you are on the wrong side of the line in the battle, you really have only one safe and right choice to make.

Millions already have. Millions more will. And God will give you the power to make that choice too.

20

• •

The book of Revelation describes the church as a pure woman. The church is the bride; Christ is the husband. Christ, the Head of the church, gives guidance and direction to His bride. The Bible pictures a pure woman as the true church; one who is faithful to her husband, one who has not committed spiritual adultery. The false church is represented in the Bible by a harlot, or an adulteress, one who has left her true lover, Jesus Christ, and united with the world.

"Now a great sign appeared in heaven: a woman clothed with the sun, with the moon under her feet, and on her head a garland of twelve stars. Then being with child, she cried out in labor and in pain to give birth." Revelation 12:1, 2. According to Scripture, this child was to rule all nations with a rod of iron. Ultimately, he would be "caught up to God and His throne" (verse 5). Obviously, this is a description of Jesus.

The Bible says that the woman stands on the moon. As the moon reflects the glory of the sun, so the Old Testament church could only reflect the glory of the gospel that blazed forth in Jesus. As the Old Testament dispensation faded away, the New Testament church, clothed with the glory of Christ, arose in splendor. The crown of twelve stars on the head of the woman signifies that the church is guided by divinely inspired apostles. So here is the true church, clothed with the righteousness of Christ, having divinely guided, spiritual administrators. What a beautiful picture of the pure, true church, unadulterated by human traditions, untouched by human doctrine, and based on the Word of God.

Revelation 17:3-5 speaks about another church: "So he carried me away in the Spirit into the wilderness. And I saw a woman sitting on a scarlet beast which was full of names of blasphemy, having seven heads and ten horns. The woman was arrayed in purple and scarlet, and adorned with gold and precious stones and pearls, having in her hand a golden cup full of abominations and the filthiness of her fornication. And on her forehead a name was written: MYSTERY, BABYLON THE GREAT, THE MOTHER OF HARLOTS AND OF THE ABOMINATIONS OF THE EARTH."

This jeweled woman passes around the wine of her false doctrines, and the world becomes drunk. She is a harlot; she has left her true lover. She is not the true church of Christ, but the false church. She is the mother of many other false churches.

The book of Revelation describes a great war that took place thousands of years ago in heaven: "And war broke out in heaven: Michael and his angels fought with the dragon; and the dragon and his angels fought, but they did not prevail, nor was a place found for them in heaven any longer. So the great dragon was cast out, that serpent of old, called the Devil and Satan, who deceives the whole world; he was cast to the earth, and his angels were cast out with him." Revelation 12:7-9.

In heaven, Satan—or Lucifer as he was then called—attempted to deceive the good and loyal angels. After he was cast out into the earth, he lied to Adam and Eve in the Garden of Eden. "Eve, you can eat of that tree, and you won't die. All the trees in the garden are the same. It doesn't make any difference whether you eat of the tree or not." Thus Satan sowed his first lie on earth.

♦ The woman in white

The Bible teaches that there are two great systems of religion. One is centered on Jesus, "the way, the truth, and the life." John 14:6. It is based solidly on the teachings of Scripture. Consequently, in Revelation 12, the true church is pictured as a woman in white. Her doctrines are pure; she is loyal to her true Master. She has not compromised the truth. Truth and error, as water and oil, cannot and do not mix.

God is looking for a church that does not mingle truth and error. He is looking for a people living in harmony with the truth of His Word. The woman in white of Revelation 12 represents God's true, visible church on earth—His faithful people through the ages who have not compromised Bible doctrine.

◆ The woman in scarlet

As we have seen, in addition to the woman in white, the Bible describes a woman in scarlet with a cup of wine—representing false doctrine—in her hand. She is the great apostate mother church, and many churches have drunk of her wine. The Bible says that she rides upon a scarlet-colored beast, and in the Bible, a beast represents a political system.

This false church, decked in scarlet and purple colors, is the mother of harlots. In other words, she has left her true lover, Jesus, by placing human traditions and the decrees of church councils above the Word of God. She is an adulteress, in the sense that she has betrayed scriptural teachings. She is the great mother church, and along with her are other churches who also have left true biblical doctrines.

Notice Revelation 17:5: "And on her forehead a name was written: MYSTERY, BABYLON THE GREAT." This apostate mother church of Revelation 17 actually retains the principles of Old Testament Babylon.

In Old Testament times, literal Babylon was a city that espoused a false religious system. The very name of the city—*Babylon*—means "confusion." (See Genesis 11:9.) God's true church was the nation of Israel. In New Testament times, the Christian church becomes spiritual Israel.

Through the apostle Paul, the Lord says, "If you are Christ's, then you are Abraham's seed, and heirs according to the promise." Galatians 3:29. So the woman in white in Revelation 12 represents true spiritual Israel, Christ's true followers. Again, the Lord says, "For he is not a Jew who is one outwardly . . . but he is a Jew who is one inwardly." Romans 2:28, 29. So men and women who accept Jesus and His doctrines become His true followers. They become His chosen people today, as Israel was His chosen people in Old Testament times.

Just as in Old Testament days literal Babylon established a counterfeit system of worship, so in Revelation, spiritual Babylon represents counterfeit worship. It continues the principles of literal Old Testament Babylon in its religious observances.

◆ Characteristics of spiritual Babylon

Who is this woman in scarlet? What are these Old Testament Babylonian principles? Revelation 17:2 describes the scarlet- and purple-clad woman as committing fornication with the kings of the earth. Fornication is an illicit union. "And the inhabitants of the earth were made drunk with the wine of her fornication."

Therefore, Revelation's picture of a woman on a scarlet-colored beast represents a union of church and state. Yet the emphasis is on the dominance of the church over the state powers—the woman riding the beast. The Bible predicted that this false church, in passing around its wine cup, would lead multitudes to drink of its false doctrines, representing the acceptance of error in the place of truth.

The Bible shows that there are two basic systems of religion—the true system outlined in Revelation 12 and the false, outlined in Revelation 17. It is true that not everyone in the true church will be saved. There are some in it who do not have a heart experience with Jesus. A denominational label does not save any individual. The Bible also says that there are many in the false church who know Jesus and love Him, but do not know all of the truth for earth's last hour. God is attempting to lead every man, woman, and child from the false system to the true system.

Notice carefully what is written on the forehead of the woman in scarlet: "MYSTERY, BABYLON THE GREAT." After the great Flood of Noah's day, wicked men defied God. They disobeyed His Word, established their own religion, and erected the Tower of Babel. It was here that God confused human languages (see Genesis 11:9). The city of Babylon was later built on the site of the Tower of Babel.

Commenting on the symbolic woman, Babylon, who rides on the scarlet beast, Robert Jamieson, A. R. Fausset, and David Brown, in their *Bible Commentary,* have this to say: "State and Church are precious gifts of God. But the State being desecrated . . . becomes beastlike; the Church apostatizing becomes the harlot."—p. 593, emphasis supplied.

◆ Babylon, a human system

Let's go back to the Old Testament and look at five identifying features of Babylon. In Genesis 10:8-10, the Bible describes the origin of the ancient city of Babylon. "Cush begot Nimrod; he began to be a mighty one on the earth. He was a mighty hunter before [against] the LORD . . . And the beginning of his kingdom was Babel." This founder of Babel (later called Babylon) was a rebel against God who led out in establishing a system contrary to God.

Daniel 4:30, speaking about a king named Nebuchadnezzar who rebuilt Babylon a thousand years after Nimrod reigned, says: "The king spoke, saying, 'Is not this great Babylon, that I have built for a royal dwelling by my mighty power and for the honor of my majesty?'"

Notice, Nebuchadnezzar asks, "Is not this great Babylon, that I have built?" So one characteristic of Babylon is that it is a man-made system of religion.

The true church of God directs men and women to Jesus Christ as its only head. The false system directs men and women to a human priesthood rather than to Jesus alone as the great High Priest. Speaking of Jesus, the Bible says, "And He is the head of the body, the church, who is the beginning, the firstborn from the dead, that in all things He may have the preeminence." Colossians 1:18.

The Bible says that the true church of God does not have an earthly head, but rather a heavenly one. Someone has said, "The true church of God is the only organization so big that its body is upon earth, but its head is in heaven." The true church of God points men and women to Jesus, who can forgive their sins and release them from the bondage of sin. Revelation's spiritual Babylon is an earthly system of religion based primarily on human tradition, with a human leader.

◆ Babylon, a system centered in image worship

Let's notice another characteristic of ancient Babylon. It is only as we understand ancient Babylon in the Old Testament that we can understand the identity of spiritual Babylon and the call to come out of her. Babylon is the source of idolatry.

Dr. Alexander Hislop states: "Babylon was the primal source from which all these systems of idolatry flowed."—*The Two Babylons*, p. 12.

In the Old Testament, Babylon was a center of image worship. In the great temples of Babylon were images of the Babylonian gods. The Temple at Jerusalem had no such images. In the New Testament Christian church, directing men and women to Christ as its head, there were to be no images. In spiritual Babylon, which directed men and women to an earthly head, images were plentiful.

The Bible plainly says, in Exodus 20:4, 5: "You shall not make for yourself a carved image, or any likeness of anything that is in heaven above, or that is in the earth beneath, or that is in the water under the earth; you shall not bow down to them nor serve them." No graven image was to be used as an object of worship, but the Babylonians worshiped their gods through images.

God intended that the true system of religion should lead men and women to worship Him directly, without the use of images, allowing His Holy Spirit to impress their minds. Babylon would lead men and women to follow the traditions of men, to give preeminence to an earthly leader, and to incorporate images in their worship.

◆ Babylonian ancestor worship

Something else about ancient Babylon that applies to spiritual Babylon is found in Ezekiel 8:13: "And He said to me, 'Turn again, and you will see greater abominations that they are doing.'" That is, greater abominations than worshiping idols. Verse 14 says: "So He brought me to the door of the north gate of the LORD's house; and to my dismay, women were sitting there weeping for Tammuz."

Who was Tammuz, and why were the women weeping? Tammuz was the Babylonian god of vegetation. The Babylonians believed that when spring gave way to summer and the summer heat scorched the crops, Tammuz died. Therefore, they wept and prayed that he might return from the underworld.

Thus the whole concept of the immortal soul came not from the Bible, but instead, it slipped into the Christian church through Babylonian sources. Its roots are in Babylon, though the doctrine became fully developed in Greek philosophy. The following quotations clearly describe the origin of the pagan doctrine of immortality:

> "This doctrine can be traced through the muddy channels of a corrupted Christianity, a perverted Judaism, a pagan philosophy, a superstitious idolatry, to the great instigator of mischief in the Garden of Eden. The Protestants borrowed it from the Catholics, the Catholics from the Pharisees, the Pharisees from the pagans, and the pagans from the old Serpent, who first preached the doctrine amid the lowly bowels of Paradise to an audience all too willing to hear and heed the new and fascinating theology—'Ye shall not surely die.'"—Printed sermon by Amos Phelps (Methodist-Congregational minister, 1805-1874), *Is Man by Nature Immortal?*

> "If you have fallen in with some who are called Christians, but who do not admit this [truth of the resurrection], and venture to blaspheme the God of Abraham, and the God of Isaac, and the God of Jacob; who say there is no resurrection of the dead, and that their souls, when they die, are taken to heaven; do not imagine that they are Christians."—Justin

Martyr (died A.D. 165), *Dialogue With Trypho*, ch. LXXX, in *Ante Nicene Fathers*, vol. 1, p. 239.

The Bible is plain about what happens to a man when he dies: "For the wages of sin is death, but the gift of God is eternal life in Christ Jesus our Lord." Romans 6:23. Psalm 146:4 (KJV) says: "His breath goeth forth, he returneth to his earth; in that very day his thoughts perish." Ecclesiastes 9:5 says: "The living know that they will die; But the dead know nothing."

It was the concept of the Babylonians that an immortal soul left the body at death and lived on. Therefore the Babylonians established a system of gods and goddesses, worshiping the spirits of those who supposedly lived on.

But among the Israelites in Jerusalem, it was not so. The prophets of Israel taught that when a man died, his breath went forth, he returned to the earth, and in that very day his thoughts perished. The Bible is a very reliable source text regarding the state of man in death. Psalm 115:17 says: "The dead do not praise the LORD, Nor any who go down into silence." Any voice that seemingly breaks death's silence is out of harmony with the Bible.

Now, friend of mine, in the book of Revelation, two great systems of religion are described. The true system of religion, referred to in Revelation 12, is based on the Word of God, with the pure doctrines of the Word leading men and women to trust Jesus alone. It leads them to understand that when they come to Christ, they are to worship Him directly, without images. It leads them to understand that when a man dies, he sleeps, and that the soul is not a conscious entity that continues on.

The Bible teaches, in Revelation 17, that there is a great apostate mother church, referred to as Babylon the great. This church is based, not on the Word of God, but on tradition. It has an earthly head who claims to take the place of Christ. It has colors of scarlet and purple. It has images in its worship service. In the place of gods and goddesses, it has those called "saints" who are worshiped. It teaches that when a man dies, he does not sleep in the earth but rather has an immortal soul that lives on after death. It passes this doctrinal wine cup around. Other churches drink the wine of false doctrine of this mother church. They too have the idea that the soul lives on outside of and independent of the body.

◆ Babylon, the center of sun worship

Another principle of Babylon—in fact, the key principle—is mentioned in Ezekiel 8:16: "So He brought me into the inner court of the LORD's house; and there, at the door of the temple of the LORD, between the porch and the altar, were about twenty-five men with their backs toward the temple of the LORD and their faces toward the east, and they were worshiping the sun toward the east."

The prophet Ezekiel saw these men following the Babylonian practice of sun worship. Turning their faces toward the east, they knelt and worshiped the sun god as the sun rose in the sky. Ancient Babylonian calendars, with the sun at the center, reveal the significance of sun worship in Babylon. The Babylonians did not believe that they were fashioned by the hands of a loving Creator, but rather that the sun, the largest luminous body in the heavens, was the source of life. Therefore, they bowed to worship it. "In ancient Babylonia the sun was worshipped from immemorial antiquity."—James G. Brazer, *The Worship of Nature*, vol. 1, p. 529.

The Israelites worshiped on the seventh day of the week—the Bible Sabbath. The Babylonians worshiped the sun on the first day of the week, now called Sunday. God's true church in Revelation 12 keeps all His commandments, including the Sabbath. The false church revives the Babylonian day of the sun and passes around its cup of false doctrines. Many churches, drinking of that cup, worship on the first day of the week—Sunday.

God has a sign of His creatorship: "Moreover I also gave them My Sabbaths, to be a sign between them and Me, that they might know that I am the LORD who sanctifies them." Ezekiel 20:12. All through the Old Testament, on into the New Testament, and until the end of time, God's Sabbath is a sign—a sign that He is the Creator.

Sun worship slipped into the Christian church in the early centuries. Arthur P. Stanley says:

"The retention of the old pagan name of Dies Solis, for Sunday, is, in a great measure, owing to the union of Pagan and Christian sentiment with which the first day of the week was recommended by Constantine to his subjects Pagan and Christian alike, as the 'venerable' day of the sun."—*History of the Eastern Church,* p. 184.

Historian Stanley says that there was a compromise measure—a union of paganism and Christianity—in the early centuries, and thus Sunday slipped into the Christian church. Church and state, the woman and the beast—united. The Babylonian principle of sun worship, that pagan principle passed down from pagan religion to pagan religion, slipped into the Christian church, not by commandment, but rather by tradition and by a wedding of paganism and Christianity in the early centuries.

Stanley further states:

"[Constantine's] coins bore on the one side the letters of the name of Christ; on the other the figure of the Sun-god, . . . as if he could not bear to relinquish the patronage of the bright luminary."—*Ibid.*

Amazing! On Constantine's coins, Christ's name was written on one side and the sun god was pictured on the other side. A wedding took place between Christianity and paganism, between the church and the pagan emperor of Rome, for Constantine was actually a Christian only in name. As a result, the Christian church was flooded with many practices that do not find their place in Scripture. Bible history bears this out.

Dr. Alexander Hislop says,

"To conciliate the Pagans to nominal Christianity, Rome, pursuing its usual policy, took measures to get the Christian and Pagan festivals amalgamated, and . . . to get Paganism and Christianity—now far sunk in idolatry—in this as in so many other things, to shake hands."—*The Two Babylons,* p. 105, emphasis supplied.

In other words, Rome was attempting to conciliate, to compromise, to bring the crumbling empire together. What is the origin of

Sunday worship? Where did it come from? How did it enter the church?

Dr. Edward T. Hiscox, author of *The Baptist Manual*, stated in a paper before a Baptist convention of ministers on November 13, 1893:

> "What a pity that it [Sunday] comes branded with the mark of paganism, and christened with the name of the sun god, then adopted and sanctioned by the papal apostasy, and bequeathed as a sacred legacy to Protestantism!"

So the door was opened as Babylonian practices flooded into the church. Catholics say,

> "Christendom is indebted to the Catholic Church for the institution of Sunday as the Sabbath day. But there is no precedence in Scripture, nor commandment in Scripture, to observe the Sunday as the Sabbath day."—*Our Sunday Visitor*, Jan. 4, 1931.

◆ A wedding between Christianity and paganism

In the fourth century, in an attempt to convert the pagans, the church opened the door. The Roman emperor Constantine, who had on the surface become a Christian, walked through that door, and church and state were thus united. Babylonian sun worship slipped into the Christian church as the wedding between paganism and Christianity took place.

E.G. Lentz says,

> "In keeping Sunday, non-Catholics are simply following the practice of the Catholic Church for 1800 years, a tradition, and not a Bible ordinance."—*The Question Box*, p. 99.

In his book *The Abiding Sabbath*, George Elliott says,

> "What is proposed, to make an erasure in the heaven-born code? Is the eternal tablet of the law to be defaced by a creature's hand? He who proposes such an act should fortify himself by reasons as holy as God and as mighty as His power."—p. 123.

Elliott says it is a dangerous thing to tamper with heaven's code. But compromise the church did in those early centuries.

Earlier, we read in Ezekiel 8:16 about the twenty-five priests of Israel who adopted the practice of sun worship. These priests turned their backs on the true God, rebelled against His law, and disobeyed His direct command to observe the seventh-day Sabbath. Ezekiel pointed out that not only did Israel's priests worship the sun, they also violated the Sabbath: "Her priests have violated My law and profaned My holy things; they have not distinguished between the holy and unholy, nor have they made known the difference between the unclean and the clean; and they have hidden their eyes from My Sabbaths, so that I am profaned among them." Ezekiel 22:26.

In the sixth century B.C., God said that the priests hid their eyes from His Sabbaths and that He was profaned among them. So in the last days, the Babylonian principle of sun worship will prevail in the Christian world, causing men and women to again "hide their eyes" from the true Sabbath. Men and women will say, "It doesn't really make any difference." My friend, it does make a difference.

James Wharey says:

> "At the end of the second century, . . . it is obvious to remark [about] the changes already introduced into the Christian church. Christianity began already to wear the garb of heathenism. The seeds of most of those errors that afterward so entirely overran the church, marred its beauty, and tarnished its glory, were already beginning to take root."—*Church History,* century II, sec. VII.

After Christ died and the apostles passed off the scene, the church drifted from its original teachings. Nevertheless, a small remnant remained loyal to God. Down through the ages, God has always had those who have said, "We will not compromise; we must stand for truth no matter what the popular masses are doing. We have submitted our lives to Christ. He has said, 'If ye love me, keep my commandments.' We will take the Word of God as our guide. We will stand loyally for Jesus."

At times that small remnant was oppressed and persecuted. Still, they would not accept the Babylonian principle of tradition above the Scriptures. They would not accept the Babylonian principle of a human, earthly head of the church rather than Christ. They would not accept the Babylonian principle of images. They worshiped Jesus directly. They would not accept the Babylonian principle that there is an immortal soul that lives on outside the body. They would not accept the Babylonian principle of sun worship. Often they were persecuted and forced to flee from the cities to the valleys, rocks, and mountains.

Friends, an understanding of what the Bible teaches leads us to see that the woman in scarlet of Revelation 17 is the Roman Church. Her daughters are the Protestant churches that have been sipping from her wine cup and accepting her errors. But even in the Roman Church, God has a people. In their commentary, Jamieson, Fausset, and Brown put it this way:

> "Even in the Romish Church God has a people: but they are in great danger; their only safety is in coming out of her at once."—p. 593.

The symbol of the harlot does not apply to Rome alone but to every church which openly rebels against the commandments of God. False Christendom—based on the traditions of men, divided into hundreds of denominations, and founded on man's ideas—is truly a Babylon of confusion.

◆ The confusion of Babylon

So today the religious world is largely confused—confused on the state of man in death, confused on the Sabbath question, confused concerning the fact that man's body is the temple of God and that what we eat and drink is to be in harmony with the Lord's will. Yes, friend of mine, the religious world tonight is confused, sipping from the wine cup of Babylon.

> "The first justification of the woman is in her being called out of Babylon the harlot, . . . when judgment is about to fall: for apostate Christendom, Babylon, is not to be con-

verted, but to be destroyed."—Jamieson, Fausset, and Brown, *Commentary*, p. 593.

I've had people ask me, "Pastor, can't I stay in my church and reform it?" God says that you are to come out of Babylon. Jamieson, Fausset, and Brown put it this way:

"In every apostate or world-conforming Church there are some of God's invisible and true Church, who, if they would be safe, must come out."—*Ibid*.

Friend of mine, perhaps you are struggling inside as you consider these things. You believe the Bible Sabbath to be true. You believe that when a man dies, he sleeps in the earth. You believe that your body is the temple of God. You wonder if you can have one foot in your church and one foot in God's true church. Friend, as we've read, in every apostate or world-conforming church, members of God's invisible, true church, if they would be safe, must come out. God calls you to come out, because Babylon is fallen.

Cardinal Gibbons put it this way:

"Reason and sense demand the acceptance of one or the other of these alternatives: either Protestantism and the keeping holy of Saturday, or Catholicity and the keeping holy of Sunday. Compromise is impossible ."—*Catholic Mirror*, Dec. 23, 1893.

◆ The evidence demands a verdict

On this point, I agree with Cardinal Gibbons 100 percent. The Catholic cardinal hit the nail on the head when he said that compromise is impossible—there is no way to compromise. These issues are too clear. They demand a choice. This evidence demands a verdict. Men and women are being called out.

Revelation 18:2 says, "And he cried mightily with a loud voice, saying, 'Babylon the great is fallen, is fallen.'" The mother church is fallen. Her traditions are fallen. This church, with vestments of scarlet and purple, is fallen. Its system of images is fallen. All systems that teach error about the state of man in death and the Sabbath are fallen.

"And I heard another voice from heaven saying, 'Come out of her, my people, lest you share in her sins, and lest you receive of her plagues'" (verse 4). There is no way to stay in Babylon without being a partaker of her sins, my friend. The most terrible scourges ever poured out are going to be poured out on Babylon. Babylon is fallen! There is no way that you can change her.

◆ Come out!

Your mission, your business, is to come out! God is calling honest-hearted men and women out of those churches that have drunk the cup of Babylon. Soon time is going to run out. Soon every human being will have to make his or her final choice, for Christ or for tradition, for truth or for error, for the Scriptures or for human substitutes.

The Bible says, "Come out of her, my people . . . lest you receive of her plagues." God is appealing to you as He appealed to Lot in Sodom: "Lot, come out, come out! Fire is about ready to fall!" Lot's children remained in Sodom. His friends stayed in Sodom. They said, "Lot, you're crazy for leaving." But Lot's family and friends were destroyed when the fire fell. The angel urged Lot, "Flee for your life." The issue was life or death. Lot's only safety was in coming out of Sodom.

My friends, your only safety is in coming out of every church based on tradition, that uses images in its worship, that has sipped the wine cup and is still practicing Sunday worship, that believes in the immortality of the soul. Friend of mine, God's appeal to you is to come out.

Jesus said, "My sheep hear My voice, and I know them, and they follow Me." John 10:27. He says, "My child, I am appealing to you. I have My sheep, My followers, in every church. I am appealing to loving, kind Roman Catholics who have never known the truth, to Protestants who haven't known that their churches have been sipping the wine cup of Babylon."

Many sincere Protestants have loved Jesus and have given their lives to Him, but they have not understood that as long as they remain in any church that is not leading men and women to full, joyful obedience to God's law and faithfulness to scriptural truth, they are supporters of Babylon—a system God condemns!

If any of you are still undecided as you read these words, I appeal to you. I appeal to you in Jesus' name to surrender your will to Him and to determine to do His will. With your Bible in your hand, tell Jesus, "I can do no other; I must come out. I hear the call of Jesus to my heart. I see how paganism and Christianity in those early centuries united together. I see the issue very clearly. I see that for more than 1,800 years, compromise has taken place. I see that God has been calling His little remnant out, and now I decide to take my stand for Jesus. I decide to stand on the Word of God; I decide to stand with Christ. I am willing to come out, even if it means standing alone."

Oh, friend of mine, will you not settle this issue in your heart right now? Will you not seal it in your mind? Will you not tell Jesus, "Lord, I hear Your call—'Babylon the great is fallen, is fallen. Come out of her, my people.'"

Tenderly and in tones of love, Jesus by His Spirit speaks to your heart at this moment. With lovingkindness, He says, "I love you, My child. I do not want you to be afflicted when the plagues fall. My child, I am appealing to you right now!" Do you hear His call? Do you hear Him speaking to your heart?

I know that right now you are willing to say, "Jesus, I love You, and I choose to follow You. Because I love You, I desire to be part of Your commandment-keeping people. I hear Your voice gently appealing to me, 'If you love me, keep My commandments.' Yes, Lord, I will follow!" ❏

All along as the war has progressed, God has provided His followers with wartime intelligence about the enemy. He has predicted the enemy's next moves, warned of his tactics, exposed his deceptions.

He has communicated with His followers directly, through His written Word, through His Son Jesus, and through His prophets.

Some say that God hasn't spoken through a prophet for a long time.

If you agree, does the Bible ever have a surprise for you! Discover what it has to say, in the chapter just ahead.

21

. . . .

Why You Never See a $3 Bill

You can't dial up God for $4.99 a minute.

We've already noted that Satan is an obsessive and pathological counterfeiter. Anything genuine God produces, he counterfeits.

So when we look around and see that he is flooding society with phony prophets, what is the logical conclusion?

Right! Somewhere—either now or just recently—a real prophet must be found.

The phonies are truly everywhere. If Satan had more self-control, maybe he wouldn't overstep himself like this. Not content with just one or two counterfeit prophets, he churns them out by the score.

For $4.99 a minute, a "psychic friend" will run up your phone bill in exchange for some vague generalities about your future. New Age channelers will happily put you in touch with ancient "spirit guides" (guess who's on the line when you choose Satan to handle your long distance?).

And that still leaves the astrologers with their horoscopes, the tabloid seers, and the readers of tea leaves, palms, and tarot cards.

The sad thing is, if we really want to know what the future holds, God has already shared it through His prophets. And He has also told us how to find the genuine among all the phonies.

21

· ·

We are witnessing a phenomenal explosion of interest in psychic phenomena, the occult, and astrology. More than 2,000 of the nation's leading newspapers carry astrology columns. Go to any bookstore, and you will find scores of books on so-called supernatural revelation.

Ruth Montgomery's book, *Gift of Prophecy* (on the life of Jeanne Dixon), sold more than a million copies. *The Sleeping Prophet*, a book on the life of Edgar Cayce, a psychic of a generation ago, continues to experience phenomenal sales.

As we come to the crisis hour of this earth's history, men and women everywhere are looking beyond themselves for an answer to the frustration, hopelessness, and despair they find so common in their daily lives. The great heart cry of humanity is for an authoritative voice from outside normal human experience—a voice that speaks with certainty.

Obviously, we need caution: Can we be sure that every so-called prophet, or voice from "beyond," is genuine? Jesus predicted that false prophets would rise in the last days: "For false christs and false prophets will rise and show great signs and wonders to deceive, if possible, even the elect." Matthew 24:24.

Earlier, Jesus had said, "Beware of false prophets, who come to you in sheep's clothing, but inwardly they are ravenous wolves." Matthew 7:15.

All around us, as a Bible-designated sign of the last generation, are false prophets, astrologers, and psychics. In an attempt to thwart and prevent men from receiving heaven's truth, Satan has attempted to counterfeit the genuine gift of prophecy by raising up false prophets.

◆ Ever see a $3 bill?

But does not the very existence of a counterfeit indicate that there must be a genuine? How many of you have ever seen a $3 bill? Why not? Not a counterfeiter in the country would waste his time making a $3 bill when there is no genuine. Thus, if there are false prophets in these last days, a genuine, authentic manifestation of the gift of prophecy must exist.

Does the Bible actually predict a manifestation of the gift of prophecy in these last days? Did the gift of prophecy cease in Bible times? How long was it to remain in the church?

Paul helps us in Ephesians 4:8, 11-15: "Therefore He says: 'When He ascended on high, He led captivity captive, And gave gifts to men'. . . . And He Himself gave some to be apostles, some prophets, some evangelists, and some pastors and teachers, for the equipping of the saints for the work of ministry, for the edifying of the body of Christ, till we all come to the unity of the faith and of the knowledge of the Son of God, to a perfect man, to the measure of the stature of the fullness of Christ; that we should no longer be children, tossed to and fro and carried about with every wind of doctrine, by the trickery of men, in the cunning craftiness of deceitful plotting, but, speaking the truth in love, may grow up in all things into Him who is the head—Christ."

Here Paul tells us that when Jesus ascended to heaven, He gave special gifts to men. Among those gifts was the gift of prophecy. Its purpose, according to the 12th verse, was to perfect a people and prepare a church for the coming of Christ. The gift of prophecy will remain in God's church, according to the 13th verse, until we all come into the unity of the faith and are changed to the measure of the stature of the fullness of Christ, a continuing growth that doesn't end until Jesus returns.

This is why Paul wrote in 1 Corinthians 1:7, KJV: "So that ye come behind in no gift; waiting for the coming of our Lord Jesus Christ."

Jesus promised that the gift of prophecy would be revived in the last generation. Knowing this, Satan has raised up false prophets to deceive multitudes. This leads us to some all-important questions. How can you tell the difference between a true and false prophet? What are the biblical tests for the true gift of prophecy? Jesus has given very plain answers to these questions. No one need be deceived. We need not turn to the writings of so-called prophets today. The Bible clearly outlines the tests of a true prophet, and these tests expose the fraudulent claims of counterfeit prophets.

◆ How to recognize a counterfeit

Some time ago, the government became concerned about a great number of counterfeit bills flooding the United States. To help deal with the problem, a six-week course was arranged. Bank tellers from all over the country met in Washington, D.C., learning how to detect counterfeit money. How many counterfeit bills do you suppose they viewed in that six-week period? Not one! They spent hours studying the minute details of the genuine one-, five-, ten-, and twenty-dollar bills. By thoroughly knowing the genuine, they could immediately detect a counterfeit. In the light of truth, a counterfeit became immediately apparent. Thus, the more we understand the truth of God's Word regarding the gift of prophecy, counterfeit manifestations will stand out like the sun at noon.

What is the biblical light that teaches us how to recognize the authentic gift of prophecy?

Before sin, God communicated with man face to face. But sin broke man's personal communication with God. Isaiah 59:2 puts it this way: "Your iniquities have separated you from your God; And your sins have hidden His face from you, So that He will not hear."

Although it may not be easy to understand at first, God withdrew His presence from man out of mercy and love. To sin, wherever found,

God is a consuming fire. Sin cannot exist in the presence of a Holy God. Thus, God could no longer communicate with man face to face, or man would be immediately consumed.

◆ A link between heaven and humanity

So God chose another method of communication— He opened another channel of revelation. We read in Numbers 12:6: "If there is a prophet among you, I, the LORD, make Myself known to him in a vision; I speak to him in a dream."

In His communication with earth, God sometimes uses a prophet as the link between heaven and humanity. This human instrument is the agent through whom God transmits messages to His people.

The Bible describes how prophets received messages from God:

1. Angels brought them visions and dreams (Revelation 1:1).
2. The Holy Spirit impressed their minds, revealing heaven's truth to them.

True prophets do not teach their own ideas. They are heaven's messengers. They are a vital part of God's channel of communication. Their message reveals God's will. They are spokesmen for the King of the universe. Since they have received a message from heaven, they can speak with certainty and conviction.

The Bible discloses two kinds of prophetic revelations. The best known are the written revelations such as those of Moses, Daniel, and John. In addition, God has spoken to His prophets through writings that have not been preserved, or through oral presentations. Enoch, Elijah, and Elisha, for example, did not contribute to the written Bible, yet they surely were Bible prophets.

In Acts 11:27, a prophet by the name of Agabus went to Antioch and predicted a great famine throughout the world. Agabus is called a prophet, but there is no book of Agabus in the Bible. Jesus said that there was never a greater prophet than John the Baptist, yet John's sermons are not recorded in the Bible.

The Bible tells us that throughout the ages, God has used women as well as men in the prophetic office. We read of Deborah, a prophetess of Old Testament times, and of Anna, a New Testament prophetess. The book of Acts mentions the four daughters of Philip, who were prophetesses to the church yet didn't write anything in our Bible.

As jewels set in a ring, God places His prophets within His church. "And God has appointed these in the church: first apostles, second prophets." 1 Corinthians 12:28.

The Bible predicts a restoration of the prophetic gift in these last days. This gift is to be found within God's true church. The book of Revelation, which focuses especially on the last days, speaks specifically to the restoration of the prophetic gift in the last-day church: "And the dragon was enraged with the woman, and he went to make war with the rest of her offspring, who keep the commandments of God and have the testimony of Jesus Christ." Revelation 12:17.

Revelation 12 contains a brief history of the church from before Christ's time to the time of the end. Here we see how the church was persecuted during the 1,260-year period and how it would flourish again at the end of time. In verse 17, we find two identifying characteristics of God's church in these last days: It is made up of a commandment-keeping people who have been given the gift of prophecy.

Can we identify this church which has been predicted to arise in these last days?

◆ The great second advent movement

The greatest religious movement of the nineteenth century was the Second Advent movement of 1844. As the 2,300-day prophecy (see Chapter 10) came to an end, tens of thousands expected their Lord to return. The movement was made up of Baptists, Methodists, Congregationalists, Catholics, and many others. Their message of the soon return of Jesus united them, and the preparation of mind and heart motivated them. But because other religious leaders resented the Advent movement, these "Adventists" were unable to remain in their former churches.

As the popular churches rejected the teaching that the Advent was near, those who accepted it either voluntarily left their churches or were disfellowshipped. Thus this little group, coming out of many denominations, united together with common purposes and beliefs.

In December of 1844, while this work of expulsion was going on, seventeen-year-old Ellen Harmon, later to become Mrs. Ellen G. White, was given her first vision. She saw the Advent people traveling an elevated road to heaven with a brilliant light illuminating the pathway.

What an encouragement this message was to this small and scattered group of Advent believers, which would later be known as Seventh-day Adventists.

From 1844 until her death in 1915, Ellen G. White received more than 2,000 prophetic visions and dreams, wrote more than fifty books, and lectured to tens of thousands on three continents. With amazing accuracy and insight, she wrote on such subjects as education, nutrition, the life of Christ, practical godliness, world conditions, general health, medical practice, the coming world crisis, and many others. Quite remarkable for a woman who had to drop out of school because of a tragic accident after only three years of formal education!

George Wharton James, in his book, *California, Romantic and Beautiful,* wrote about Ellen White. She had lived her last years in California, and her influence was felt in that state. Wharton said:

"This remarkable woman, though almost entirely self-educated, has written and published more books in more languages which circulate to the greater extent than any other woman in history."—p. 319.

Let's look at six biblical tests of a true prophet and then ask if Ellen White passes these tests. Does she meet and fit the biblical criteria for a true prophet? The Word of God is our only safeguard. We cannot accept any so-called prophet who does not meet the biblical tests. But dare we reject a prophet who meets these tests? Since Ellen White was raised up within a movement that exalts Jesus as its Saviour and His law as its guide, we cannot pass her by lightly. We cannot dismiss this gift without examining the evidence.

◆ 1. Prophetic accuracy

In prophecies that are not conditional—that is, prophecies the fulfillment of which does not depend on how people respond to them— a true prophet must be 100 percent accurate. With the exception of conditional prophecy, a true prophet's predictions always come to pass. A true prophet does not guess about the future. He foretells what God has revealed to him: "As for the prophet who prophesies of peace, when the word of the prophet comes to pass, the prophet will be known as one whom the LORD has truly sent." Jeremiah 28:9.

What is the prophetic accuracy of some prophets of our time? How does Jeanne Dixon fare? A leading newspaper recently concluded that, after a careful survey, she was around 30 percent accurate. Other reports indicate she is 60 percent accurate. Assuming she is 60 percent accurate, do we then assume God is wrong 40 percent of the time? Do we assume that the prophetic revelation from heaven is so muddled and confused that even the prophet cannot understand it 40 percent of the time?

Ralph Blodgett, in an article in *These Times* magazine, compared the predictions of the leading psychics at the beginning of a given year with their accuracy quotient at the end of the year. He discovered that on average, they were 16 percent accurate.

What about Ellen White? What is her percentage of prophetic accuracy? Let's look at some of her predictions.

A century ago, she cautioned about the dangers of too much fat and sugar in the diet. Almost seventy years before the surgeon general's report on smoking and health, she warned, "Tobacco is a slow, insidious, but most malignant poison."—*The Ministry of Healing*, p. 327. It was not until 1964 that the surgeon general reported that tobacco was linked with cancer. Yet, in love, God had warned His people more than seventy years in advance.

Ellen White also discussed the important effects of prenatal influence during pregnancy. It is exciting to sense that God revealed prophetic insights for the benefit of His people. Since He is interested in their health, He has sent these messages in love. Medical science today is just catching up with the gift of prophecy.

Today, spiritism is sweeping the world, leaping across denominational boundaries. For many, it appears as a great world power that will one day unite all religions. More than a century ago, Ellen White predicted an explosion of interest in the occult, psychic phenomena, and astrology just before the end.

◆ 2. The prophet's relationship to the Bible

At times, keen observers of human nature may make some predictions that appear to come true. Yet their teachings may not be in harmony with biblical principles. One of the great tests of the true gift of prophecy is whether or not the prophet's life and teachings are in harmony with the Scriptures.

Moses gave us this help: "If there arises among you a prophet or a dreamer of dreams, and he gives you a sign or a wonder, and the sign or the wonder comes to pass, of which he spoke to you, saying, 'Let us go after other gods'—which you have not known—'and let us serve them,' you shall not listen to the words of that prophet or that dreamer of dreams, . . . You shall walk after the LORD your God and fear Him, and keep His commandments and obey His voice, and you shall serve Him and hold fast to Him." Deuteronomy 13:1-4.

What was Ellen White's attitude toward the Bible? Does she pass the test? Did she consider her writings a second Bible? In referring to the importance of the Bible, she wrote:

> "In our time there is a wide departure from their doctrines and precepts, and there is need of a return to the great Protestant principle—the Bible, and the Bible only, as the rule of faith and duty."—Ellen G. White, *The Great Controversy*, pp. 204, 205.

The writings of a true prophet always agree with the Bible. You can read the writings of Ellen White and not find a single instance in which they contradict the Bible. Her writings complement the Bible. Like a telescope which does not put more stars in the sky but brings out the ones already there, the writings of Ellen White magnify and bring out the precious gems of truth in Scripture.

◆ 3. The prophet's relationship to the law of God

A true prophet exalts the law of God and calls all men to obedience. Isaiah 8:20 states clearly: "To the law and to the testimony! If they do not speak according to this word, it is because there is no light in them."

For more than seventy years, God's last-day prophet, Ellen White, called men and women back to obedience to all ten commandments, including the Sabbath. As we study the prophets of the Old Testament, we note this common thread: They were raised up in periods of apostasy to call men from commandment breaking to commandment keeping. Elijah called Israel from idolatry focused on sun worship. Nehemiah called for a reform in Sabbath keeping, and John the Baptist challenged Herod to repent of his adultery.

Each biblical prophet exalted God's law. Truly, Ellen White passes this test. The law of God was indeed exalted in her speaking and writing. False prophets often attract others with their spectacular predictions, but their relationship to God's law and the teachings of Jesus will not stand the light of truth. Since light is what we are to follow, we must turn away from any prophet or movement that does not exalt the law.

◆ 4. The prophet's relationship to Christ

Since the spirit of prophecy is the testimony of Jesus Christ (Revelation 19:10), a true prophet witnesses to Christ. Thus we can expect that the central focus of the prophet's ministry would be on exalting Christ. Many of the prophets of our day fall far short on this point. Self is exalted rather than Jesus.

What about Ellen White? Her books *The Desire of Ages, Christ's Object Lessons, Thoughts From the Mount of Blessings, Steps to Christ*— all testify to the fulfillment of this test.

An official in the Library of Congress in Washington, D. C., was asked which book in that vast library he felt was the best one on the life of Christ. His answer:

"My preference or choice would be guided by what I wish to get from the book or books to be read, but let me put it this way: I would put *The Desire of Ages*, by Ellen G. White first for spiritual discernment and practical application."

Throughout her ministry, Ellen White exalted Jesus. In her book *Gospel Workers*, she wrote,

"Lift up Jesus, you that teach the people, lift Him up in sermon, in song, in prayer. Let all your powers be directed in pointing souls, confused, bewildered, lost, to 'the Lamb of God.'"—p. 160.

◆ 5. Physical tests

God has placed many tests in His Word to help us distinguish the true from the false. Among these are certain physical criteria to evaluate the genuine gift. We shall examine three:

A. Prophets experience visions with their eyes open—their eyes remain open throughout the vision (Numbers 24:4).

B. In vision, prophets have no strength (Daniel 10:8).

C. Prophets, in vision, do not breathe (Daniel 10:17).

Repeatedly, Ellen White was examined by physicians and others during her visions. Like the prophets of old, throughout her visions her eyes were open, she retained no strength, and her breath was gone.

A Dr. Drummond—a physician who, before he saw Ellen White in vision, was skeptical about the authenticity of her visions—declared that he could hypnotize her and give her a vision. In his presence, God gave Ellen White a vision. Dr. Drummond stepped forward and examined her thoroughly. Turning pale, he exclaimed, "She doesn't breathe!" This convinced him the visions were from God.

Sometimes her visions lasted for hours, sometimes for only a few minutes. The physical phenomena surrounding Ellen White's visions indicate that they were supernatural.

◆ 6. Spiritual fruit

Jesus declared in Matthew 7:20: "Therefore by their fruits you will know them." After many decades, what is the fruit of Ellen White's life and teachings? What did she accomplish? What have her teachings done for God's church? How have they benefited mankind?

As a result of God's messages through Ellen G. White, Seventh-day Adventists have established over five hundred hospitals, dispensaries, and clinics throughout the world. Some years ago, millionaire Charles Kettering, after having been treated in one of these hospitals, was so impressed with the caring service he received there that he gave ten million dollars to start a new Adventist-operated hospital near his home in Ohio.

The Seventh-day Adventist medical center at Loma Linda University in southern California was established as the result of one of Ellen White's visions. When application was first made for accreditation, the Council on Medical Education tried to persuade the new medical college not to apply, since an adequate staff was not available. But the school insisted, so it was given the lowest rating of "C." However, it wasn't long before the school received full accreditation, and its graduates were welcomed everywhere.

In recent years, the United States government has sent the Loma Linda Heart Team to various countries on good-will tours. The medical school of Loma Linda University is well-known throughout the world.

Because of the guidance of Ellen White, Seventh-day Adventists over the years have become a world-wide yet unified religious presence—at work in more countries than any other Protestant denomination. In the 1870s, Ellen White counseled that the time had come to establish overseas mission centers from which the last-day messages of the three angels of Revelation 14 would expand with new and greater intensity. As a result, in 1874, the first Seventh-day Adventist foreign missionary sailed from Boston Harbor. In little more than a hundred years, our work has grown so that now, the sun never sets on the work of Seventh-day Adventists.

In a time when most churches are cutting back on their mission budgets, Seventh-day Adventists are moving forward. A few years ago, some 100,000 people in the Kasai area of Zaire approached Seventh-day Adventist leaders and asked, "Can you send teachers to instruct us? We want to become Adventists." Thousands have been baptized, and thousands more are preparing for baptism.

◆ The people of the Book

A number of years ago, in the desert wastes of Bechuanaland, South Africa, lived a primitive bushman named Sukuba. A member of a wild, nomadic people, he lived an isolated life. One winter night he crept into his shelter and retired for the evening.

Suddenly the night became brighter than day. A shining being appeared to him and told him to find the people of the "Book." He must find a people who worshiped God. What did it mean? How could he read a book?

The language of the bushman contained clicks and guttural sounds quite unlike the language of other African tribes. It has never been reduced to writing. "The Shining One," as Sukuba called the angel that appeared to him, said, "The Book talks. You will be able to read it." His family, now very much impressed, traveled with him until, days later, they reached the hut of some Bantu farmers and asked one of them for the people with the "Book."

The tribesman was startled to hear a bushman speaking his language. Immediately, he took him to his pastor. The pastor, deeply moved by the story, said, "Your journey is over."

Sukuba was very happy. But that night "The Shining One" appeared again to Sukuba and told him that these were not the people he was looking for. He must find "the Sabbath-keeping church and Pastor Moye." Pastor Moye would have a Book, and also "four brown books that are really nine."

The next day Sukuba prayed that God would give him a sign to lead him on his journey. When he did, a cloud appeared in the sky. For seven days Sukuba followed it. It disappeared over a village. There Sukuba asked for Pastor Moye and was quickly directed to his home.

After Sukuba told his story in the local dialect, Pastor Moye brought out his worn Bible. "That is it!" said Sukuba. "That is it! But where are the four books that are really nine?" (Years before, Ellen White had written nine volumes of instruction to God's church called *Testimonies to the Church,* which were later combined into four books.)

Sukuba's search was over. He had found the people of the Book, a Sabbath-keeping people, a people blessed with the prophetic gift. Eventually, he and his family were baptized, and he became a missionary to his own people.

God is working in a marvelous way to lead men and women to His true church. The fact that you are reading this book is no accident. Like Sukuba, God is guiding you to the truths that will give you courage to face the future.

You have been divinely guided. Perhaps you have been searching for truth for years. You, like Sukuba, can exclaim, "This is it! God's church!" Your search is ended. This book will introduce you to a people who keep the commandments of God and have been blessed by a prophet to guide them through the difficult, often perplexing, issues of these last days. ❏

If you are convinced that you have finally found the people of the Book, what should you do next?

In fact, the Bible says there is something very specific you should do. And once you do it, your life will never be the same.

Learn what it is in Chapter 22.

22

· ·

How to
Start Life
Over Again

A radical solution.

Selfishness is potent stuff.

Once infected with it in Eden, our original parents found selfishness more natural than love. They were suddenly out of tune with God. And they began to die.

Selfishness has cascaded down through the generations ever since. Every one of us is born selfish to the core.

Yet God and His love are bigger—more powerful—than selfishness. If we choose, He can change us. From the inside out.

But His solution is radical. He doesn't just refurbish us. He insists that we die. Not physically, of course, but rather that we agree to let Him put to death our old self-centered hearts.

Then He creates inside of us a whole new person, no longer controlled by selfishness, but controlled by love.

When this change has taken place, He asks us to go public with this dramatic change by symbolically dying, being buried, and then rising again to a whole new life. That symbol is the subject of this chapter.

Once changed, we are truly ready to report for duty in the ongoing war over God's character of love.

22

● ●

W hen the former Soviet Union opened its doors, in its recent "religious awakening," a flood of pamphlets and
preachers overwhelmed the country—each claiming to
have "truth" for the long-oppressed people.

On almost every Moscow street corner, as well as in most other
cities throughout the former Soviet Union, religious voices called out
their messages, offering their solutions for the "new day." The spiritual "answers" to a nation denied religion for so long fell into four
basic categories.

Islam, the youngest of the four great world religions, proclaims,
"There is one God, Allah, and Mohammed is his prophet." Born in
Mecca, in A.D. 570, the religion's founder, Mohammed, claimed to
have been visited by the angel Gabriel in vision and given the words
of the Koran, the Muslim's ultimate authority. For centuries, the ultimate joy of the Muslim has been in making a pilgrimage to Mecca,
the "holy city" of Mohammed's birth.

Mohammed died at 61. Today, parts of his body are enshrined in
various mosques throughout the Middle East, and his grave in Medina
is tightly guarded around the clock.

A second world religion in the Middle East is Judaism. The Jewish
religion today is a way of life and has no formulated creed, or articles
of faith. Its adherents conform to certain teachings, sometimes called

doctrines or dogmas, which are considered obligatory. The fundamental doctrine is that God is One. To the Jew, the Godhead cannot be divided into different personalities or powers.

The founding father of Judaism, Abraham, died about 1900 B.C. at the ripe old age of 175 years, according to the Old Testament. He was buried in Canaan in the Cave of Machpelah.

The third great world religion, Buddhism, was founded by Siddhartha Gautama, known as "The Buddha," or "The Enlightened One" among his followers. Buddha gave to his adherents "four noble truths":

1. Life is suffering.

2. All suffering is caused by ignorance of the nature of reality.

3. Suffering can be ended by overcoming ignorance.

4. The path to the suppression of suffering consists of morality, wisdom, and concentration.

Buddha died in 483 B.C. Relics of his body, including hair and teeth, have been enshrined in pagodas throughout the Buddhist world.

The fourth great world religion is Christianity. Based on the life and teachings of Jesus Christ, Christianity teaches that men and women can do no good thing on their own. Their peace of mind and strength for overcoming weaknesses of mind and body depend entirely on the life and death of the Son of God.

◆ The fourth tomb is empty!

Unlike the often-visited tombs of the founders of other world religions, the grave of Jesus Christ contains no well-preserved relics for today's tourists. While the followers of other religions often challenge Christians to show them where their leader is enshrined, they are pointed only to an empty tomb.

Yet the very fact that the body of Jesus Christ is not decaying in an earthen grave speaks of the power of Christianity. While the tombs of Mohammed, Abraham, and "The Buddha" bear witness to the final end of these "great men," the empty tomb of Christ is evidence of

His power over death! The Bible states that an angel spoke to those seeking to visit His grave after His death with these words: "Why do you seek the living among the dead? He is not here, but is risen!" Luke 24:5, 6.

No shrine anywhere in the world can boast of owning one part of the body of Christ. The Roman seal could not hold Him in the tomb. Armed guards could not keep Him there.

One enormous difference between Christianity and every other religion in the world is an empty tomb! Only Christians claim the resurrection of their founder. The apostle Paul stated that if there is no empty tomb or returning Lord, the inhabitants of Planet Earth are doomed to a life without meaning: "And if Christ is not risen, your faith is futile; you are still in your sins! Then also those who have fallen asleep in Christ have perished." 1 Corinthians 15:17, 18.

When the Jewish religious leaders asked Jesus to give them a sign of His divinity—proof that He was the Son of God as He claimed— He said that His resurrection would be the only sign. He staked His authority on His resurrection.

In His unique way, Jesus announced His death and resurrection when He said, "Destroy this temple, and in three days I will raise it up." John 2:19. Assuming that Jesus was speaking of their Jerusalem Temple, the Jews scoffed at Him, saying, "It has taken forty-six years to build this temple, and will You raise it up in three days?" John 2:20.

These religious leaders missed the point completely! Jesus did not speak about bricks or stones but about His body temple. The miracle of His resurrection authenticated His claims to divine Messiahship. Only after His death did the disciples fully realize the extent of His mission. "When He had risen from the dead, His disciples remembered that He had said this to them; and they believed the Scripture and the word which Jesus had said." John 2:22.

Many others besides the disciples witnessed Christ's resurrection. At least five hundred New Testament witnesses either saw Him, talked with Him, walked with Him, or ate with Him after His resurrection (1 Corinthians 15:6). Even angels testified that Christ had risen!

The last few hours of Friday, the day of the crucifixion, were unparalleled in meaning and intensity. As three bruised bodies hung from crosses on Calvary's hill, the skies darkened, lightning flashed, the ground shook, and the veil in the temple split from top to bottom as Jesus triumphantly cried out, "It is finished!"

Later, Pilate consented to the request of Joseph of Arimathea to bury Jesus' body before sunset that Friday. Remembering Jesus' prediction to rise on the third day, the chief priests, too, went to Pilate with their request. "Sir, we remember, while He was still alive, how that deceiver said, 'After three days I will rise.' Therefore command that the tomb be made secure until the third day, lest His disciples come by night and steal Him away, and say to the people, 'He has risen from the dead.'" Matthew 27:63, 64.

Pilate sent a legion of Roman soldiers to guard the tomb, but all the soldiers in the world could not have kept Jesus in it! Sometime before dawn on Sunday morning, "there was a great earthquake; for an angel of the Lord descended from heaven, and came and rolled back the stone from the door, and sat on it. His countenance was like lightning, and his clothing as white as snow. And the guards shook for fear of him, and became like dead men. But the angel answered and said to the women, 'Do not be afraid, for I know that you seek Jesus who was crucified. He is not here; for He is risen, as He said. Come, see the place where the Lord lay.'" Matthew 28:2-6.

◆ Many eyewitnesses

Later that day, Christ appeared to the disciples and showed them His nail-scarred hands and pierced side. "The disciples were overjoyed when they saw the Lord." John 20:20, KJV. Christ then encountered a number of people at various times and places. Paul, a contemporary of Christ, mentions some of these eyewitnesses of Christ after His resurrection, citing Peter (1 Corinthians 15:5), the Twelve (verse 5), "more than five hundred of the brothers" (verse 6), James (verse 7), all the apostles (verse 7), and finally, himself (verse 8).

Such eyewitnesses to Christ's resurrection certainly give ample evidence that He lives! Numerous first- and second-century historians add their testimony regarding the resurrection. Josephus, a Jewish historian of the first century A.D., writes this fascinating passage:

"Now there was about this time Jesus, a wise man, if it be lawful to call him a man; for he was a doer of wonderful works, a teacher of such men as receive the truth with pleasure. He drew over to him many Jews, and also many of the Greeks. This man was the Christ. And when Pilate had condemned him to the cross, upon his impeachment by the principal man among us, those who had loved from the first did not forsake him, for he appeared to them alive on the third day, the divine prophets having spoken these and thousands of other wonderful things about him. And even now, the race of Christians, so named from him, has not died out."—*Antiquities*, 18:3.3.

Josephus was a Jew, writing to please Romans. Yet he records this historical information which would hardly be considered pleasing to the very ones who sought the final demise of Christ. Josephus surely would not have included such controversial information unless it were true.

And what motivated the disciples, cowering in despondence and doubt, hiding as they did behind locked doors, to rally and go forth proclaiming a crucified, risen, and returning Lord with unmitigated zeal and boldness? Surely, it could not have been a wrapped corpse in a tomb! It had to be a risen Christ!

What caused hundreds of thousands of Christian martyrs down through the centuries to courageously face death rather than recant? They believed the promise made by a risen Lord, "Because I live, you will live also." John 14:19.

The resurrection of Christ and the promised resurrection of His followers became the heart of the message they proclaimed. In fact, on the day of Pentecost, Peter and the disciples set the city Jerusalem aflame by boldly preaching a risen Christ. Addressing the "men of Israel," Peter stated, "This Jesus God has raised up, of which we are all witnesses. "This man was handed over to you . . . and you, with the help of wicked men, put him to death by nailing him to the cross. But God raised him from the dead, . . . and we are all witnesses of the fact." Acts 2:24, 32, KJV.

Stunned and deeply moved by Peter's inspired words, the crowd responded, "Men and brethren, what shall we do?" Acts 2:37. Peter replied, "Repent, and let every one of you be baptized." Acts 2:38.

To show that they believed in Christ's resurrection and His victory over sin and death, three thousand individuals "gladly received his word" and were baptized (verse 41).

Baptism, to the early Christian, was a public demonstration of his or her belief in the death, burial, and resurrection of Christ. Through baptism, the believer enters into the crucifixion of Christ, putting to death the "old man of sin" (see Romans 6:6).

◆ Start life over again!

Have you ever wished you could bury the past? Wipe out the mistakes and guilt and start over again? That is exactly what baptism is all about. Through this sacred ceremony, God gives us the opportunity to be "born again" (see John 3:3).

When a baptismal candidate repents and confesses his sins, he is placed under the water—a symbol of the death and burial of the old life of self and sin. Then he is raised up out of the watery grave to a new life in Christ, symbolizing the resurrection of our Lord.

What could more beautifully symbolize death to sin and the beginning of a new life than baptism by immersion? For the Christian church, baptism had its origin with John the Baptist, a rugged man who appeared in the wilderness of Judea boldly preaching repentance. All roads leading to Jordan were crowded with people going to listen to him, and ultimately, to be baptized.

Closing the door to His carpenter shop and bidding His mother farewell, Jesus also made His way to the Jordan. And when John caught sight of Jesus, he recognized Him and said, "Behold! The Lamb of God who takes away the sin of the world!" John 1:29.

When Jesus asked to be baptized, John refused, saying, "I need to be baptized by You, and are You coming to me?" Matthew 3:14. But Jesus insisted, saying, "Permit it to be so now, for thus it is fitting for us to fulfill all righteousness" (verse 15).

John certainly recognized that Jesus had no sinful past to confess, and He did not need to demonstrate His belief in His own resurrection. But Jesus wanted to identify with men and women—He wanted to leave us a perfect example of right-doing to follow.

So according to Christ's request, John immersed Him in the Jordan. As soon as He was baptized, He "came up immediately from the water; and behold, the heavens were opened to Him, and He saw the Spirit of God descending like a dove and alighting upon Him. And suddenly a voice came from heaven, saying, 'This is My beloved Son, in whom I am well pleased.'" Matthew 3:16, 17.

As Jesus walked up out of the water and stood with dripping clothes on the muddy banks of the Jordan, God publicly introduced Him as His Son—the Anointed One. Christ's baptism marked the beginning of His public ministry. "God anointed Jesus of Nazareth with the Holy Spirit and with power, who went about doing good and healing all who were oppressed by the devil, for God was with Him." Acts 10:38.

In Christ's last recorded command just before His ascension, He admonished His followers to go and teach all nations, baptizing them in the name of the Father, Son, and Holy Ghost, and teaching them to observe all the things He had taught His disciples.

Jesus' followers took these words seriously. In the book of Acts we find a detailed account of a baptism conducted by Philip, the evangelist. As Philip walked the dusty road to Gaza, he saw an Ethiopian treasurer riding in an official chariot of the queen of that country. When the chariot stopped, Philip noticed that the official was reading from the scroll of the prophet Isaiah. The Ethiopian invited Philip to ride along with him and explain the meaning of Isaiah 53, which gave the details of the crucifixion of the Messiah. Philip, "beginning at this Scripture, preached Jesus to him." Acts 8:35.

Not only did Philip tell about Jesus, but evidently he explained the significance of baptism, for the Bible says that when they came to a pool of water, the Ethiopian asked, "See, here is water. What hinders me from being baptized?" (Verse 36.)

Nothing, Philip replied. "If you believe with all your heart, you may" (verse 37).

The Ethiopian official then ordered the chariot to stop. The two men dismounted, and Philip performed the baptism, immersing the Ethiopian treasurer in the water just as John had immersed Christ when He was baptized.

◆ New Testament baptism is by immersion

It is clearly seen here that the mode of baptism practiced by the early church was immersion. In fact, there is no evidence in the New Testament for any other method of baptism. The writings of early church historians and the discoveries of archaeologists both provide evidence that immersion was the mode of baptism until the twelfth and thirteenth centuries.

James Cardinal Gibbons wrote:

> "For several centuries after the establishment of Christianity baptism was usually conferred by immersion: But since the twelfth century, the practice of baptism by infusion (pouring) has prevailed in the (Roman) Catholic Church, as this manner attended with less inconvenience than Baptism by immersion. . . . The Church exercises her discretion in adapting the most convenient mode, according to the circumstances of time and place."—*Faith of Our Fathers*, 94th ed., p. 277.

There are dozens of cathedrals with large baptismal fonts in Europe. Sixty-six are found in Italy alone that were constructed between the fourth and fourteenth centuries.

In A.D. 988, Grand Vladimir I was baptized by immersion in Kiev. In the "Cathedral Vladimir," a beautiful mural on the wall depicts his baptism. It is reported that he invited the whole city to come and be baptized in the Dneiper River, saying that anyone who refused to come would be his enemy, whether they were "rich or poor, beggar or slave."

Obviously the idea of forcing the masses to enter into this most sacred rite would negate its meaning, as Christ asks for our hearts as an exercise of our own free will. But the importance of baptism for the Christian is not to be underestimated. As Christ told Nicodemus,

"I tell you the truth, unless a man is born of water and the Spirit, he cannot enter the kingdom of God." John 3:5 NIV.

No doubt Nicodemus, the proud Pharisee, anticipated entrance into God's kingdom as a natural-born, devout Jew. However, Jesus made it clear that anything less than a complete transformation of the life by the power of the Holy Spirit as demonstrated by water baptism was inadequate.

Jesus said, "He who believes and is baptized will be saved." Mark 16:16. Nothing less than a total belief in Christ will do. Anyone stepping into the waters of baptism does so with the full assurance that Christ forgives all past sins.

On another occasion, Jesus told His disciples that before baptism comes instruction. The sacred rite of baptism is not something to be entered into lightly, but comes after a person has become fully acquainted with God's truths in the Bible.

But more than a mere knowledge of doctrines is needed. There must be a commitment of one's whole life to Christ. When a person unites with Jesus, he naturally begins to live Christ's way. He does not want to do anything unacceptable to the One who gave His all for him.

Along with commitment comes repentance. Peter said, "Repent therefore and be converted, that your sins may be blotted out." Acts 3:19.

Repentance involves a deep sorrow for sins committed and a turning away from the errors of the past. Beholding Jesus, a sinner's heart is touched and softened by the incredible price paid for sin on the cross of Calvary.

The rite of baptism is the hallmark of the Christian life. For those who have not yet made the decision to follow Christ all the way and join with His body of believers on earth, the apostle Paul asks, "Why are you waiting? Arise and be baptized, and wash away your sins, calling on the name of the Lord." Acts 22:16. ❏

The radical spiritual change discussed in this chapter is not an option for those of us who are alive when the War Behind All Wars reaches its final battle before the King returns in triumph.

That great battle—the Bible calls it Armageddon—is ushered in by seven catastrophic plagues.

The final battle of the long war—previewed in the next chapter.

23

....

A Preview of
Earth's Final
Headlines

"We interrupt this broadcast . . . "

Finally, the world's media are jolted from their endless, narrow preoccupation with the local politics of Earth and forced to report events of truly cosmic significance.

Network anchors ponder the meaning of an unprecedented series of worldwide catastrophes. Newspapers write headlines that signal to alert Christians that the Great War has reached its final battle. The cable headline news is about to circle the world for its final half hour.

Those who have thrown in their lot with Satan will reap a harvest of intense suffering as they reel under the impact of serial plagues. But God will miraculously protect and provide for His loyal followers throughout this time of trouble and terror.

Then, just as headline writers are searching their dictionaries for the spelling of "Armageddon," the battle is interrupted by what would be history's greatest headline ever—if anyone were around to read it!

Which astronomer will be the first to sight the cloud closing in on Earth and growing brighter by the second? Will it turn out that it is first picked up as a mysterious light racing Earthward through the yawning vault of Orion's Great Nebula?

From all indications, we won't be waiting long now for the answers.

23

● ●

I was sitting in my living room conducting a Bible study recently, when a young woman related an interesting story. The night before, while driving home from shopping, a meteor shower had suddenly lit up the night sky. Unaccustomed to such a starry display, she anxiously pressed down on the accelerator. "All I wanted to do was to get home and be with my son," she told me. "I was sure Jesus was coming that very minute!"

Linda, like many people today, had the mistaken idea that Jesus might come at any moment—something like Russian roulette. Although the Bible teaches that Jesus is coming soon, specific events will take place before He comes. A significant part of being ready for His coming involves an understanding of what the Bible teaches regarding what will occur in Earth's last days.

This sequence of events—this preview of Earth's final headlines—begins in Revelation 14:9, 10: "Then a third angel followed them, saying with a loud voice, 'If anyone worships the beast and his image, and receives his mark on his forehead or on his hand, he himself shall also drink of the wine of the wrath of God, which is poured out full strength into the cup of His indignation. He shall be tormented with fire and brimstone in the presence of the holy angels and in the presence of the Lamb." Revelation 14:9, 10.

Before Jesus comes, the mark of the beast will be enforced upon men and women throughout this world. We read in Revelation 13 that "the mark or the name of the beast, or the number of his name" (verse 17) will be forced upon all classes of people—rich and poor, small and great, free and bond. Only those with the mark will be allowed the privilege of buying and selling.

Those who do not have the mark become the objects of an economic boycott. Ultimately they will be threatened with death. Before Jesus comes, the whole world will be tested in the area of worshiping the Creator on the true Sabbath.

The entire issue of the great controversy will focus on the question of loyalty. In the days of Daniel, the test of loyalty for the three Hebrew worthies was the second commandment, forbidding the worship of graven images. Since the three Hebrews would not bow down to the image and violate the second commandment, they were threatened with imprisonment and death.

In the last generation, the issue will not be the second commandment, but the fourth. After the mark of the beast is enforced, there will be two classes of people—those who receive the mark of the beast, and those who receive the seal of God; those who are disloyal, and those who are loyal. Each person will be on one side or the other. After each person has made a final, irrevocable decision, God's wrath unmingled with mercy will be "poured out full strength into the cup of His indignation." Revelation 14:10.

The wrath of God, poured out without mercy! What a picture! We find in Revelation 15 that God's wrath, in earth's last hour, will come in the form of the seven last plagues, reserved for those who receive the mark of the beast. Those who yield to human traditions and human laws, selling out their devotion to Christ, will ultimately experience the unmitigated wrath of God.

But what of God's people during this time of calamity that is unlike any other crisis in human history? God's Word assures us that His children will be alive during this time but protected by His grace. While the plagues will be falling all around them, they will not be touched. God's church will go through the tribulation and emerge triumphant.

Thus the sequence of events in the time of the end is clear according to the Bible. Before Jesus comes, the mark of the beast will be enforced. This will lead to the outpouring of the seven last plagues. At the end of the plagues, Christ will come to deliver His people and take them home.

Revelation 15 tells us that "no one was able to enter the temple till the seven plagues of the seven angels were completed." Revelation 15:8.

Thus the popular teaching of the "secret rapture" is not supported by scripture. If God's people were to be raptured or taken to heaven before the plagues were poured out, they would obviously have entered the heavenly temple. But the Bible clearly says that nobody—no man—can enter the temple in heaven until the seven last plagues are fulfilled.

Prior to the beginning of the plagues, the solemn announcement will be made: "He who is unjust, let him be unjust still; he who is filthy, let him be filthy still; he who is righteous, let him be righteous still; he who is holy, let him be holy still." Revelation 22:11.

Then and only then will Christ's work as our High Priest in heaven be ended. Every case will have been decided for eternal life or eternal death. The door of God's mercy will be shut, ushering in the "time of trouble" spoken of by the prophet Daniel (see Daniel 12:1).

The most vivid description of this period of earth's history cannot approach its reality as the wicked drink the cup of God's wrath unmixed with mercy. John was given a preview of this terrible time of trouble that would take place just before the coming of Jesus and the deliverance of His people. "Then I heard a loud voice from the temple saying to the seven angels, 'Go and pour out the bowls of the wrath of God on the earth.'" Revelation 16:1.

◆ Plague One

In John's description of the plagues, we find a striking similarity between the plagues of the last days and those that fell upon Egypt. The first plague to fall upon the wicked is "a foul and loathsome sore," (verse 2) possibly resembling the boils and blains suffered by the Egyptians during their seventh plague. Many scholars believe them to have been some type of cancerous lesion. But whatever the diagnosis, we do know that the sores under the first plague will be painful, and they will fall on all those who have chosen to follow the dictates of man instead of the commands of God.

Can you imagine the impact such a plague would have? Schools would close. Factories would shut down. Stores would not be able to open. Hospitals would be overflowing with people seeking emergency treatment, but most of the doctors and nurses would be suffering from the same affliction.

◆ Plague Two

And then, while people are still suffering from their sores, another calamity strikes! "Then the second angel poured out his bowl on the sea, and it became blood as of a dead man; and every living creature in the sea died" (verse 3). What a sight—and what a stench, as the creatures of the sea wash ashore. People will be stumbling over one another in their speedy exodus from the beaches.

◆ Plague Three

The third plague is closely associated with the second: "Then the third angel poured out his bowl on the rivers and springs of water, and they became blood" (verse 4).

Just think! A person turns on the faucet to get a drink—and instead of water, blood flows! What havoc! Could anything be worse?

But, ghastly and frightening as the seven last plagues may be, God's justice is fully vindicated. For the angel declares, "You are righteous, O Lord, The One who is and who was and who is to be, Because You have judged these things. For they have shed the blood of saints and prophets, And You have given them blood to drink. For it is their just due" (verses 5, 6).

At this time, when the wicked are perishing of thirst and have nothing to drink but blood, the promise is made to him who walks righteously that "Bread will be given him, His water will be sure." Isaiah 33:16. This promise may sound like poetry now, but then it will be worth more than the wealth of all the world's banks.

◆ Plagues Four and Five

Then the fourth angel pours out his bowl, scorching men with fire and great heat. The fifth angel follows, spreading darkness through-out the land, while men continue to suffer from the earlier plagues, gnawing their tongues in pain. This text indicates that the plagues are not all universal, nor are they all immediately fatal, since those under the fifth plague are still suffering from the sores of the first plague.

Apparently the plagues fall successively, instead of simultaneously, as their effects overlap; the accumulation of dreary trouble becomes unspeakable!

◆ Plague Six

The sixth plague includes the great final battle, Armageddon.

Revelation 16 describes "three unclean spirits like frogs coming out of the mouth of the dragon, out of the mouth of the beast, and out of the mouth of the false prophet" (verse 13)., These unclean spirits, symbolizing "spirits of demons," will "go out to the kings of the earth and of the whole world, to gather them to the battle of that great day of God Almighty" (verse 14).

The whole world is to be involved in this final conflict.

The Battle of Armageddon focuses on the final offensive of the combined forces of rebel religious powers, as they mobilize against God's people. The aim of these rebel forces is to completely destroy those loyal to God. All of us will be involved in the Battle of Armageddon.

In the last moment of time, when it looks as if God's people will be annihilated, the last phase of the battle occurs. Christ, the King of the east, returns, accompanied by His armies from the sky. The wicked are themselves slain under the artillery from heaven. This is Armageddon!

◆ Plague Seven

"Then the seventh angel poured out his bowl into the air, and a loud voice came out of the temple of heaven, from the throne, saying, 'It is done!' And there were noises and thunderings and lightnings; and there was a great earthquake, such a mighty and great earthquake as had not occurred since men were on the earth . . . Then every island fled away, and the mountains were not found." Revelation 16:17, 18, 20.

This catastrophic convulsion of the earth levels the cities as well as the mountains. Next comes a "great hail" out of heaven, "each hailstone about the weight of a talent" (verse 21). Most scholars place the weight of a talent at about fifty-seven pounds. The devastation from such a hailstorm is beyond human comprehension. But the Bible tells us that the Lord Himself will interrupt the conflict as He rides forth with the armies of heaven to deliver His people from a planet in rebellion.

We can learn a lesson for the future from the past. After the children of Israel had been held captive by the Egyptians for many years, the time arrived for God to fulfill His promise to deliver them from bondage. Sending Moses and Aaron to Pharaoh with the message, "Let my people go" (Exodus 5:1), God's wrath was kindled with the response of this haughty earthly official: "Who is the LORD, that I should obey His voice?" (Verse 2.)

In the ten plagues that fell on Egypt just before God's people were delivered, God answered Pharaoh's question in a graphic way.

In the final chilling plague, all the firstborn in Egypt were slain, beginning with the Pharaoh's family. With an aching heart, Pharaoh learned to take the warnings of God seriously.

But what was happening to the children of Israel during this time of great suffering and turmoil throughout the land? While Moses and Aaron had requested Pharaoh to deliver God's people from bondage, they had also instructed their fellow Israelites as to their response to this remarkable intervention by the Lord. On the fourteenth day of the first month, the Israelites were to slaughter a lamb and sprinkle its blood on the doorposts of their houses. Such a sign was not done lightly. It clearly differentiated between those willing to trust the God of Israel and those who were either hesitant or afraid to declare themselves, fearing Egyptian reprisals. It was a night of testing for Israel as well as for the Pharaoh.

Just as God had warned, at midnight the destroying angel passed through the land, visiting death upon the homes of all those without God's identifying mark—the blood on the doorpost—and sparing those families who had declared their loyalty to the God of Israel, regardless of the consequences. That night the children of Israel left for the promised land under God's protection.

Just so in earth's last hours, the final plagues will fall on those who have rejected or neglected God's deliverance and salvation. But those who have chosen the blood of the Lamb for forgiveness and cleansing from their sins will be delivered.

By our lives we are choosing today which side we will be on—God's side or the side of a rebel angel. When the destroying angels begin their work, it will be too late to change sides! Probation's door will have already closed forever.

◆ Under the wings of safety

The story is told of an Australian lumberman who built a simple cabin at the edge of a forest. One day, returning home from work, he was stunned and heartbroken to find his home reduced to a heap of smoldering ruins. All that remained were a few pieces of charred lumber and some blackened metal. Walking out to where his old chicken coop had stood, the lumberman discovered only a mound of ashes and some burned wire. Aimlessly, he shuffled through the debris. Then, glancing down at his feet, his eye caught a curious sight—a mound of charred feathers. Idly he kicked it over. Four little fuzzy, baby chicks scrambled out, miraculously protected by the wings of a loving mother.

In the most beautiful and meaningful language of Scripture, God describes what He longs to do for every one of His children on earth when the plagues fall. "He shall cover you with His feathers, And under His wings you shall take refuge." Psalm 91:4.

God has given wonderful assurance to those who choose to follow Him. Down through the ages, Christians have memorized the words of Psalm 91, taking courage in God's promise: "A thousand may fall at your side, And ten thousand at your right hand; But it shall not come near you. . . . No evil shall befall you." Psalm 91:7, 10. The good news of the Bible is that while the plagues will be falling all around those loyal to God, He will give His angels charge over them (see verse 11).

So in the words of the hymn writer:

> *Give to the winds your fears;*
> *In hope be undismayed:*
> *God hears your sighs and counts your tears,*
> *God shall lift up your head.*

We already know how the Battle of Armageddon will turn out. We know who will walk away, shaken perhaps, but with a song on their lips. John the Revelator names the song, "The Song of Moses and the Lamb." (See Revelation 15:3.)

The valiant heroes of earth's final conflict—those qualified to sing this victory song—are described as "those who keep the commandments of God and the faith of Jesus." Revelation 14:12. What a group to belong to! The invitation to join that group is ringing around the world today. And you are invited! ❏

Armageddon is cut short by Christ's return. But it will be another thousand years before the Great War is forever over. Yet for God's people, it will be the first thousand years of eternity—a millennium spent with the King in Heaven.

Satan, on the other hand, will spend ten centuries confined to the hell he has made of Earth.

24

....

A Workaholic's
Long Vacation

Millennial interlude.

For those of us born during the Great War, we can't imagine anything else. It's all we've ever known.

But really, it is just a temporary aberration of a few thousand years—preceded by a perfect eternity before and followed by a perfect eternity after.

Imagine what life would be like without sickness, disease, pain, fear, endless stress, violence, temptation, conflict, and death. Imagine perfect happiness, perfect health, perfect peace of mind.

Imagine living forever, never needing sleep, traveling the universe, realizing every dream.

That's how God intended we should live. And beginning with His return to Earth, that's just how it will be—if we are His.

Our first thousand years of eternity will be spent with our Maker and Saviour in the place called Heaven.

The enemy will still be alive, but confined to Earth. We will already be forever beyond his reach. Never again after Christ returns can he ever tempt or harass us.

Those thousand years for him will grind away with maddening slowness. Time will hang heavy indeed on his hands.

But even a thousand years of reflection leave him unrepentant— more confirmed in his rebellion against his Creator than ever. He plots one last assault on love. It will be his last, desperate act.

24

· ·

The world was spellbound when Soviet astronaut Yuri Gagarin circled the planet in just over eighty-nine minutes on April 12, 1961. And that was just the beginning. Space technology had "lifted off." On July 21, 1969, astronauts Neil Armstrong and "Buzz" Aldrin walked on the moon, as countless millions sat transfixed before their television sets.

Have you heard about the multimillion-dollar satellite dish that sends a variety of signals millions of miles into space and waits for a friendly response? A responsible group of scientists is hoping to contact "alien beings" from outer space, who could conceivably provide clues for living peacefully on Planet Earth.

Yet not all Americans respond to these space exploits with ecstatic wonder. Some are concerned about the billions spent on space exploration when so many problems on earth still cry out for attention. Others wonder where the new technology may lead. One man wistfully remarked, "Wouldn't it be wonderful if our scientists would discover a beautiful, habitable, fertile planet somewhere out there in space where mankind could slip away and escape all the problems we have on earth?"

Not a bad idea! Wouldn't it be a relief to escape the pollution, the crime, the sickness, sorrows, and heartaches we have here on this earth? That would be wonderful—even if it were just a long, long vacation!

312 • BEYOND ORION'S GATES

When the routine of life begins to tire us out as if we were on a treadmill running faster and faster, we long for something different—a break from the expected and the exhausting. Vacations are a refreshing change of pace, but how would you feel about a vacation lasting a thousand years? This might be difficult for today's classic workaholic to swallow! But the Bible tells us that the greatest workaholic of all time has a thousand-year enforced vacation ahead, from which he cannot escape:

"Then I saw an angel coming down from heaven, having the key to the bottomless pit and a great chain in his hand. He laid hold of the dragon, that serpent of old, who is the Devil and Satan, and bound him for a thousand years." Revelation 20:1, 2.

◆ The greatest workaholic ever

Bound for a thousand years! Talk about a change of pace! If ever there was a workaholic, Satan fits the description. He never punches a time clock. He has been on the job around the clock, seven days a week, month in and month out, for thousands and thousands of years. No coffee breaks. No holidays. No sick time. And no vacations, ever!

And talk about production! Everywhere, every day, we see the diabolical accomplishments of this fallen angel.

We see it in hospitals and nursing homes. In prisons and refugee camps. In earthquake-shattered and tornado-devastated cities. In crime and war zones.

If anyone ever earned a vacation, Satan has. Yet strange as it may seem, he is not anxious for one—he would have to be forced to sit down on the job!

Let's briefly review the background of this once-beautiful angel. The Bible tells us that Satan was aspiring, arrogant, and anxious for heaven's top position. He was not content to glorify his Lord. We find him eventually stirring up strife and contention among his heavenly companions. Revelation 12:7, 9 describes the outcome of his behavior: "And war broke out in heaven. . . . So the great dragon was cast out, that serpent of old, called the Devil and Satan, who deceives the whole world; he was cast to the earth, and his angels were cast out with him."

Cast out! Guess where he landed? Planet Earth, fresh from the Creator's hand, became Satan's headquarters. By deceit, he gained control of this planet from Adam and Eve. Then began his mission of destroying humanity. With Satan as director, Earth became a theater in the universe, illustrating what happens when God's commands are ignored, when man chooses to do his own thing, to go his own way!

Yet before Satan rebelled, before sin and crime and pain and sorrow existed, our all-wise God had a plan to rescue mankind. It involved sending one member of the Godhead to earth to live the life of a human being, enduring all the liabilities every child of humanity must face, and eventually, at thirty-three years of age, offering Himself as a sacrifice on Calvary for all humanity.

In His life and death, our Lord Jesus faced Satan down and rescued this hijacked planet and its inhabitants from Satan's control. What a contrast! Ultimate love, face to face with ultimate rebellion and hate!

When Christ returned to heaven as the victor over death and sin, Satan knew his time was running out. That is why Peter cautioned men and women, "Be sober, be vigilant; because your adversary the devil walks about like a roaring lion, seeking whom he may devour." 1 Peter 5:8.

◆ A long, forced vacation

For more than six thousand years now, Satan has been perfecting the art of perverting and destroying the lives of men and women. How long will this last? Will he ever quit?

The war begun in heaven will end on Earth only after Satan's forced vacation—a vacation lasting one thousand years—has come to an end. This time period is often referred to as the "millennium" (a union of two Latin words, *milli* and *annum*, translated as "one thousand years").

"But," someone asks, "when will the millennium, or Satan's vacation, begin? Can we know?"

Indeed we can! Let's take a look at the events surrounding Christ's second coming. "For the Lord Himself will descend from heaven with a shout, with the voice of an archangel, and with the trumpet of God." 1 Thessalonians 4:16.

And what will happen on that great day, when the Son of God descends to the Earth in all His glory with His retinue of angels? Jesus Himself tells us: "Do not marvel at this; for the hour is coming in which all who are in the graves will hear His voice and come forth—those who have done good, to the resurrection of life, and those who have done evil, to the resurrection of condemnation." John 5:28, 29.

The Bible refers to two general resurrections: (1) The resurrection of life for those who have done good; and (2) the resurrection of condemnation for those who have done evil.

Further, the Bible reveals that one resurrection takes place at the beginning of the thousand years, and the other resurrection at the end of that time.

The apostle John describes those who will comprise the first resurrection: "Blessed and holy is he who has part in the first resurrection." Revelation 20:6.

Paul, too, points to this first resurrection (1 Thessalonians 4:16) when he tells us that the dead "in Christ" will rise first. Clearly, Jesus doesn't want His dear friends, the sleeping saints, to wait any longer than necessary! His promise to us is: "He who believes in Me, though he may die, he shall live." John 11:25.

◆ Don't miss this!

Imagine with me the scene: Graves opened! Families reunited! Babies put back into the arms of their mothers! Lovers together again, never to part! And in the midst of all this excitement, another thrilling event takes place.

"Then we who are alive and remain shall be caught up together with them in the clouds to meet the Lord in the air. And thus we shall always be with the Lord." 1 Thessalonians 4:17. The righteous living, the righteous resurrected—all are gathered into one exulting, ecstatic group in the swirling winds, rushing heavenward! And there's still more!

At that moment the redeemed will be changed! Bodies that once bore the marks of old age will surge forth with new life. These bodies once beaten down by disease or injury will once again be restored by the friendly Creator—who is very good at what He does! The Bible promises in 1 Corinthians 15 that we shall all be changed, that the dead will be raised incorruptible, that the mortal will put on immortality! Can anything be more exciting to think about?

I don't know about you, but I look forward to that day! The prognosis for all of us on Planet Earth isn't that good. As much as we try to avoid birthday celebrations (at least after we pass a certain age), the years do go by. Once-clear eyes become blurred. Joints ache. Knees and backs give out.

◆ Never again!

But let's listen to the rest of the story! The Bible tells us that the redeemed will, one day soon, have perfect bodies never again subject to disease or death. What a promise! Talk about something to anticipate! No more cancer, heart attacks, leukemia, AIDS. Lifting some words from a recent United States president: "Read my lips: No more suffering. No more pain!"

And isn't it just like Jesus to do all this first for those who have fallen asleep in Him? The first people to experience the exhilaration of renewed life surging through them are those who have been sleeping in their graves, waiting for His return:

"For this we say to you by the word of the Lord, that we who are alive and remain until the coming of the Lord will by no means precede those who are asleep. For the Lord Himself will descend from heaven. . . . And the dead in Christ will rise first." 1 Thessalonians 4:15, 16.

All the righteous—both the living and those resurrected at Christ's coming—will be taken to heaven at the same time, "And thus we shall always be with the Lord." 1 Thessalonians 4:17.

But before relaxing in the bliss of eternity, the Bible tells us that the righteous will have a job to do. While Satan is taking his forced vacation on Earth, the saints will be putting in overtime in heaven! Wrote John: "They shall be priests of God and of Christ, and shall reign with Him a thousand years." Revelation 20:6.

What an experience! It's almost too much for our finite human minds to grasp. A thousand years with our Lord and loved ones in the New Jerusalem without fear of death or separation! A thousand years to accomplish a specific mission! John the Revelator describes this auspicious occasion as he viewed it in vision: "And I saw thrones, and they sat on them, and judgment was committed to them." Revelation 20:4.

The all-wise, all-powerful God of the universe has included feeble men and women in the solemn task of judging fallen angels and the unsaved! As Paul asked, "Do you not know that the saints will judge the world? . . . Do you not know that we shall judge angels?" 1 Corinthians 6:2, 3.

What part will the righteous play in the judgment process? How meaningful a role can anyone play when it appears that the judgment has already been completed at the return of Christ? Hasn't everyone's fate already been sealed before the millennium begins?

The Bible clearly states that the redeemed will be looking at the books and, as it were, "judging" for themselves during this one-thousand-year period. The realization will become clear—once and for all—that God is just and good and right. For thousands of years Satan has leveled the accusation that God is unfair, unloving, and unjust. The years of the millennium will put this notion to rest, vindicating God's character before the entire universe.

Have you ever wondered what your reaction might be if you looked for someone in heaven whom you expected to find there—only to discover they are lost forever? You might call the fairness of God's justice into question. During the millennium, the records of the lost will be opened. The most carefully guarded secrets and purposes harbored in each mind will be exposed. God's love and justice will be affirmed. Those inspecting the records will be left with only one response: "Even so, Lord God Almighty, true and righteous are Your judgments." Revelation 16:7.

But what are the lost doing while the redeemed are so busily engaged for a thousand years? Let's go back again to that dramatic picture of the Lord's return to Earth. While the righteous are being raised, reunited, and renewed, the wicked are involved in a totally different scenario. To them, the return of the Lord is a time of terror, not joy!

Desperately seeking shelter, they run for cover, crying to the rocks and mountains: "Fall on us and hide us from the face of Him who sits on the throne and from the wrath of the Lamb!" Revelation 6:16, 17.

An awesome picture! The prophet Jeremiah adds these vivid details: "And at that day the slain of the LORD shall be from one end of the earth even to the other end of the earth. They shall not be lamented, or gathered, or buried." Jeremiah 25:33.

What an overwhelmingly sad end—to be stricken down with none even to mourn one's passing! And what about the rest of the wicked—those in the grave at Christ's return?

The Bible clearly states that Christ's second coming does not disturb the wicked dead: "The rest of the dead did not live again until the thousand years were finished." Revelation 20:5.

◆ Utter desolation

What then will Planet Earth look like during the millennium? Across the earth, everywhere, will be devastation and emptiness. Probably the sound of wind and storm, no more. While the redeemed are actively engaged in the judgment process in heaven, the wicked lie dead across a scarred, burnt Earth, with no one to grieve their passing. Even their fearless leader, now handcuffed by circumstances beyond his control, has abandoned them.

Wrote the prophet Jeremiah: "I beheld the earth, and indeed it was without form, and void; And the heavens, they had no light. I beheld the mountains, and indeed they trembled, And all the hills moved back and forth. I beheld, and indeed there was no man, And all the birds of the heavens had fled. I beheld, and indeed the fruitful land was a wilderness, And all its cities were broken down At the presence of the LORD, By His fierce anger." Jeremiah 4:23-26.

What chaos! The desolation and ruined condition of the Earth at that time is now unimaginable. John uses the metaphor of a "bottomless pit" to describe the emptiness of the planet at that time: "Then I saw an angel coming down from heaven, having the key to the bottomless pit and a great chain in his hand. He laid hold of the dragon, that serpent of old, who is the Devil and Satan, and bound him for a thousand years." Revelation 20:1, 2.

The Greek word for bottomless pit is "abussos." This same Greek word is used in the Septuagint (the Greek translation of the Hebrew Old Testament) to describe the chaotic condition that existed on the first day of creation, when the Earth was "without form and void."

So Satan spends a forced vacation on a devastated planet! Certainly a fitting place for Satan and his evil angels, wouldn't you say?

◆ A dragon in chains

And what better symbolism could God use to describe Satan's condition than being "chained" or "bound" during that time? Think for a moment: The redeemed are in heaven. The wicked are dead. Everyone is gone. Ruin everywhere!

Evidently, the great chain with which Satan is bound is a chain of circumstances. No one is alive to deceive. No lives to twist or destroy. No human minds with which to toy. His hands, as it were, "are tied." He would love to continue his sinister work, but no one is around. He is "bound" to a lonely existence on a devastated planet.

Satan has nothing to do but wander to and fro reflecting on the results of his rebellion against God. No doubt he will also ponder with terror his eventual punishment—the bitter end to his self-promoting life.

But this thousand-year vacation does end, as the "the holy city, the new Jerusalem, come[s] down from God out of heaven." Revelation 21:2, KJV.

What a sight! A city perfectly square, 375 miles on a side, "floating" down from heaven in all its splendor and settling upon the Earth!

Almost simultaneously, as the city descends with Christ and His followers, another dramatic event takes place: "The rest of the dead did not live again until the thousand years were finished." Revelation 20:5.

The wicked dead also have their resurrection, but oh, how different it is from the first resurrection! All those in the second resurrection have gone to Christless graves. From Adam's day to the second advent, the rebellious unsaved, "whose number is as the sand of the sea," (verse 8) will rise up with one mighty purpose.

Following their leader, who "will be released from his prison and will go out to deceive the nations" (verses 7, 8), this enormous army of rebels will plan their attack on the Holy City. Of all the ruthless armies this Earth has ever known, this final group of warriors will surpass them all in hate and their thirst for revenge. The greatest military strategists of all time will organize them; the most passionate leaders of hate and power this world has ever known will drive them into their last great frenzy. They will probably take as much time as they feel necessary to manufacture their assault weapons, whether nuclear, laser, or chemical.

Then the day arrives when all is ready. Bent on taking the New Jerusalem by force, the mighty army advances under the master rebel of all time: "They went up on the breadth of the earth and surrounded the camp of the saints and the beloved city" (verse 9). Grasping his last opportunity to seize world dominion, the archenemy feels confident, with the vast army and their nuclear armament, that they are capable of capturing the city of God. Evil knows no limits to its self-deception.

However, John makes it clear that this desperate attempt will not succeed. In what is called His "strange act" (Isaiah 28:21, KJV), God will finish the battle. "And fire came down from God out of heaven and devoured them" (verse 9).

Notice that the fire comes down from God out of heaven. Hell is not a hot spot burning in the center of the earth. Hell is not some subterranean cavern imprisoning the lost who are tormented in the flames, shrieking in horror. Hell is God's final judgment at the end of this world as we now know it. According to Hebrews 12:29, "Our God is a consuming fire." An all-righteous, holy God "consumes" or "devours" sin. The fires of hell proceed from heaven. His righteousness, in harmony with all-embracing love, destroys all evil. It banishes all sin. It defeats all wickedness. The Bible does not picture an angry God tormenting sinners. It presents a righteous, holy, just God, cleansing the universe from the consequences of sin. The most loving act a gracious Lord could do!

◆ Reaping the consequences of selfish choices

From God's viewpoint, the destruction of sinners is a deeply sorrowful event. Yet He has no choice if He is to respect their freedom of choice. Sin is self-destruction. Every person is free to choose his or her future—and then to accept the consequences. The wages of rebellion is death, not because God is arbitrary, but because inherent in the rebel thought and act are the seeds of self-destruction. The seeds of sin are ultimately death. God allows sinners to reap the results of their choice. A loving, just, all-wise God with the best interests of the universe in mind could do no other.

Viewing this final fire in vision, Peter writes: "The heavens will pass away with a great noise, and the elements will melt with fervent heat; both the earth and the works that are in it will be burned up." 2 Peter 3:10.

Although hell was prepared for Satan and his angels, those who have rejected Christ's salvation will also be destroyed in the final conflagration. The whole universe will understand then Christ's heart-rending words, "Depart from Me, you cursed, into the everlasting fire." Matthew 25:41.

Does this verse mean that God will torture His victims unmercifully throughout all eternity? In our next chapter, we'll seek a Bible answer to that question!

Out of the ashes of a charred world, cleansed from the deadly virus of sin, God recreates a new world. A world where weeping is heard no more. A world where you will never again be misunderstood, hurt, abused, lonely, or confused. "For behold," our Lord promises us, "I create new heavens and a new earth; And the former shall not be remembered or come to mind. . . . The voice of weeping shall no longer be heard in her . . . They shall build houses and inhabit them; They shall plant vineyards and eat their fruit. . . . And My elect shall long enjoy the work of their hands." Isaiah 65:17, 19, 21, 22.

What a glorious eternity God promises the redeemed! The human mind cannot comprehend the glory and the beauty of the paradise God is preparing for those who love Him and are willing to follow Him wherever He leads. "Eye has not seen, nor ear heard, Nor have entered into the heart of man The things which God has prepared for those who love Him." 1 Corinthians 2:9.

The most glorious vacation spot on Earth will be nothing compared to the vacation land God has prepared for the saved in the Earth made new. And think—all of this the wicked could have enjoyed! But the price tag seemed too high. They were unwilling to choose Christ as their Saviour and Lord. They exchanged eternal life in paradise for "the passing pleasures of sin." Hebrews 11:25.

What an exchange! So much for so little! As John reminds us, "For what profit is it to a man if he gains the whole world, and loses his own soul? Or what will a man give in exchange for his soul?" Matthew 16:26. ❏

The millennium is over. God prepares to move the capital of the universe from Heaven to Earth. Yet the war isn't over. Satan and his followers must finally reap to the fullest what they have sown.

But can it possibly be true—as multitudes today believe—that God will consign the devil and his followers to spend eternity in the agonies of an ever-burning fire?

Or is that just another of Satan's own lies?

25

....

Who
Framed God?

The God who never was.

Satan's constant effort in his war against Heaven is to hold up before himself a mirror, and then try to persuade us that the reflection we see there is God. Don't be taken in.

God is not the destroyer. Satan is.

God is not the author of death. Satan is.

God is not to blame for suffering and sorrow. Satan is.

One of Satan's most contemptible lies is that at the end, God will burn sinners forever in the fires of hell. Can you imagine a more warped, unspeakable, brazen lie? No wonder some have found this picture of God so revolting they have abandoned all belief in His existence! But what a tragedy that the God they repudiated has never existed—that such a God is the devious product of the devil's own perverted imagination.

What, then, is the real truth about the end of Satan and the confirmed sinners who have chosen him? Can God still be all love, yet bring the Great War to its end?

See if this chapter helps answer those questions.

25

● ●

C an we find the love of God in the fires of hell? If God is love, why would He want to burn sinners throughout eternity, and then some? Is God pleased in some way to torment sinners in hell? In some way, does getting even bring Him happiness? Some churches and their pastors obviously think so.

Samuel Hopkins, a Calvinist preacher in the late 1700s, wailed,

"The smoke of their torment shall ascend up forever in the sight of the blessed. There before their eyes this display of divine character and glory will be in the favor of the redeemed, and most entertaining, and will give the highest pleasure to those who love God."—*The Works of Samuel Hopkins, D.D.,* pp. 457, 458.

Can you identify with that statement? Do you think that one of the great "entertainments" of heaven will be to watch agonizing sinners thrashing in hell?

Hopkins then continues, "Should the eternal torment and fires be extinguished, it would in great measure put an end to the happiness and glory of the blessed."

Samuel Hopkins proclaimed that hell is a hot spot in the center of the earth where millions now suffering provide entertainment for those in heaven. He pictures the fires of hell and the burning of the wicked as some kind of sport for the spectators in heaven.

Is hell a hot spot in the middle of the earth with millions of people crying in unimaginable pain, with no end ever in sight? And does God watch it all? Is heaven so close to hell that those in heaven can actually look into hell's fire and see their loved ones crying out in agony? Most of us wouldn't torment our worst enemy this way.

◆ A false picture of God

This picture of a God of love tormenting people for endless trillions of years has caused many thousands in every generation to become infidels.

Robert Ingersoll, one of the best-known infidels of the past century, was born into the home of a minister. After hearing his father preach on the fires of hell, Ingersoll said, "If God is like that, if God would burn millions and trillions of people, men, women, children and babies, I don't believe He exists. I believe He is a figment of human imagination."

Robert Ingersoll concluded that a God who would torment people for millions of years must not be a loving God at all. Further, he decided that such a God must not really exist at all.

And Ingersoll was right. A vengeful God who delights to inflict and witness suffering doesn't exist. Unless, that is, we're talking about the one who fancies himself to be the god of this world. The charge that this world's Creator is a tormenting, vengeful God is just one more of Satan's appalling lies.

The devil himself invented the idea of eternal torment, and ever since, he's enjoyed great success in painting God as the villain of this diabolical doctrine. Once again, Satan tries to frame God for his own crime.

What does the Bible actually teach about hell? Down through the ages, pagan practices and human tradition have often replaced Bible truth. Many human imaginations have slipped into the Christian church in place of Scripture. The subject of "hell" is one sad example.

You may be surprised at what the Bible really teaches about hell.

You will discover that the truth in the Bible may be what you always imagined it should be, but never thought it really was.

For the truth about hell, the only safe place to look is in God's Word. Peter helps us to put this subject of hell into its proper setting. The Lord, Peter wrote, "is longsuffering toward us, not willing that any should perish but that all should come to repentance." 2 Peter 3:9.

God does not delight in the death of the wicked! Does heaven rejoice when people are destroyed at the end of this present world? Certainly not! Jesus longs for us to be saved. What more could He have done to get that message across?

Jesus discussed this subject with His disciples in His classic parable of the sower: "The kingdom of heaven is like a man who sowed good seed in his field; but while men slept, his enemy came and sowed tares among the wheat and went his way. But when the grain had sprouted and produced a crop, then the tares also appeared. So the servants of the owner came and said to him, 'Sir, did you not sow good seed in your field? How then does it have tares?' He said to them, 'An enemy has done this.'" Matthew 14:24-28.

What is this parable teaching us regarding the final destruction of the unsaved? In this parable, Jesus likens His kingdom to a farmer's field. The good seed was sown by the master, or owner, of the field. Then, Jesus added, "his enemy came and sowed tares." In God's world, the enemy, or Satan, sows the evil.

Jesus then makes this startling statement: "At the time of harvest I will say to the reapers, 'First gather together the tares and bind them in bundles to burn them, but gather the wheat into my barn'" (verse 30).

Then Jesus explains the meaning of the parable in these clear words: "The field is the world, the good seeds are the sons of the kingdom, but the tares are the sons of the wicked one. The enemy who sowed them is the devil, the harvest is the end of the age, and the reapers are the angels" (verses 38, 39).

Note carefully: The Bible says that the wheat and the tares grow together until the harvest at the end of the world. Then Jesus makes His point:

"Therefore as the tares are gathered and burned in the fire, so it will be at the end of this age" (verse 40).

Could Jesus have said it any clearer? The destruction of the wicked—the harvest of tares in the parable—will take place at the end of the world. Does this mean then that a place called hell doesn't yet exist?

Jesus made it abundantly plain that it was at the end of time, at an event known as the harvest, that the wicked would be burned.

The Bible gives us a consistent account of what Jesus taught:

"For the wicked are reserved for the day of doom; They shall be brought out on the day of wrath." Job 21:30.

Further, the Bible does not teach that people are now burning in hell with the redeemed in heaven looking down on their suffering. The Bible teaches, as we have already studied, that death is a sleep. Death is a silent rest until Jesus comes—for the redeemed as well as for the unsaved. God's final judgment will occur only at the second coming of Jesus Christ.

Matthew helps us understand: "For the Son of Man will come in the glory of His Father with His angels, and then He will reward each according to his works." Matthew 16:27.

All men and women will be rewarded for their works at the end of this present world, at the return of Jesus. The Bible teaches that the wicked are "reserved" until the day of judgment. The apostle Peter puts it this way: "The Lord knows how to deliver the godly out of temptations and to reserve the unjust under punishment for the day of judgment." 2 Peter 2:9.

The wicked who rejected Christ are reserved in their graves until the time of the second resurrection, after which they will be mercifully destroyed, according to Scripture.

But someone might ask, "When Christ destroys the wicked at the end of the world, does that mean that He will burn them for millions of years?"

To answer this question, let us look at the Bible illustration of Sodom and Gomorrah. The Bible describes Sodom and Gomorrah as becoming increasingly wicked with each passing year. Finally, God sent angel messengers to warn Lot to leave Sodom, along with anyone else who would believe him: "Escape for your life . . . lest you be destroyed." Genesis 19:17.

Unless they hastened out of Sodom, they would be destroyed with it. God made that urgent appeal in love. After God gave them that opportunity to leave Sodom, "the LORD rained brimstone and fire on Sodom and Gomorrah, from the LORD out of the heavens." Genesis 19:24.

◆ What is "eternal fire"?

According to God's Word, the fire that destroyed Sodom and Gomorrah was an eternal fire: "As Sodom and Gomorrah, and the cities around them in a similar manner to these, having given themselves over to sexual immorality and gone after strange flesh, are set forth as an example, suffering the vengeance of eternal fire." Jude 7.

Question: Is the fire that consumed Sodom and Gomorrah—the fire that came from God out of heaven—burning today? Obviously not! These cities were soon covered by the Dead Sea. In modern times, some of the sea has receded, and the cities are being excavated by archaeologists. But Sodom and Gomorrah aren't burning today. Yet they suffered the vengeance of what the Bible calls "eternal fire." What is the explanation?

Let the Bible explain itself as to what is meant by "eternal fire."

We read in Matthew 25:46: "And these will go away into everlasting punishment, but the righteous into eternal life." What did Jesus mean when He said "everlasting punishment?" Notice, it doesn't say everlasting punishing—rather, it says "everlasting punishment."

The Bible makes the matter even clearer in 2 Peter 2:6: "And turning the cities of Sodom and Gomorrah into ashes, [God] condemned them to destruction, making them an example to those who afterward would live ungodly."

Jude 7 says that Sodom and Gomorrah were burned with eternal fire; Peter adds that they were turned into ashes. An eternal fire, according to the Bible's own definition, is one that turns into ashes.

The *results* of "eternal fire" are eternal, not the *duration* of its burning. Do Sodom and Gomorrah ever need to be burned again? Certainly not, because they were completely destroyed.

An eternal fire is not one that eternally, perpetually burns. Eternal fire consumes, completely and utterly. Eternal fire turns what it burns into ashes—it completely destroys. Everlasting punish*ment* is not everlasting punish*ing.* Everlasting punishment is a punishment so final, so complete, so totally destructive, that it never has to be repeated. The punishment is everlasting.

We have difficulty picturing a loving God whose greatest pleasure is to burn people in unimaginable anguish for billions of years without end. But we have no difficulty accepting the biblical picture of a loving God who, after making countless invitations to sinners to forsake their evil ways, consumes sin wherever it is found. God consumes the world before the evil, rebellious world destroys itself in some horrific manner. He consumes it before the wicked, who want to "do it their way" destroy those loyal to God. The biblical picture is the only just and merciful solution God can choose.

The Bible further describes the fires of hell as being so hot that they totally destroy sin and purify this planet. Then God recreates the world. The Bible puts it this way: "Anyone not found written in the Book of Life was cast into the lake of fire. Now I saw a new heaven and a new earth, for the first heaven and the first earth had passed away." Revelation 20:15 - 21:1.

Let us look at additional texts that speak of hell fire: "If your hand causes you to sin, cut it off. It is better for you to enter into life maimed, rather than having two hands, to go to hell, into the fire that shall never be quenched." Mark 9:43.

Jeremiah 17:27 provides insight into the meaning of the expression "unquenchable fire: "But if you will not heed Me to hallow the Sabbath day, . . . then I will kindle a fire in its gates, and it shall devour the palaces of Jerusalem, and it shall not be quenched."

In A.D. 70, Jeremiah's prophecy was fulfilled when the Romans set fire to Jerusalem. The city was burned with unquenchable fire. Again I ask, is Jerusalem burning today? Obviously not! What, then, is an unquenchable fire? Simply this: An unquenchable fire cannot be put out by human hands. In Bible language, an eternal fire is one that turns what it burns to ashes. Everlasting punishment is punishment that is so full and complete that it need never be repeated.

◆ Nothing left of the wicked

Malachi gives additional insight regarding the final end of the unsaved: "'For behold, the day is coming, Burning like an oven, And all the proud, yes, all who do wickedly will be stubble. And the day which is coming shall burn them up,' Says the LORD of hosts, 'That will leave them neither root nor branch.'" Malachi 4:1.

In highly figurative language, Malachi emphasizes even further the final end to sin and sinners: "You shall trample the wicked, For they shall be ashes under the soles of your feet" (verse 3).

Notice how the Bible repeats this truth again and again: "May sinners be consumed from the earth, And the wicked be no more." Psalm 104:35.

"Let them be blotted out of the book of the living." Psalm 69:28.

The wicked are "reserved for fire until the day of judgment and perdition." 2 Peter 3:7. "Perdition" means destruction. They're not burning—they are "reserved" until the day of judgment.

The wicked are "cut down and thrown into the fire." Matthew 3:10.

"The wicked shall be no more." Psalm 37:10. God is not going to allow wickedness to go on and on—for the sake of the universe, as well as for the sake of sinners themselves. Wickedness comes to a final end. Sin and sinners will be consumed.

"Into smoke they shall vanish away." Psalm 37:20.

"The future of the wicked shall be cut off." Psalm 37:38.

"The soul who sins shall die." Ezekiel 18:4. The Bible does not say that the soul who sins will continue to live in the fires of hell forever and ever. The Bible says in Romans 6:23 that the wages of sin is death. And death is not continual life in hell. Death is the absence of life. Sin pays its own wages, sooner or later. Sin is self-destructive; it destroys all who cling to it. The Bible says in Revelation 20:14: "This is the second death."

You may wonder about the expression "forever and ever" in the book of Revelation. What does that little phrase mean? Does "forever" mean something other than forever? Let's consider the passage. The wicked, "shall be tormented with fire and brimstone in the presence of the holy angels and in the presence of the Lamb. And the smoke of their torment ascends forever and ever; and they have no rest day or night." Revelation 14:10, 11.

Here, in highly symbolic language, John is emphasizing that the "smoke" of their punishment indicates that the fire has done its work—its smoke wends its way into the universe forever—in a statement of finality. When fire does its work, without human intervention, nothing but ashes remains. Long after what is burned is fully consumed, the smoke arises, figuratively speaking, forever. The destruction is permanent—forever.

Let us look at another Bible passage where this expression "forever" is used: "But if the servant plainly says, 'I love my master, my wife, and my children; I will not go out free,' then his master shall bring him to the judges. He shall also bring him to the door, or to the doorpost, and his master shall pierce his ear with an awl; and he shall serve him forever." Exodus 21:5, 6.

The Old Testament slave would have an ear pierced, indicating that he would serve his master "forever." How long would the slave serve his master? The Revised Standard Version translates this text, "He shall serve him for life." So the term forever as used in the Bible doesn't mean existence without end; it means "until the end of the age"—or as long as life shall last.

Another good example of the use of this term and its meaning is found in 1 Samuel 1:22, 28. Here Hannah dedicated Samuel to the Lord "forever." Then she says she has lent him to the Lord "as long as he lives."

The wicked will be consumed and reduced to ashes—burned up. The fire that burns will last as long as it takes to cleanse the earth. In the biblical sense, that means "forever." The day will come when sin and its consequences will have been destroyed, when God will usher in a new age with no more suffering or heartache. That day will be the beginning of "forever" in the sense that we use that term today.

The Bible makes plain that the fires of hell destroy both the body and the soul, or the life, of a person. The word *soul* simply means the whole person. Sometimes, Bible writers—as we still do today—used "soul," however, to refer to the character, to the inner spirit, of man. We seem to sense when we use "soul" in this way and when we use it in the more correct way, as referring to a whole person, in harmony with Genesis 2:7.

Jesus said, in Matthew 10:28: "Do not fear those who kill the body but cannot kill the soul. But rather fear Him who is able to destroy both soul and body in hell."

That is, the sinner who experiences the fires of hell is totally destroyed, both soul and body—the whole life.

Isaiah put it another way: "Behold, they shall be as stubble, The fire shall burn them; They shall not deliver themselves From the power of the flame; It shall not be a coal to be warmed by, Nor a fire to sit before!" Isaiah 47:14. When the wicked are destroyed, there won't even be a coal left. When God burns up sin, it's gone forever. There is no place for sin and sinners any more—not a trace remains!

◆ The only solution to contamination

A tragic experience, recently recorded in the book *Bitter Harvest*, describes an event that took place in Michigan when an employee in a large grain company mixed in with the grain a substance known as PBB. The employee mixing the feed mistook the deadly poisonous PBB for a vitamin supplement.

The cattle, chickens, and pigs on the many farms which bought the deadly grain were contaminated. The farmers were deeply troubled as they realized that they had no choice but to isolate the contaminated animals, kill them, and burn the bodies to prevent the contamination from spreading. Grown men were moved to tears as they burned their own cattle.

God's beautiful planet has become contaminated with sin. God has done everything He could to save every human being from its poison. Any human being who clings to sin, who knowingly and willingly rebels against God, is contaminated. And for the sake of all, redeemed and the wicked, God must destroy the contamination. Sin is like a spreading cancer that must be cut out of the universe. My mind could never understand a loving God who would delight in burning people for millions of years. But my mind could understand the justice of a loving God who decided to eliminate sin from the universe before it continued to spread.

Suppose you were in heaven and decided to take a flight over a certain section of earth, and you saw some smoke. Coming closer, you hear familiar voices—but this time they are cries of anguish as people suffer the dreadful fate of never-ending fire. Cries of your friends, maybe your loved ones!

How do you think you would feel? Would that experience add to your heavenly bliss? If possible, you would be distressed even more when you realized that their intense agony would never end. Be glad today that God would never put the redeemed—or the unsaved—through such horrific experiences!

God has done everything He can to save us for eternity. Can you think of anything more He could have done? God will even erase the memory of that destruction from the minds of the redeemed: "For yet a little while and the wicked shall be no more; Indeed, you will look carefully for his place, But it shall be no more." Psalm 37:10.

Again, we are reminded that the wicked will be utterly removed from the universe. Obadiah 16:16 reminds us that "they shall be as though they had never been."

◆ God will bring sin and Satan completely to an end

God's way is the best way. His original plan for this world will be accomplished (see Isaiah 45:18). There will not be some remote corner where sin remains forever, boiling in a hell fire that will never go out! No, sin will not perpetually exist!

"But," you ask, "What about Satan? Will he be destroyed?"

Ezekiel wrote: "I will destroy thee, O covering cherub, from the midst of the stones of fire. . . . therefore will I bring forth a fire from the midst of thee, it shall devour thee, and I will bring thee to ashes upon the earth, . . . and never shalt thou be any more." Ezekiel 28:16, 18, 19, KJV.

When God makes an utter end to Satan, he will never again arise to torment the universe. The redeemed will have already settled the question of God's fairness and wisdom. Never again will the question be cherished anywhere in the universe—especially among the redeemed—as to whether created beings may be better able to run their lives than God is. The tragic results of sin will never be forgotten—though those results will be gone.

The God that we serve is a God of love. He's done everything He could to save us. God would not be a God of love if He allowed sickness and suffering to go on forever. He would not be a God of love if He allowed murder, adultery, and stealing to continue. The only way God can destroy sin is to destroy those sinners who cling to sin. Sin is combustible. Men and women who choose to cling to their sins will be consumed along with their sin.

Jesus appeals to men and women to be saved, for this world is soon to go up in flames as sin and sinners are destroyed. The invitation is still open: "Let the wicked forsake his way." Isaiah 55:7. Jesus cannot save us while we cling to our sins. Jesus cannot save us if we know that the Bible Sabbath is Saturday—the seventh-day of the week—yet continue to knowingly, willingly break it. Jesus cannot save us if we understand that our body is the temple of the Holy Ghost, yet continue to willingly destroy it. Jesus cannot save us if we continue to live willingly in known sin.

The door of mercy is still open. Jesus is still knocking on the door of our hearts. Perhaps in reading these pages, you hear Him speaking to you. Do you hear Him knocking? Think of what it would be like to be lost—to be as though you had never been. But that need never be. Jesus—if you answer His knock—will make sure of that! ❏

At last, the war is really over! In the contest between love and selfishness, love has emerged triumphant.

Now Earth, the primary battlefield of the Great War, must be purged of every trace of the conflict and made new and better than ever.

Those of us who weren't around when Earth was first created will watch in speechless awe as God creates it new again. Then, like children racing through the rooms of a new house, we will fan out over Earth II to explore our new and permanent home.

You and I simply must be there, friend!

We simply must.

26

. . . .

The Incredible Wonders of Earth II

The land of no limits.

Those of us who survive the war will have spent only a few decades—at the most—here on a sin-wracked planet.

Ahead of us will stretch an eternity.

Maybe 70 years here. Then 70 thousand, 70 million, 70 billion trillion gazillion years on Earth II—and we'll have only just begun!

If that's true, maybe we ought to spend a bit more time thinking about eternity and a little less thinking about the here and now. If we really believe that the New Earth is more than a distant mirage, maybe we ought to start making some concrete plans for what we'd like to do there.

Remember that it will be the land of no limits. The place of possible dreams.

Consider the incredible wonders of Earth II brought to view in this chapter. Let what you read here launch your imagination on a flight to your permanent home.

Soon, very soon, the dream will become real!

26

• •

As the golden desert sun began to sink behind the ancient Egyptian pyramids, a secret that had been perfectly kept for 3,265 years was about to be unfolded!

On November 26, 1922, the eight-year search led by Howard Carter for the missing pharaoh in the Valley of the Kings was drawing to a close. With his wealthy patron, Lord Carnavon, Carter broke the time-honored seal of the tomb, and the fabulous treasures of the boy king, Tutankhamun, lay strewn before them!

No one had even begun to comprehend the staggering wealth, the dazzling art, or the glories of the past, that lay hidden in the sand, until this moment of discovery. No royal tombs had ever been found intact in the burial grounds of the kings. King Tut's tomb held treasure unimagined.

A life-sized statue of King Tut—mace and rod in hand—stood at the door of the burial chamber. His death mask of beaten gold revealed the handsome features of the boy-king who ruled only nine years and died under mysterious circumstances at the age of nineteen in 1350 B.C. Effigies of gods and goddesses, jewels, chests, vases of ivory, furniture, and coins gleamed in the new light of the sun.

In all, more than 5,000 priceless treasures were found in the tomb, taking Carter more than nine years to remove and transfer to the Egyptian Museum in Cairo.

A dazzling collection—an extravagant burial. But contrast this with the burial of another ruler in Egypt two hundred years before—a ruler destined for something better than mere gold and finery.

During the time that Egypt was presided over by Thutmose I, a son was born to two Israelite slaves—Amram and Jochebed. Moses' arrival in the world came at a very inopportune time. Alarmed at the increasing strength of his captive people, Thutmose had ordered that every Israelite baby boy be thrown into the Nile River.

Determined that their little son should not die, Jochebed succeeded in hiding the child for three months. Then, fearing for his safety, she wove a basket, made it watertight, carefully placed her precious baby inside, and carried it to the river, where she and her daughter, Miriam, hid it among the rushes at the water's edge.

Miriam hid herself a short distance away to watch and see what would happen. Soon Princess Hatshepsut, daughter of the Pharaoh, came to the river to bathe with her servants. Spying the little basket floating among the bulrushes, the princess instructed her maid to bring it to her.

◆ A very willing nurse

As she opened the basket's lid, she read the story at a glance. Some unknown mother had resorted to this means of attempting to save her baby's life. Quickly determining to save the infant, Hatshepsut decided to adopt him. Since she had no male heir, this baby would become ruler when her father, Thutmose I, died. The princess named the child Moses, which means "drawn out of the water."

When Miriam, watching from her hiding place, saw how tenderly Hatshepsut held her baby brother, she ran and asked if she could get a nurse for the baby. The princess agreed, and Miriam ran to get her mother.

For nearly twelve years, Hatshepsut paid Moses' own mother to care for him. During that time, Moses was taught to obey and trust in the God of heaven. Then, from his humble home, Moses was taken to the royal palace, where he became the son of the princess.

Determined to make his adopted grandson his successor to the throne, Thutmose I saw to it that Moses was educated for his high position. In the court of pharaoh, Moses received the highest civil and military training of his day.

All steps led to eventual occupation of the royal throne. All the wealth, influence, and power of the then-civilized world lay at Moses' feet. It was his for the taking if he would cast his lot with the Egyptians and forget the God of heaven. The Palace of Pharaoh would be his home—the Valley of the Kings would be his final resting place. His body would be wrapped in a hundred yards of fine linen. His burial would be dazzled by gold coins, intricately carved vessels, exquisite pieces of furniture.

◆ The passing pleasures of sin

But no archaeologist's spade has ever unearthed a staggering display of King Moses' burial. And no expedition ever will. For no tomb was ever built. No earthly position was ever gained. Moses never became the Pharaoh of Egypt. Instead, he chose something better.

While the relics of Egypt's past are impressive, they cannot compare with the future Moses chose.

"By faith Moses, when he became of age, refused to be called the son of Pharaoh's daughter, choosing rather to suffer affliction with the people of God than to enjoy the passing pleasures of sin." Hebrews 11:24, 25.

Moses looked beyond the palaces, beyond the pleasures of earthly wealth and ease, to a future that made Egypt's fortunes fade into insignificance. He chose to become the son of the Mighty King—the son of the God of Heaven!

Moses died alone atop Mount Nebo—without royal fanfare, without an elaborate funeral marker. An unfair exchange, you say? This life for the one he could have enjoyed at the royal palaces in Egypt? This insignificant ending for all of the extravagance that could have accompanied him to his grave?

Moses knew that the wealth and glitter of a lifetime are nothing compared to the vastness of God's riches in eternity. He wanted to be among the faithful who would enter the City of God; he longed to hear the voice of Jesus, richer than any music, saying, "Come, you blessed of My Father, inherit the kingdom prepared for you from the foundation of the world." Matthew 25:34.

Like Abraham, Moses had his eyes firmly fixed on a city "which has foundations, whose builder and maker is God." Hebrews 11:10.

And this same city to which the ancient patriarchs looked with such longing is held out before us today, still waiting for the moment when faith becomes sight.

"In My Father's house are many mansions," Jesus promises. "I go to prepare a place for you. And if I go and prepare a place for you, I will come again and receive you to Myself; that where I am, there you may be also." John 14:2, 3.

While John was exiled on the little island of Patmos off the coast of Turkey, God showed him the heavenly city in vision. Astounded by the happiness and beauty before him, John compared the scene to a "bride adorned for her husband." Revelation 21:2.

His description did not stop there. "Now the wall of the city had twelve foundations, and on them were the names of the twelve apostles of the Lamb. . . . The foundations of the wall of the city were adorned with all kinds of precious stones" (verses 14 and 19).

John even specified the size of the New Jerusalem. "The city is laid out as a square; its length is as great as its breadth. And he measured the city with the reed: twelve thousand furlongs" (verse 16).

The city is square and 1,500 miles in circumference—or 375 miles on each side. One mathematician has estimated that the New Jerusalem could house two billion people. In other words, there will be room enough for every person who wants to be a citizen.

The city itself is built of pure gold. "The twelve gates were twelve pearls. . . . And the street of the city was pure gold, like transparent glass" (verse 21).

If such a city existed on Planet Earth today, everyone would be packing up, trying to get reservations on the next plane, regardless of the cost! But there is good news! Soon that city will be the capital of this Earth made new. John saw it, "coming down out of heaven from God" (verse 2) to a new and perfect Earth where sin no longer exists, "for the first heaven and the first earth had passed away" (verse 1).

Planet Earth—the future home of the saved? Is that to say that heaven will not be some wispy bank of clouds "way beyond the blue?"

Throughout Scripture, the earth is promised to those who are faithful. In the Sermon on the Mount, Jesus assured His people, "Blessed are the meek, For they shall inherit the earth." Matthew 5:5. In the Old Testament, Abraham was promised that his seed would inherit the Earth.

◆ Earth II

But the Earth of promise is not the land we know today, ravaged by violence, corruption, pollution, disease, suffering, and heartache. In its present state, this world would not be much of a gift! The Earth that awaits us with such beauty and wonder is the "earth made new"—Earth II, if you will—purged by fire and remade into a pristine, Edenic paradise.

"But the day of the Lord will come as a thief in the night, in which the heavens will pass away with a great noise, and the elements will melt with fervent heat; both the earth and the works that are in it will be burned up," Peter wrote. "Nevertheless we, according to His promise, look for new heavens and a new earth in which righteousness dwells." 2 Peter 3:10, 13.

The prophet Isaiah describes the new Earth that God has for us in these words: "The wilderness and the wasteland shall be glad for them, And the desert shall rejoice and blossom as the rose." Isaiah 35:1.

What flower could better describe the beauty and perfection of the Earth made new than the rose? Our promised home is a haven where pain cannot exist. There will be no cancer, no heart attacks, no arthritis, no colds, no illness—forever!

"And the inhabitant will not say, 'I am sick.' . . . Then the eyes of the blind shall be opened, And the ears of the deaf shall be unstopped. Then the lame shall leap like a deer, And the tongue of the dumb sing. For waters shall burst forth in the wilderness, And streams in the desert." Isaiah 33:24; 35:5, 6.

Yes, man's relentless search for the fountain of youth will finally be over. Perfect bodies will surge with boundless energy to be used in exploring the wonders all about us. Drinking the pure water from the river of life, we will be refreshed. Eating from the tree of life, we will be filled.

"And he showed me a pure river of water of life, clear as crystal, proceeding from the throne of God and of the Lamb. In the middle of its street, and on either side of the river, was the tree of life, which bore twelve fruits, each tree yielding its fruit every month. The leaves of the tree were for the healing of the nations." Revelation 22:1, 2.

◆ The legacy of sin—gone forever!

The Bible is filled with promises about the home that awaits us. Isaiah tells us, "Violence shall no longer be heard in your land, Neither wasting nor destruction within your borders." Isaiah 60:18.

No violence! Just peace and harmony and love! Even the animal kingdom, motivated on earth today by instincts of fear and survival, will be filled with a new and trusting spirit. "The wolf also shall dwell with the lamb, The leopard shall lie down with the young goat, The calf and the young lion and the fatling together; And a little child shall lead them. The cow and the bear shall graze; Their young ones shall lie down together; And the lion shall eat straw like the ox. . . . They shall not hurt nor destroy in all My holy mountain, For the earth shall be full of the knowledge of the LORD As the waters cover the sea." Isaiah 11: 6, 7, 9.

No need for burglar alarms. No need for locks and bolts on doors and windows. No need for safety-deposit boxes. But the promise that means the most is found in the book of Revelation. "And God will wipe away every tear from their eyes; there shall be no more death, nor sorrow, nor crying. There shall be no more pain, for the former things have passed away." Revelation 21:4. The inhabitants of the New Earth will never fear death. That chilling thought, awakening us in the night; that gripping, haunting realization that someday it will be over; that tearing, sudden rendering of our life from those we love—none of this will ever be part of reality in the Earth made new.

Our bodies will serve us well. The process of deterioration that is a natural part of the life cyle on this Earth will not be programmed into bodies designed to never grow old. "But those who wait on the LORD Shall renew their strength; They shall mount up with wings like eagles, They shall run and not be weary, They shall walk and not faint." Isaiah 40:31.

Exhaustion, fatigue, burnout, depression will be things of the past. Renewal, energy, new life, exuberance, optimism will be ours forever more.

◆ A tapestry of fulfilled dreams

But how will we channel all this energy? What will keep us busy in such a place of peace and tranquillity? How will we occupy ourselves with no evils to combat, no rent to pay or food to buy! With every faculty developed, our existence will be a creative tapestry of fulfilled dreams.

Have you ever let the creative juices flow and mentally designed your "perfect dream house"? Huge living room, sunken swimming pool, lush gardens? Isaiah tells us that heaven will be a place for the actualization of such dreams. "They shall build houses and inhabit them; They shall plant vineyards and eat their fruit. They shall not build and another inhabit; They shall not plant and another eat; For as the days of a tree, so shall be the days of My people, And My elect shall long enjoy the work of their hands." Isaiah 65:21, 22.

Our hands, designed by God to build, create, and work out the visions of our minds, will be enabled to produce anything we can conceive! And our energy will be renewed, each week, through a special service of worship and communion with our Creator: "From one Sabbath to another, All flesh shall come to worship before Me," says the LORD." Isaiah 66:23.

Just as the Sabbath celebration brings us new life and vision on this marred old Earth, so will it continue to energize us in the splendors of heaven. But the sense of community and praise will exceed anything we have ever witnessed here below. Voices will rise in perfect harmony. Musical notes will float and blend in tune and pitch, in a silver strain never before sounded. "And the ransomed of the LORD shall return, And come to Zion with singing, With everlasting joy on their heads. They shall obtain joy and gladness, And sorrow and sighing shall flee away." Isaiah 35:10.

As we study the history of Planet Earth in relation to the rest of God's creation, we find that this earth is the prodigal world in the universe—the one world where the plague of sin has spread its ugly disease for 6,000 years. God has promised that one day soon, this earth will be the center, or the capital, of God's universe!

"And I heard a loud voice from heaven saying, 'Behold, the tabernacle of God is with men, and He will dwell with them, and they shall be His people. God Himself will be with them and be their God. . . . They shall see His face." Revelation 21:3 and 22:4.

Just think of taking hold of a hand—and finding it our Lord's! Could anything be more awesome? Just think of waking up—and finding it home! Our eternal home!

How can we make certain we are citizens of the Earth made new? How can we know that our name is on one of those mansions in the New Jerusalem? The answer is so simple—yet many try to make it so complex! God promised Abraham many years ago that his seed would inherit the earth. He referred not to direct lineage, not to genetic lines, not to nationality or race. The symbol of Abraham's seed comes to fruition in the New Testament. "And if you are Christ's, then you are Abraham's seed, and heirs according to the promise." Galatians 3:29.

If you belong to Christ—if you have accepted Him as Lord and Saviour—then you are Abraham's seed, heir to the promised land, heading for heaven. The journey may seem long, the trek hazardous at times, the road rough, but with Christ to guide you, your arrival is secure. ❏

So we reach the end of the story. We've followed the great War Behind All Wars from its outbreak to its sad conclusion. We've considered our personal role in the conflict.

And it's still true that somewhere out there . . .

> *beyond our solar system,*
> *beyond our home galaxy,*
> *beyond the vast emptiness of intergalactic space,*
> *beyond the portals of some starry constellation—*

is the very throne of God Himself.

Do you know Him, my friend?

Do you truly know Him?

You are invited . . .

. . . to contact the publisher of *Beyond Orion's Gates* if you would like to order additional copies of this book (inquire about quantity discounts)—or to learn about other Christian outreach materials available through Hart Research Center.

To order, or for information, call toll-free
1-800-487-4278